Your Complete Guide to College Success

Your Complete Guide to College Success

HOW TO STUDY SMART, ACHIEVE YOUR GOALS, AND ENJOY CAMPUS LIFE

DONALD J. FOSS

AMERICAN PSYCHOLOGICAL ASSOCIATION • *Washington, DC*

Published by
American Psychological Association
750 First Street, NE
Washington, DC 20002
www.apa.org

To order
APA Order Department
P.O. Box 92984
Washington, DC 20090-2984
Tel: (800) 374-2721; Direct: (202) 336-5510
Fax: (202) 336-5502; TDD/TTY: (202) 336-6123
Online: www.apa.org/pubs/books
E-mail: order@apa.org

In the U.K., Europe, Africa, and the Middle East, copies may be ordered from
American Psychological Association
3 Henrietta Street
Covent Garden, London
WC2E 8LU England

Typeset in Meridien by Circle Graphics, Inc., Columbia, MD

Printer: Edwards Brothers, Lillington, NC
Cover Designer: Naylor Design, Washington, DC

The opinions and statements published are the responsibility of the authors, and such opinions and statements do not necessarily represent the policies of the American Psychological Association.

Library of Congress Cataloging-in-Publication Data

Foss, Donald J., 1940-
 Your complete guide to college success : how to study smart, achieve your goals, and enjoy campus life / by Donald J. Foss.
   pages cm
 Includes bibliographical references and index.
 ISBN-13: 978-1-4338-1296-5
 ISBN-10: 1-4338-1296-7
 1. College student orientation. 2. College students—Psychology. 3. Study skills. 4. Learning strategies. 5. Academic achievement. 6. Educational attainment. I. Title.

 LB2343.3.F67 2013
 378.1'98—dc23
                                    2012045434

British Library Cataloguing-in-Publication Data
A CIP record is available from the British Library.

Printed in the United States of America
First Edition

http://dx.doi.org/10.1037/14181-000

This book is dedicated to Cordelia and Colton,
and to all other future college students.

Contents

II

V

Conquering Challenging Courses   191

Preface

My great hope is that you will be happy you picked up this book or were assigned it—and for two big reasons. First, because you'll find that the information and tips presented here will genuinely increase your chances of college success when you put them into practice. And second, because the writing routinely provides you with what a colleague once called the "click of comprehension." My goal has been to write each chapter in an informal way such that it can easily be digested with your dinner, while at the same time honoring the fact that you deserve college material that meets high standards of accuracy.

This *Guide* can be read as a stand-alone document, picked up by a lone reader either before starting college or after classes have begun. It also may be used as a textbook in college courses devoted to helping students stay on the path to college success. To help in either case, I have provided end-of-chapter learning aids that typically ask you to "Take Action" and "Explore Your Campus." Further, nearly every chapter ends with a set of "Self-Test Items." If you are an instructor using this book as part of a First-Year Experience or other college success course, please consult the instructor's webpage associated with this book at http://pubs.apa. org/books/supp/foss/. There you will find additional ideas for classroom discussion and activities.

If you are glad that you read this book when you're done, then I owe thanks to many people who have helped make that so. No one can be an expert in all the topics I've covered, so I've leaned on friends and colleagues who have given generously of their time and constructive criticism. If you are not glad, it's my fault. In addition, any errors that remain are my responsibility.

Professor Randolph Bias used a draft of this book in a course he taught at The University of Texas at Austin. The 40 students in that class provided evaluation and useful critiques of the chapters. The book is much improved because of their feedback. I'm grateful to them and to Randolph for causing that to happen.

Throughout the *Guide* I've made liberal use of quotes, the vast majority of which are from new college students writing about their experiences and reflections as they begin college. These quotes come from a huge collection of student writings gathered by Professor James Pennebaker, also on the faculty at The University of Texas at Austin. My thanks to Jamie for allowing me to read those materials and to quote from them. These snippets of reality add a great deal to the text.

Other colleagues provided encouragement, pointers to relevant research that I needed to know about, and constructive criticism. In particular, I want to thank Robert Bjork, Robert Olen Butler, Marjorie Chadwick, Kim Fromme, Arturo Hernandez, Leigh Hollyer, Thomas Joiner, Clayton Neighbors, Peter Norton, Christiane Spitzmueller, Ron Thurner, and Alan Witt. Many staff members, particularly at the University of Houston, met with me to discuss issues of student life from their "on the ground" perspective; this book is better because of their advice and input. Thanks, too, to Kim Thompson; she made the fortune cookie drawing in Chapter 2. Also, a number of anonymous reviewers provided both encouragement and very helpful feedback, and I wish to give them a most friendly wave. The editorial staff at APA Books, in particular, Susan Herman, Linda Malnasi McCarter, Caroline Barnes, and Edward Porter, kept me on the proper path as I tried to bring this project to a safe landing—and they did so in a most professional and cheerful way.

Finally, thanks a ton to Lara Foss, who produced the tables and figures, and to Melissa Foss Zdyb, whose comments improved the text. They exemplify what college success can mean.

ORIENTATION

From Green to Grad

1

This is my new home and I am comfortable. . . . College is GREAT!!!

I can handle it, but it is just so stressful it is unbelievable.

After the first week of school I was ready to quit. It's slowly getting better, I guess!

I like thinking about college, but it seems like that is all I have been thinking about lately. I wish I could have something else on my mind other than did I make the right decision. Did I choose the right school? Am I going to succeed? I wish going to college was less stressful. I feel happy, stressed, tired, hot, small, and insignificant. I have always felt big and important, but now that idea is far from my mind. Life is strange, life is strange.
—Students' reflections on starting college

Where Are We Going?

You've been thinking about college for a long time, whether you are a first-time student, returning after some time off, or transferring to a new school. College success requires a big commitment, and in turn, the experience will have a big impact on you. The goal of this book is to help you get the most out of your college years. In this chapter, I introduce some

http://dx.doi.org/10.1037/14181-001
Your Complete Guide to College Success: How to Study Smart, Achieve Your Goals, and Enjoy Campus Life, by Donald J. Foss

of the opportunities you'll be given and discuss some of the threats to success you may face—both academic and personal. By the end of the chapter, you'll discover what many of your college issues actually are, and you'll learn what's ahead: These are the core topics of this book. You'll also learn that many of the "obvious" ways to succeed in and out of the classroom may not be true.

You're walking across your new campus, perhaps heading to one of your first classes. It's glorious outside, and, yes, you look the part of a confident new student. You're very happy to be there, and you should be. But inside, is that all you feel? Are you sure about college and where it will take you? Are you convinced that you'll do well this year and for the next few years? And are you certain that what you do in college will ensure success as you move into the world of careers and commitments?

I remember being in your shoes, walking with two friends, Tom and Nick, on our first orientation day. We had chosen the same college, and that particular day was sunny and crisp—the kind that makes you want to be outside to view the passing scene, especially the other students. We all had fairly confident or even cocky looks, but guess what? I didn't feel entirely confident. If asked, I would have said I felt better than great; inside, though, I definitely felt some anxiety. You may feel the same.

In school you made good or even excellent grades, and it's likely you did well on standardized tests. But you've heard the troubling news that college is harder; you've been told repeatedly that good students don't always make it and that college teachers are famous for not having much concern about their students. And though some old friends may be attending your new college, you may feel troubled about leaving others behind and anxious about making new ones. In addition, you may not feel sure about your new living arrangements, how your family will adjust to your role as a student here, or how you'll get along with a new roommate. So although you are excited to be on campus, you may also be uneasy about surviving the next 4 years. That's okay; it's natural for some anxiety to accompany your confidence—after all, there are legitimate things to be concerned about.

After meeting some of the other new students on that beautiful fall day, my worries bloomed. Rich said he wanted to be a doctor and knew what it took to get into med school. Antonio was confident that he would be a neuroscientist—I wasn't sure what that even meant. And Liz quickly became known as one of the smartest and most able people around. They all seemed at ease in dealing with others, whether joking or flirting or talking about a class they were registered for. I wasn't completely comfortable with all those new people, and I admired them for their ability to meet and greet.

With respect to my college future, I wasn't sure if I had what it took to get through the courses I'd signed up for, and I had only a vague idea of what I wanted to major in, let alone what I would do with that major. That last problem turned out to be a real one; it took me a long time to settle on a degree plan that I stuck with and an even longer time to see where it might take me after college. In the meantime, I somehow had to stay motivated to do the work.

Though I didn't know it then, many students are wandering these same dark woods. For example, it's common to be worried about your first college math course. And for some students it may be beneficial, if somewhat scary, to change directions during the early college years. However, there are smart and not-so-smart ways to deal with the tough classes and to explore alternative majors and careers.

You may also be concerned about another real problem: money. I had enough from savings and financial aid for that first year, but I wasn't sure I'd have the money to keep going even if I did manage to get through year 1. So, like many new students, I secretly had a bundle of concerns slung over my shoulder with my backpack, but trust me, I was walking tall so no one could tell.

What Are the Confident People Thinking?

Later I learned that many of those seemingly confident people had their own issues, some more serious than mine. It turned out, for example, that it was Rich's father who wanted him to be a doctor; it wasn't what Rich himself wanted. Once he struck out on his own, which was a struggle for him, he ended up an economics major and then got an MBA. Also, a couple of the people who had big reputations as being super smart were gone at the end of the year, their GPAs so shattered that it would have taken a miracle for them to get back in school. And one of the apparently most socially able and self-confident of my new friends got into so much trouble with alcohol that he dropped out midway through the first semester. His family had to take him back home. In addition, many of my new friends were also worried about paying for college. So I wasn't the only one whose confident look that brilliant afternoon was somewhat forced.

Most of those new friends did fine in college and even better in their later careers. But life being what it is, we all had some bumps in college, some much harsher than others. You can avoid many of those jolts. With a little planning, and by adopting some proven problem-solving techniques, you can steer around the serious ones, those that can tear up your college career.

Naturally, you want to avoid the major threats to your college success; you certainly have better things to do than bailing yourself out of trouble. But more than just avoiding problems, you want to maximize the benefits and the enjoyment of your college years. Although we cannot forecast the future with certainty, there are some predictable issues you will have to deal with as you adjust to college and make your way through it. Your success and your eventual happiness, both in college and after, depend to a large extent on how you deal with these key issues. This book will guide you through them. More than that, it will show you how to be an effective and efficient student, how to succeed in less time than most of those around you, and how to get a better education while adding time for other activities.

College and the "Real World"

Many people refer to a distinction between *college* and the *real world*. Outsiders, sometimes even the old grads whose memories have faded, talk as though college is an easygoing, ivy-covered environment in which the stakes are low, the fun quotient is high, the hours are few, and the consequences of one's actions are slight, especially if those consequences might have been unpleasant. "Oh," they'll agree, "there can be some messiness, but nothing like it is out there, beyond the ivy, in the real world. It's really tough out there." Of course, most students do not go to movie-set, ivy-covered colleges. The vast majority of students attend community colleges or large state universities. But even many graduates of those schools would likely endorse the college versus real world distinction. Does that difference really hold up?

Sometimes there is a modest truth to the college versus real world distinction—for example, you might get an extra chance after an academic mishap, a chance you would not get "out there." But it's far from the whole truth. In reality, the level of pressure, the impact of looming deadlines, the need to stay motivated day in and day out, and the requirement to juggle multiple obligations are not that different from what you will face after college.

As we discuss the various opportunities and possible threats that will come your way over the next few college years, you'll notice that I often refer to the fact—and it is a fact—that how you handle certain college challenges is good practice for life after college. The attitudes, habits, and skills you develop inside the university will also apply outside it. This will be discussed in more depth as we go along, but for now my point is this:

Learning how to thrive in college is good practice for later success in almost any career. College is life, not just preparation for it.

A Voyage of Self-Discovery

Before you read on, I urge you to try the following exercise, and for reasons I'll tell you shortly, I believe you'll be glad you did. This exercise will take just about 20 minutes total; to be sure, set aside half an hour of uninterrupted time to devote to it. First, get out some paper and a pen (you can use a computer, but this little project is said to work better if you do it by hand) and make sure that you are in a quiet and private spot. You will be writing for 5 minutes, taking a 3-minute break, and then repeating that sequence twice for a total of three 5-minute writing sessions with two 3-minute breaks in between. Got your paper and your quiet place?

Then for 5 minutes, follow these instructions:

During this session, I want you to let go and write about your very deepest thoughts and feelings about coming to college. College, as you know, is a major transition. In your writing, you might want to write about your emotions and thoughts about leaving your friends or your parents; about issues of adjusting to the various aspects of college such as roommates, classes, or thoughts about your future; or even about your feelings of who you are or what you want to become. The important thing is that you really let go and dig down to your very deepest emotions and thoughts and explore them in your writing. The only rule is to write continuously for the full 5 minutes. If you run out of things to write about, you can repeat what you have already written, choosing the same or different words. Don't worry about spelling—you are writing just for yourself.

Ready? Begin. Don't read on until you have finished writing for 5 minutes.

I hope you took the time to write. If not, please reconsider and do so before you continue; you will learn something of high interest. You don't have to show anyone what you wrote. You can keep it or eventually delete it. For the moment, just turn it over or save it.

Now, I want you simply to take a break for about 3 minutes. Get up, walk around, take a drink of water, and stretch. Keep your eye on the time, and come back in 3 minutes. Then read on.

Now, sit down again, take a clean sheet of paper or open a new document on your computer, and write for 5 more minutes. Again, write about your deepest thoughts and feelings about coming to college. You can write on the same topic or topics you wrote about last time or on something else. However, whatever you write about, really let go and explore your deepest thoughts and feelings about coming to college. Once again, write continuously for the full 5 minutes. Go ahead, begin.

When you are done, just turn the paper over or save this second document in a file. Later you can dispose of it however you wish—file it or delete it—but not just yet. Now take another 3-minute break. Give yourself a quick breather. After that, read on.

Finally, write for one more 5-minute session. You can add a new topic or not, whatever comes to you, as long as it reflects your thoughts and feelings. This time, though, at some point during the session try to write something about how you will deal with the issues you have raised in these writings. In other words, go beyond description and write about your thoughts and feelings, what you have learned about yourself from this exercise, and what you can do about the issues you've identified as important. Write for a full 5 minutes, starting now.

You now have three sets of honest writing about yourself. It might be worthwhile to let a day go by to get a bit of distance from what you've done, but either now or tomorrow, or both, you should attentively read through what you have written.

What Are Other Students' Deepest Concerns About Coming to College?

Psychologists, led by the work of Professor James Pennebaker, have asked thousands students to write essays revealing their deepest concerns about coming to college (with instructions just like those presented previously), guaranteeing to those students that what they wrote would be kept anonymous. What do they write about? You can look over your writing to see whether your topics are on the list in the table on the facing page, which is taken from one such study (Pennebaker, Colder, & Sharp, 1990). The numbers add up to much more than 100% because each student could write about more than one topic, as you may have done, and those students wrote longer—for about 20 minutes on each of 3 days.

Topics Discussed in Students' Reflections About Starting College

Topic	Percentage of students
Isolation and loneliness	54%
Absence of family	51%
Absence of friends back home	45%
General worries about the future	42%
General academic concerns	41%
Issues surrounding identity (such as "Who am I?")	39%
Problems with boyfriend or girlfriend	31%
Conflicts with parents	26%
Feeling different from others	23%
Problems with roommate	19%
Conflicts surrounding religion	16%
Conflicts surrounding money	11%
Thoughts about suicide	11%
Conflicts involving sexuality	8%

Note. Data from Pennebaker, Colder, and Sharp (1990).

The most commonly addressed topics included feelings of isolation and loneliness; 54% of students in the study discussed this in at least one essay. Did you? The table shows the frequently mentioned issues and the percentage of students who wrote about each one.

It's clear that if you could look into your heart and those of the students in just one of your classes, you would find concern about many vital issues.

By carrying out this simple writing exercise, you can learn some important things about yourself. To make an analogy, you are explicitly mapping some important aspects of yourself. It's wise to draw this map because understanding "what's up" with you and your family, your friends, your relationship with your religion, or whatever is at the core of your concerns can help you. It is better to have these issues visible (to yourself) than to pretend they don't exist. As you can see from the table of results, many other students are also confronting them. And if you wrote about some positive steps you can take to deal with the matters that are on your mind, that's all the better. But the most important thing for now is simply to begin developing an understanding of your issues in an explicit way; that's why I emphasized the importance of writing things down.

I should quickly point out that it does no good to just go over and over your feelings, especially if they are negative. Writing down negative thoughts and expressing negative feelings again and again doesn't get rid of those feelings. In fact, it probably does more harm than good to do that—a topic we'll discuss more thoroughly later. But if the writing helps you to sort out your thoughts, to look at yourself "from the outside" (more about that later, too), and to think things through, then that's an indication it will help you in many ways, including improving your study effectiveness. On average, the students in Pennebaker's studies got higher grades and even made fewer visits to the health center the next semester if they wrote about themselves as you have just done (e.g., Pennebaker & Chung, 2007; Pennebaker, Mehl, & Niederhoffer, 2003). That is, they did better than students who wrote about much more casual topics.

As shown in the table of results, a huge number of students are concerned about social isolation and other interpersonal matters. Similarly, a huge number are concerned about their academic success and their future lives. Many have both on their minds. In this book we'll address these grand topics, letting you know what's known about how best to deal with them.

Before we go on, also take this quick little quiz:

True or False?

1. You should set aside one evening a week and devote it to the material from your most difficult class.
2. The more hours that students study, the better grades they get.
3. A college-level term paper will be better if you begin by making a detailed outline.
4. If you absolutely need money to continue, it is better to "step out" for a semester and go to work than it is to get a student loan.
5. When your friend deserves it, it is better to vent your anger than to bottle it up inside.
6. A 1-hour paper-and-pencil test is of no use in predicting anything about the career you might find to be a "best fit" for you.
7. If you want to stay on the good side of your professors, only go to their office hours when you are in trouble in a course. Otherwise they'll think you are wasting their time.

The correct answers to these statements are sometimes more complicated than a simple true or false. However, in all seven cases the correct answer is closer to false than to true. You'll learn why as you read on.

What's Up Ahead?

The next sections provide a preview of what you'll find in this book. I start with academic topics that affect how you'll do in the classroom. Your academic performance can deeply affect how you feel and how you interact with other significant people in your life. Doing well in school will boost your confidence; it's contagious. I then move on to topics dealing with your attitudes and feelings, and with weighty decisions you'll have to make about your major, your career path, and other issues of core importance to you.

Please note that this book does not address things in chronological order—that is, in the order you will come across them. Feel free to use the table of contents or the index if you want to read ahead for information on how to make best use of a faculty member's office hours, or for tips on taking multiple-choice tests, or for information on other specific issues.

Also, please note that most topics apply to just about everyone—for example, the advice on how to read a textbook and how best to organize your study time. However, other topics may primarily apply to a subset of readers. There are about 20 million college students in the United States, so it's not surprising that there is great diversity among them and among their primary challenges. Students differ in age, economic resources, ethnicity, political beliefs, willingness to ask for help when needed, the extent to which they have family responsibilities, and just about any other dimension we can imagine.

To take one example, students who are the first in their family to go to college (as I was) may not have the same knowledgeable support system at home as those who come from families with college experience. As a result, first-generation students should pay particular attention to the pointers directing them to the campus resource people who can advise and help them. Also, commuter students and those who live on campus must deal with somewhat different issues (Chapters 13 and 14 explicitly deal with some of them). As noted, most of the advice in this book is meant to be general—that is, it's intended to apply to nearly everyone, but from time to time I'll talk about special cases as well.

TIME AND SPACE

No matter what you do later in life, you will be miles ahead if you learn how to manage your time effectively and efficiently. This is a critical skill for both college years and after. We'll soon spend some of your valuable time on this topic because many students who get to college have not had to worry about time management. Even though you've led a very active life, school has been relatively easy, and the last-minute cram has often worked. It's even a point of pride for some college students to say that they never study and yet make excellent grades. That's just bravado, though; it's almost never true. Oh, a few rare, quick-study birds may come close sometimes; my friend Austin claims he spent more time on the basketball court than in the lecture hall at some points in his undergraduate years. But for most of us, what worked in high school will not work in college and certainly will not work after college—even Austin will tell you that.

Chapter 2 will show you an easy way to become an efficient time manager. In addition, it will introduce a useful way to think about problem solving, which is also a fundamental skill that you'll use constantly. In addition, I'll talk about finding your way around both physically (simple) and in the "space" that makes up the campus culture (not so simple). If you learn to manage your time and to become a successful problem solver, and you are good at navigating complex organizations, you stand an excellent chance of college success and of moving up in your career even long after many of the particular things you learned during college have been forgotten or become obsolete.

CLASSES AND STUDYING

Nearly half the students who wrote about their thoughts and feelings talked about general academic concerns (and another large group listed general worries about the future). Perhaps you mentioned something that fits in these categories, including possible unease about your courses, your major, or even your preparation for college work.

As I focus on the academic side of college life, I'll provide useful tools to deal with threats to your success. For example, you've already spent a great deal of time reading and studying, but it's quite likely you aren't as efficient at these tasks as you could be. To quote expert scientists (e.g., Pashler, McDaniel, Rohrer, & Bjork, 2008) who study these topics: "Basic research on human learning and memory, especially research . . . carried out in the last 20 years or so, has demonstrated that our intuitions and beliefs about how we learn are often wrong in serious ways" (p. 117). They go on: "People [frequently] manage their own learning and teach others in non-optimal ways" (p. 117). In this book, I'll make use of these recent discoveries to answer the question, "How can I learn most efficiently and effectively?" Chapter 3 will show you the best ways to study so that you maximize your chances of mastering and remembering the course materials. Studying smarter is better than studying longer.

We'll also take a look at your reading assignments and introduce you in Chapter 4 to a "strategic reading" technique. Many students are surprised to discover both how much reading they have to do in certain college courses and the level of detail they are expected to grasp from those reading assignments. Of course, you're a good reader, but you can be better. You'll get there by being a strategic reader.

In addition to reading, you'll get substantial information from your professors. Indeed, you will spend hundreds of hours in classrooms listening to and interacting with them. The chance to do that is a main reason why you've come to college. But you can't just listen to the lectures; you need to write down the important points to help you review and remember the material. That's not always easy. Scientists who study what students actually do in college courses have found that "one of the major cognitive challenges that most college freshmen face is developing the listening and note-taking skills they need to survive in . . . introductory courses" (Armbruster, 2009, p. 221). In addition, there are published estimates that "college students probably only record somewhere between 20% and 40% of lecture information" (Armbruster, 2009, p. 225). In Chapter 5, I'll show you how to do much better than that—how to get the most out your classes, including how to take effective notes, and then how to use them to your best advantage.

When I talk about how best to study I'll also emphasize the importance of honest self-assessment. Seeking out, and not being afraid to face, accurate self-knowledge is one of the most valuable lifetime skills you can acquire. You'll learn how to figure out whether you know what you need to know—no fooling. You'll also learn how self-assessment can be aided by working with other students. Along the way I'll provide many other concrete recommendations that will help you develop into an excellent student. When you put these tips into practice, you'll get better grades, have more time for other things, and feel good about yourself.

WILL THIS BE ON THE TEST?

You've taken hundreds of tests, and by now you know a lot about what to expect from them; you may be "test wise." Still, some of the most common questions that students ask, or wish they had asked, are the tried and true ones: "What will be on the test?" or "Will this be on the test?" It is, of course, essential for you to do well on the exams, papers, lab reports, or artistic performances that lie in front of you. You are going to be quizzed, questioned, examined, evaluated, tested, and in general assessed many more times in college and afterward. It does not stop. In Chapter 6, I'll make sure you know what to do so that you can shine on those assessments. In addition, many students have substantial fear about being assessed; they're said to have *test anxiety*. I'll explain how test anxiety works and give you tips for both avoiding and dealing with those feelings.

Although you no doubt look forward to most of your courses, anticipating one or two of them may make you quite uneasy. Some classes are known to be stumbling blocks for a lot of students. In particular, college mathematics courses (discussed in Chapter 11) and, to a lesser extent, basic writing courses (Chapter 12) have developed that reputation. I remember sitting and staring at both math problems and writing assignments. That "blank stare" time was a waste of time. I'll provide separate chapters on these potentially killer topics, with specific guidelines for how to master them—tips that fit right in with the general approach we'll take to studying. For example, you've probably been advised to begin a paper by making an outline. But that's not what professional writers typically do. There are better ways to solve the "writing problem." By learning these techniques you will greatly reduce or even eliminate the time you spend just spinning your mental wheels without getting anyplace.

HOW FEELINGS AND MOTIVATION AFFECT YOUR ACADEMIC SUCCESS

The writing exercise also showed that students like you have a bundle of personal concerns about family, friends, loves, their identities, and other issues. And in addition to the cares you bring with you, at some time during college an event beyond your control—perhaps something social, emotional, or financial—may lead you to think you've come to a dead end. Or you might find yourself highly anxious because you're in serious academic trouble—if, for example, you simply ignore the advice given here! Just as worrisome, you may find yourself losing your motivation and commitment to your college work. Or perhaps you already feel apprehensive about your future career and the choice of major that you hope will open the door to that career, whatever it is.

In all these cases, you have to learn to cope with your feelings and, as well, find ways to carry on with your studies, your work, and other aspects of your daily life. You need to keep going in spite of problems. This book will tell you about concrete, tested ways to deal with the negative events that come up in your college years. I can tell you now that some of the most effective coping strategies turn out *not* to be the most commonly used (or "common sense") ones. For example, venting your anger is not an effective way to handle that emotion. Chapter 7 will be particularly useful in sorting out what to do in those cases, but relevant information is provided in other chapters, too. Of course, it's certain that there will be unpleasant challenges in your life after college. Once again, then, what you learn to do while in college will help you handle many of those later difficulties.

RESOURCES FOR LIFE PLANNING

I've already mentioned that I had a difficult time picking a major and a career. Many students today have the same problem, whereas others start by being sure about their career goals but lose that certainty as they go along. These students are also at risk for losing their motivation and dropping out of college. That needn't happen. Most likely there are first-rate resources on your campus (and, for sure, there are good resources on the Internet) that can help you work through questions about both course selection and career planning. I'll cover these topics in Chapters 8 and 9. I'll also discuss some highly practical issues—for example, how much you can safely work while going to college and ways to think about serious financial decisions that may come your way.

A NEW CULTURE

No matter what you do later, you will have to learn your way around complex institutions, and your college is one. If you start a new company in a garage, as the founders of Apple Computer famously did, your company will not last if you cannot work with and around large organizations. Even rebels have to understand the systems they want to change.

In Chapter 10, we'll take a quick tour around the university so that you understand the way it is organized, and we'll meet some people who can help you be a successful student and help you reach your wider goals. We'll see that the university's organization is more than just an annoying bureaucracy; how it is structured affects how its citizens (and now you are one of them) can effectively attain their goals. Therefore, learning something about the overall system will help you work through it; or to put it differently, knowing the system can help you beat it.

Your success depends to some extent on how you deal with a great variety of people. Some of them will have a certain authority over you. For example, professors can demand attendance or not, can give a comprehensive final examination (one that covers material from the entire course) or not, and usually can fail you if you are caught cheating on an exam or plagiarizing a paper. Because the vast majority of professors want students to succeed, you can help yourself a great deal if you learn how to approach and deal with them. When you do, you'll feel good both about the interaction and about each other.

You will also meet many new students this year, and some of them may be outside your comfort zone in what they believe and how they behave. Learning to adjust to them while being true to your core values, and learning how to work with the people who work for the university, pose separate sets of challenges. These may not be problems for you; you may be a person who enjoys the stimulation that comes from interacting with smart people who are not like you. In addition, you may already know how to adjust your behavior appropriately to the various situations and people you must deal with. Maybe. Realistically, though, you may still be developing your people skills. College will provide a learning experience in social behavior, and this book will give you some fresh ways to think about and adjust those skills.

We also know that students who are actively engaged in college life tend to do better academically as well as socially. In Chapters 13 and 14, I'll provide some guideposts for successful involvement whether you are a full-time student who lives on campus or a part-time commuter student. And for many (including me when I was in college), money squawks as often as it talks. In Chapter 14, I'll present some novel ways to think about your financial health, as well as your physical and mental health.

TAKING ACTION, EXPLORING, AND TESTING

At the end of each chapter, you'll find sections called Take Action and Explore Your Campus. In addition, you'll see some test items and suggestions for self-reflection. Carrying out the actions and giving yourself the tests will help ensure that you are getting the most out of your reading, and therefore out of your college experiences. As I will discuss soon, one of the most important things you can do to maximize the chances of meeting your goals is to honestly assess how far away from them you are at any given time. When you actively participate in your own learning, and frequently assess how you are doing, you can greatly improve how much and how quickly you learn.

Where Does the Advice in This Book Come From?

Finally, I want to let you know where my advice comes from. It has two major sources. The first and by far the more important one is that, insofar as possible, it is based on evidence, not just opinion. When you get medical advice you want it to be based on the best evidence around, not just on what someone thinks makes sense. For example, doctors know that giving certain drugs in combination with others can lead to bad results, even if each drug by itself leads to a good outcome. In such cases, they do not jump to the "obvious" conclusion that if drug A is good and drug B is good, then A and B together must be better. Instead, the evidence guides them. Similarly, I'll draw on existing research when providing advice, even though the results are sometimes surprising.

We are fortunate because there is substantial research on topics such as how we learn and retain both information and skills, on how best to take notes and how to study, and on a variety of other issues with everyday relevance to your success in the classroom. There is also research on other important topics, for example, on coping with personal problems that are bothering you and on the relationship of self-esteem to the quality of your work. These personal issues can affect your success in college, the amount of fun you'll have, and your growth as a person.

That said, I also have to tell you that it isn't possible to take what's known about learning, for example, and then tell you how to learn any topic quickly and with little effort. Indeed, what we know about learning suggests that it really isn't possible to become an expert quickly and effortlessly, though some ways definitely are better than others. For example, I can assure you that recording the lectures and playing them back while you sleep does not work! And sometimes the evidence points in a direction that may not appear to be the shortest route to success. But just because "everyone knows" something does not guarantee that it is correct. Some of the things that seem obviously true turn out to be false when they are studied carefully. Common sense is common, but it's not always sensible. The important point for you is that, when possible, the advice presented here is based on state-of-the-art knowledge.

In addition to reading the relevant research papers on our topics, I've talked with experts who work with students professionally (career counselors and residence hall advisors, for example), and I do draw on my own experience, which extends from freshman to academic vice president. In my administrative roles I've dealt with student issues of every imaginable kind, so my experience-based opinion does play a role, but a secondary one. Also, I'm on your side. I've seen too many students carried out on academic stretchers and others who scrape by but who are all but wasting their years in college. I do not want you to be in either of those groups.

Many advice books present recommendations in the form of to-do lists and lists of things to avoid. These may be accurate and useful, and I'll give a few here. However, there are two problems with lists: They can't cover everything, and the number of items on lists can overwhelm your memory. This book takes a different approach; it is based on the belief that a useful guide provides an understanding of the big picture and of the reasons behind the recommendations. Once you understand the reasons for things, you can often produce the specific lists yourself. That's the college way—to become a self-sufficient problem solver, someone who will make decisions that maximize chances for success. In short, this book is not just a list of "how to" items; it is also a "why to" guide.

Summary

For most first-year students, college begins with a combination of happy anticipation and genuine concern about what's ahead. That's realistic because college success requires both working smart and working hard. It is a sample of the real adult world as well as preparation for it. Many students are worried about their readiness for college and their eventual major and career path. Even more are uneasy about being on their own (including feeling lonely) and about their family and friends. This chapter explored your concerns via a written voyage of self-discovery. It also provided a look at what's ahead by briefly summarizing some of the key topics and issues that will be explored in the succeeding chapters. This book's commitment is to provide advice based on the best evidence available about what actually works.

TAKE ACTION— ANOTHER VOYAGE OF SELF- DISCOVERY

You learn more rapidly, and retain material longer, when you actively participate in the learning process. In light of that fact, many chapters in this book will ask you to carry out concrete activities, either within the chapter itself or right after it, in a section called Take Action. You've already started doing that by writing about your feelings as you start college. Some of the exercises are learning experiences in themselves. Others ask you to practice the techniques recommended in the book. Still others ask you to put the tips into practice in some of your other college courses.

In carrying out the next exercises, please think about your goals— what might keep you from them and what you can do to increase the chances that you will, in fact, meet those goals. Keep copies of this writing. You'll want to compare it with some things I'll ask you to write later.

1. An ancient instruction, sometimes attributed to the philosopher Socrates, is: Know Thyself. This is good advice; there is evidence that people who do not have an accurate view of themselves experience negative consequences. To quote psychologist Timothy Wilson (2009), "It thus seems to be to people's advantage to discover what is under their mental hoods" (p. 387; see also T. D. Wilson, 2002). It turns out, though, that it is not as easy as it first seems to get accurate information about yourself. One way is to watch carefully what you actually do. For example, suppose you believe you are not prejudiced against, say, gay people, but you avoid socializing with them. Your actions may be more revealing of yourself than

your words are. Even so, a quick writing exercise can help. In the next 10 minutes, then, write a one-page note on this topic: my most important goals for my college years. Just write down (a) what you now believe are your goals and (b) also say what you think college will provide to you as you work toward them. You don't have to do any research; just write from your heart as well as your head.

2. List three "threats to your success" that you are concerned about. Rank the items on your list in terms of how big a threat to success they seem to be at this point.

3. What do you believe is the one most important thing you can do that will increase your chance of being a successful student? The important word here is *do*. We're not looking for a statement of an attitude or belief, but of action.

4. What do you do when you study? Again, the important word is *do*. Jot down the things you do and the order in which you do them. Your answer will probably depend on the type of class; how you study math may differ from how you study in, say, a history class. That's okay. Just specify the class and then write down what you think are the most important things you do when you study for it. After you've listed what you do, then add what percentage of your study time you spend on each activity. We'll come back to your answer later.

5. On a more immediate and practical note: Make a list of the new things you have to do as you come to college, from personal items such as doing laundry and buying books to choosing courses and thinking about a major and a career. See how many you can list in 10 minutes.

EXPLORE YOUR CAMPUS

Many colleges have numerous activities in the days before and after classes begin, including orientation programs for both first-year and transfer students. Some orientation programs are required. If your program is not, I highly encourage you to attend it.

Campus activities continue at a high level in the first week or two of classes. Again, I urge you to explore the possibilities provided by your school. Select some events or meetings that sound interesting and go to them. Of course, participation is a good way to meet people. But more than that, we know that getting involved on your campus helps you do well as time goes by. The events may be listed on your school's website. Your campus newspaper probably has a "Back to School" edition. My experience is that these issues are thick with opportunities and well worth browsing with your calendar in hand. Take a look.

The Mental Maps to Success
Space and Time

2

I took seventeen hours and worked. I hardly had time to do anything but study and work, and try to catch up on sleep.

At freshman orientation, when I registered for 15 hours I thought it would be an okay amount to have for the first year of school. When school started, I felt like I was going to fail. Especially after going to each class the first day and reading the syllabus. But you know what? I know that I can do it and succeed.

—*First-year students writing about starting college*

The half of knowledge is to know where to find knowledge.
—*Anonymous. Inscription above
the entrance to Dodd Hall,
Florida State University*

Where Are We Going?

This chapter will show you how to manage your most important college resources—yourself and your time. By the end of the chapter, you will know how to predict (some of) the relevant future, and you will construct a tool that will get you through your course assignments by their due dates while also giving you more time for other things. In addition, you will be able to look beyond individual course assignments

http://dx.doi.org/10.1037/14181-002
Your Complete Guide to College Success: How to Study Smart, Achieve Your Goals, and Enjoy Campus Life, by Donald J. Foss

and construct a "goal and subgoal tree," a system that will help you develop your organizational and critical-thinking skills, and one that will help you clarify—and then reach—your college objectives.

College can be an enormously productive and fulfilling experience. It's a sad fact, though, that lots of students drop out during the first year; about 35% of those who start at 4-year colleges do so, as do nearly 45% of those who start at 2-year colleges (ACT Educational Services, n.d.). Indeed, by Thanksgiving a surprising number have made the decision to leave. In many cases, that decision need not and should not have been made. It is the result of some unhappy experiences, most of which could have been avoided or repaired: feeling that you don't fit in, financial struggles, early difficulties in coursework, powerful homesickness for family or other love, getting overwhelmed with the tasks of living independently, or the total impact of all these things. Homesickness usually passes in a couple of weeks, and the other issues can effectively be dealt with if you know how.

Let's jump in by asking some simple questions and showing you how to answer them. Because dealing with strange territory is easier if you have a map, let's provide the perspectives you need via a set of them—I'll call them *big PICTure maps*. In this shorthand, P stands for a familiar tool; it's the *physical map* of the campus. I and C stand for maps of less concrete things: the way that the *institution* is organized and structured and the *culture of the college*, especially its academic culture. Finally, T represents *time*, a critical and nonrenewable resource. The institutional and cultural components of college are highly related, and we'll discuss them later. Let's start with P, the simple, familiar map, and quickly move on to T in this chapter.

Four Big PICTure "Maps"

P: Physical Place Map
   Helps you literally find your way around.
I: Institutional Organization (Chapter 10)
   Shows you "who's who" and who can help you.
C: Culture of the College (throughout the book)
   Understanding the informal rules of behavior can increase your chances of success.
T: Time Map
   A critical "map" that you draw yourself (this chapter).

Your Place and Space

It takes only a few days to get the lay of the land in the literal sense. You will quickly learn your way around. Nevertheless:

Pick up or print out a campus map and locate the buildings where your classes will be held.

You can find the campus map by searching the website of your college; it's usually only a click or two from the home page. Also, your college may have a map app you can download that shows buildings, bus routes and times, etc. Looking at the map helps you learn the overall organization of your new environment, which speeds up your feeling of belonging there. On large campuses such a simple step can help you be on time to those first classes—highly advisable! Mark the buildings and rooms that hold your classes and stroll by them before classes start; doing a little exploration can pay off. When I was a student at the University of Minnesota, some of the big tunnels that carried steam pipes were open to student foot traffic if you knew how to find them. It was a sign of sophistication in campus lore if you knew your way around the tunnel system.

Those tunnels have long been closed, so that way of ducking the February blizzard is no longer available. However, another mark of campus savvy was to know about certain quiet and even lovely places where one could study or read. These still exist. On most campuses there are out-of-the-way areas in the library, or in a campus art gallery, or in a departmental reading room, or in the student union. Exploration will turn them up. It's nice to be the person who knows about such places; it gives you the sense of being an expert in your environment. Then you can give directions rather than ask for them—a sign you belong.

While we're talking about being on time to your first classes and other simple things that can get you off to a good start, at many schools the real trick for those living off campus is to learn about parking and how to find a parking place. Trust me, if you must drive to campus, or choose to do so, and if parking is a problem on your campus during your first week of classes, it will be a problem during your graduation week. The problem can be managed but will not be solved while you are a student.

Do not assume you can drive up the first day of class and find a place to park, even if you could do so the week before classes started.

You might burn through a quarter tank of gas, a half hour of extra time, and a full dose of frustration while circling the campus and missing your first class. If your university runs a shuttle bus service, get the map and timetable for it. Most likely you will save time by using it. It's a green choice, too.

However, if you are going to park on campus, make sure that you look through your registration materials, or check out the campus website, for information about parking before you pay your fees. On many campuses, generally those in urban areas, you will have to pay for a parking permit of some kind. Quite often there are more permits sold than there are actual parking spots—students call them "hunting licenses." They allow you to park in certain locations but do not guarantee that there will be a spot in your favorite location. This is particularly true during the first 2 or 3 weeks of class.

A Guide to Managing Time and Predicting the Future

> Things that worked for me in high school, I discovered, don't work for me in college. I really was unprepared for the amount of material that is presented here and the speed at which it is presented. It was a bit of a shock.
>
> I still haven't purchased the textbook for this class . . . I wonder when the first exam is going to be so I don't fail it. Ahh, I'll deal with it later.
>
> —*Students writing about starting college*

At first it seems like a long time from Labor Day to the winter break. Although you are making many adjustments, most things academic may seem just fine in those first few weeks. Perhaps classes don't strike you as that hard; there's plenty of time for socializing, and if you work off campus, your job isn't interfering with school. Given the freedom to set your own schedule, your waking hours may be sliding later and later: "It's almost 10 p.m.; time to start thinking about going out."

Later, though, when midterms are upon you, when you have three exams in 7 days and the draft of a paper due the same week, your stress level may soar. With a hint of alarm in her voice, a student in my class said, "If I can just get through this week, I'll have it made." Most do, but too many don't. Let's be sure you do.

Tomas joined a fraternity and had an active social life; he liked to enjoy himself and he wasn't about to give that up. But he'd been admitted to the Architecture College, which was known to be a very time-consuming major. Tomas had to learn to design both buildings and his social schedule. One characteristic got him through architecture school in good time while he had a good time: He was organized. Unlike the freshman student just quoted, Tomas always had the right books, and he knew for sure when exams were scheduled.

People say that you can't predict the future. But with high probability you can predict some of it. For example, if I go to your college's website or look in the course guide, and if I know what classes you've signed up for, I'll be able to predict with great accuracy when you will be sitting in a chair taking a final exam. So can you. This is a stunningly simple observation, but a tremendously important one. Ignoring it will cost you.

Note. Copyright by Donald J. Foss 2013. Printed with permission.

Why is it that some undergraduates make the transition from high school to college smoothly, whereas others have much more trouble? One research study (Light, 2004) addressed this question by interviewing two groups of sophomores: One group had an outstanding first year, whereas the other struggled. The interviewers "quickly discovered that one difference, indeed a single word, was a key factor . . . . The critical word is *time*" (p. 24). The successful students thought about time management, and they were explicit about it. The less successful students rarely even mentioned it.

One of the most important recipes for college success is to be prepared for the events you can accurately forecast, such things as exams and papers as well as an off-campus work schedule, certain family responsibilities, and regular meetings of a social or social service organization. Tomas did that; he organized his life so that he was ready for the predictable, and predictably, he was successful. It's amazing what a difference it makes; being ready for what's coming up not only improves your academic performance, but also reduces your stress level. Also, learning to plan for the foreseeable parts of the future is one really important way that college prepares you for your future life. All successful people in the professions, in business, and even in sports have to master The Rules of Time Management:

- Prepare for the predictable.
- Allow time for the unpredictable.

If you do not respect the Rules of Time Management, you are guaranteed to increase your stress level. It's easy to get overwhelmed, especially if you are working as well as going to school. Life sneaks up on you; all of a sudden things pile up. Soon you feel you're not prepared for anything and are going to do poorly at everything. It once seemed like a long time from Labor Day to the winter break, but suddenly there is no time at all, and a sense of panic can overtake you. These feelings lead many students to spiral down. They can't see how they can do it all, so in frustration and with a certain air of false bravery they do none of what is needed; they go out for a beer instead. That may dull anxiety for the moment, but that anxiety will rise blazing with the sun the next day.

STEP 1: THE TIME MAP

The way to reach your academic goals—for example, to graduate and enter the profession that interests you—is to follow the first Rule of Time Management: Prepare for the predictable. Let's start with the academic sources of time pressure, those things that must be a high priority for you. It's easy in the first week of classes to lay out the major events that you can forecast for the rest of the term. It is not only easy; it's necessary.

Every course will provide you with a *syllabus*—an outline of the course and its requirements. The syllabus may be written and handed out in class, posted on a website, or both. Normally the syllabus will tell you the aims of the course; perhaps it will also provide a statement of "learning outcomes," the knowledge and skills you are expected to acquire from the course. It will inform you about the required books and other readings, and crucial for your planning purposes, it will specify the dates for reading assignments and the due dates for key events such as exams and papers. You should:

> **Collect together the information from each course syllabus and transfer the dates of the major events (e.g., midterm exams, due dates for papers and their drafts, dates for lab reports) to one master calendar.**

For any day that something is due, transfer onto the master calendar the name of the course and the assignment or exam that will occur on that day. If an instructor changes the date of an exam, don't forget to update it on your master calendar. Many electronic calendars and time planners are available free on the web or come with computers, smart phones, and other digital devices. Such programs may update your master calendar wherever it resides electronically. That feature is particularly handy because you easily can check your schedule and your course obligations before making spontaneous plans with your new friends.

If you print out or write out your master calendar, it might look something like the one on the following page.

The one simple step of building a master calendar will help you control your time. You are making a time map; it is the most important map we'll discuss. Unlike space, you cannot retrace your steps in time, except in your memory. Those memories can be happy or sad; you don't want them to be bitter. Students who do not plan their time often end up with bitter memories because they wasted it, and thereby they wasted opportunities that have long-term consequences. You don't want to be like the student quoted at the beginning of this section, the one who concluded, "Ahh, I'll deal with it later." He just blew off the need to organize his time, and eventually he regretted it. Simply said, don't let things pile up and then get buried under them when they topple onto you.

OPPORTUNITIES FOR REGRET AND THE FALLACY OF THE EXPANDING FUTURE

Let's linger a moment on the topic of regret; it's a nasty emotion over the long haul. Psychologists have asked people to look back over their

October

September
S	M	T	W	T	F	S
	1	2	3	4	5	6
7	8	9	10	11	12	13
14	15	16	17	18	19	20
21	22	23	24	25	26	27
28	29	30				

November
S	M	T	W	T	F	S
						1
2	3	4	5	6	7	8
9	10	11	12	13	14	15
16	17	18	19	20	21	22
23	24	25	26	27	28	29
30						

Sunday	Monday	Tuesday	Wednesday	Thursday	Friday	Saturday
28 September	**29**	**30**	**1** October 9 AM Coll Algebra 10 AM Composition II 11 AM (Algebra homework) 3 PM US Hist 7 PM (Draft Comp II paper)	**2** 9 AM **Jog with Marj 11:30 AM **Early lunch 12 PM Psych 1:30 PM Gen Biology 3:30 PM (Study Psych) 7 PM (Read/Study History)	**3** 9 AM Coll Algebra 10 AM Composition II 11 AM Work on comp paper 2 PM Do Algebra practice test 3 PM US Hist 8 PM Movie with ?	**4** 10 AM (Laundry / shop) 12 PM Work at Rec Center till 5 7 PM Football game
5 1 PM (Finish composition paper) 4 PM (Read History assign)	**6** 9 AM Coll Algebra 10 AM Composition II -- 11 AM (Algebra homework) 3 PM US Hist 7 PM Club meeting	**7** 10 AM Bio Lab 12 PM Psych 1:30 PM Gen Biology 3:30 PM (Write lab report) 7 PM (Study Algebra) 8 PM (Read History) *More...*	**8** 9 AM Coll Algebra -- EXAM 10 AM Composition II 11 AM (Study bio) 3 PM US Hist 7 PM (Study Bio)	**9** 9 AM **Jog with Marj 11:30 AM **Early lunch 12 PM Psych 1:30 PM Gen Biology 3:30 PM (Study Psych) 4 PM (Study Bio)	**10** 9 AM Coll Algebra 10 AM Composition II 3 PM US Hist 9 PM Nails on the Blackboard Concert!!!	**11** 10 AM (Exercise / shop) 12 PM Work at Rec Center till 5
12 2 PM (Read / study History) 4 PM (Study Psych)	**13** 9 AM Coll Algebra 10 AM Composition II 11 AM (Algebra homework) 3 PM US Hist 7 PM Club meeting	**14** 10 AM Bio Lab 12 PM Psych 1:30 PM Gen Biology 3:30 PM (Write lab report) 7 PM (Take Psych practice... 8 PM (Study/Test re Algebra)	**15** 9 AM Coll Algebra -- QUIZ 10 AM Composition II 11 AM (Algebra homework) 3 PM US Hist 7 PM (Study Psych)	**16** 9 AM **Jog with Marj 11:30 AM **Early lunch 12 PM Psych -- MID-TERM... 1:30 PM Gen Biology 3:30 PM (Study Psych) 7 PM (Bio Practice test)	**17** 9 AM Coll Algebra 10 AM Composition II 3 PM US Hist 4 PM (Study Bio) 7:30 PM Rally at auditorium	**18** 8 AM Work at Rec Center till noon 1 PM Football game
19 2 PM (Read / study History) 4 PM (Study Psych) 7 PM (Study Bio)	**20** 9 AM Coll Algebra 10 AM Composition II 11 AM (Algebra homework) 3 PM US Hist 7 PM Club meeting 10 PM (Review Bio)	**21** 10 AM Bio Lab 12 PM Psych 1:30 PM Gen Biology -- EXAM 3:30 PM (Write lab report) 7 PM (Study Algebra) 8:30 PM (Study History)	**22** 9 AM Coll Algebra 10 AM Composition II 11 AM (Algebra homework) 3 PM US Hist 7 PM (Research Comp paper)	**23** 9 AM **Jog with Marj 11:30 AM **Early lunch 12 PM Psych 1:30 PM Gen Biology 3:30 PM (Study Psych) 7 PM (Study History)	**24** 9 AM Coll Algebra 10 AM Composition II 3 PM US Hist -- EXAM 4 PM (Study Bio)	**25** 10 AM Laundry / Exercise 12 PM Work at Rec Center till 5
26 2 PM (Read / study History) 3 PM (Study Algebra) 4 PM (Draft paper for Composition)	**27** 9 AM Coll Algebra 10 AM Composition II 11 AM (Algebra homework) 3 PM US Hist 7 PM Club meeting	**28** 10 AM Bio Lab 12 PM Psych 1:30 PM Gen Biology 3:30 PM (Write lab report) 7 PM (Algebra / Practice test)	**29** 9 AM Coll Algebra -- EXAM 10 AM Composition II 11 AM (Algebra homework) 3 PM US Hist 7 PM (Write Comp II paper)	**30** 9 AM **Jog with Marj 11:30 AM **Early lunch 12 PM Psych 1:30 PM Gen Biology 3:30 PM (Study Psych)	**31** 9 AM Coll Algebra 10 AM Composition II -- PAPER DUE 3 PM US Hist	**1** November

An example master calendar.

lives and to pick out the most important sources of their regrets. Many are surprised to hear that the single biggest source, on average, involves education. Formal education provides tremendous opportunities for change and advancement. That's great, of course, but it also puts you at risk for regret if you don't take advantage of those chances. To quote experts who have studied this topic:

> People's biggest regrets are a reflection of where in life they see their largest opportunities; that is, where they see tangible prospects for change, growth, and renewal. . . . The top six biggest regrets in life center on (in descending order) education, career, romance, parenting, the self, and leisure." (Roese & Summerville, 2005, p. 1273)

If I had to pick a single skill that would best reduce your chances to feel regret over missed educational opportunities, it would be time management.

Your time map permits you to determine your schedule in a thoughtful way rather than letting the whims of the moment capture you. For one thing, you'll see at a glance that in 6 weeks you have, say, a math midterm, a biology lab report, and a draft of a paper in a composition course all due on that Monday or Tuesday. It's obvious, isn't it, that it's not a good idea to plan on attending an out-of-town game the previous weekend. Your master calendar almost shouts at you: Do Not Make That Plan! You might believe that you will arrange your time so that you're ready for these deadlines days before they are due. But if you plan to work ahead in that way, will you actually be able to do it?

We are all subject to what I'll call the *fallacy of the expanding future*. For example, if you ask me whether I can help you move into your new apartment this coming weekend, I might have to tell you that I've got other commitments and deadlines, and sorry, I just can't do it. But if you ask me to help you move in 3 months, I readily imagine that I'll finish all the things on my deadline list by then and be able to help you. I'm sure I'll have more spare time in the future; it seems that time expands out there. And that's the fallacy. What I'm forgetting is that other deadlines

Biggest Sources of Regret in Life

1. Education
2. Career
3. Romance
4. Parenting
5. The Self
6. Leisure

and commitments will no doubt crop up between now and then. If I agree to help you, I'll do it, but only by putting off some other activities that by then will be important. Therefore, given the fallacy of the expanding future, I advise you to be cautious about planning on that out-of-town game the weekend before midterm exams are scheduled, especially during your first year in college. It's your decision, of course. And, of course, actions have consequences.

Another problem with time management can come up because one or another of your acquaintances will go out nearly every night, and you may frequently be invited to go along. But if one set of friends goes out on Wednesday, and another on Thursday, then it's not just one night for you. Can you afford the time to join them both? Then you learn that on Friday your favorite band, Nails on the Blackboard, is playing a local concert, and you certainly can't miss them. Again, your calendar with its list of goals can come to the rescue. The calendar insists that Wednesday night you have to get that lab report done. Listen to that message; after all, it's from you. If you ignore it you are setting yourself up—first for panic, and then for regret.

STEP 2: THE SUBGOAL TREE

Once you've got a master calendar, you can move to the second step: setting and reaching subgoals. It's a truism to say that Rome wasn't built in a day. But not even Podunk, a one-stoplight town, was built in a day. Every construction project, indeed anything worthy of the term *project*, has many steps, some of which have to happen before others and all of which take time. The need to sequence the parts of a job is obvious, of course. Yet many students ignore the fact that successfully getting to the end of a course requires successfully getting to the middle of it, or that writing a quality paper entails doing the necessary research and writing a first draft. Oh, in some sense of the word *know*, they know this obvious fact, but their actions demonstrate that they work hard to ignore it. That may have worked in high school, especially for the top students, but it rarely works in college even for them.

To successfully accomplish your important assignments (goals), you should figure out in advance the major steps needed to reach each of them. Let's call each of these big, intermediate steps a *subgoal*, something you have to accomplish to reach the goal. Of course, accomplishing a subgoal takes time. Therefore:

Put your subgoals on your master calendar as well.

Got a paper due? You need time to write it. Before that, though, you need time to do the library or Internet research. When will you do it?

And after doing the research, but before you've written the final version, you need time to try out the various ways you can organize the paper; time to draft it; and yes, time to rewrite the draft. Put each of these subgoals on the calendar at the date you expect to complete it. If you then follow the expanded time map, now including the subgoals, you will reach the main goal. (Chapter 12 will show you how to write a successful paper.) Not only that, you'll reach it with much less stress than students who wait until the last minute, and the product will be better, too.

ENDS AND ACTIONS

The goal and subgoal way of thinking is most effective if you make a mental distinction between (a) goals as ends—I want to get an *A* in this course, I want to get the required paper done and get an *A* on it, or even I want to graduate and become a high school teacher; and (b) subgoals as means to those ends—the actions that will get you there. When you set up your subgoals, be sure you specify the concrete actions needed to accomplish them. To meet the subgoal, you must carry out those actions: Read the relevant materials, or complete a draft of the paper, or carry out some other specific task. Those actions (subgoals) are the means to the end (the goal). A simple way to say it is that you should develop a plan and an associated timetable to implement your goal. Research has shown that you are more likely to reach a difficult goal if you furnish that goal with concrete actions that will get you there.

Most projects are large enough that reaching a subgoal takes a number of steps and a fair amount of time. For example, successfully "doing research" for a term paper is not a one-step process. It may involve Internet searches, conferring with a librarian, taking notes on what you read, etc. In that case, the subgoal itself has subgoals; we could call them sub-subgoals! Even they could branch into yet smaller tasks, which is why I labeled this way of thinking a *subgoal tree* at the beginning of this section. For now, I'll stick with just one "level" of subgoals. Because few students carry out even this degree of planning, you'll be way ahead of the game if you are one of them. Why put it off? Successful managers and executives in the after-college world think this way all the time. Deadlines are a fact of life. Learning to cope with them effectively is another skill that will help you no matter what you do after you graduate.

Construct your master calendar by the end of the first week of classes. It will display your academic goals for the term and their subgoals. When you first try, you may not be very good at determining how much time the subgoals take. In that case, you'll need to make adjustments as the semester proceeds. That's okay; it's a living document. I advise you to overestimate the time you think you will need for each major subgoal. There is an ironic "rule of life" that comes into play here:

Things take longer than they do.

Given this "rule," it makes sense to allow for the likelihood that, indeed, it will take you longer than one Thursday afternoon to gather and read the research materials for your paper on, say, the method of financing railroads during the American Civil War. Like the generals of that or any other war, by developing a goal and subgoal time map you will be using the time-honored strategy of divide and conquer. Major projects can be overwhelming, but if you divide them into subgoals, then the smaller pieces become manageable—especially if you complete them on time. Here is another benefit of such an approach: You will soon get a reputation for reliability, for being someone others can count on. That, too, is a highly valuable trait that will follow and aid you in your career after college.

CRITICAL THINKING AND THE SUBGOAL TREE

To construct and schedule your subgoals, you will have to clarify and analyze the problem (i.e., determine your goal) as well as the steps and timetable to reach it. Evaluating problems and coming up with a solution strategy is a key feature of what commonly is labeled *critical thinking*. By itself, the term *critical thinking* conjures up something abstract and perhaps mysterious. In contrast, determining a goal and setting up the needed subgoals and timetable involves concrete steps. You know when you've done it. You readily can practice the skill of setting up goals and subgoal trees in your college assignments. Doing so will increase your chances of success. More important, it is one of the most valuable skills you can develop during your college years because it applies to huge numbers of situations and challenges you'll deal with later. To be a critical thinker is to be a valuable member of any group.

Time Urgency

Constructing your master calendar can be a sobering experience even when done at the end of the first week of classes. Students tell me that they often get a sense of time urgency just by carrying out this simple organizational task. It becomes apparent that if they want to do well in their courses, then they have to do something toward one of their subgoals *now*, today. That's good. It's much better to get some time urgency early in the term when you can deal constructively with it than to panic about it later. No one is around anymore to tell you to study after dinner;

you left that life when you graduated from high school, if not before. Your calendar, with its subgoals telling you what you have to accomplish this week, is the needed substitute—and the sign of an executive's approach to managing something really important: your time.

While we are speaking about the *now,* I want to underscore something about this book. I urge you to immediately implement the tips provided here. Unlike some courses in which the application of what you learn occurs later on life's calendar, the material we're discussing is appropriate for your current courses, your current calendar, and how you use your time today. The sooner you put the tips into practice, the sooner you will benefit.

And also with respect to *now,* remember that you can predict now when your final exams will occur. Make sure they are on your master calendar (both time and place), and put sizeable blocks of time on it to prepare for each one. Also, once you've got the syllabus you'll know more about the nature of each final exam; for example, will it be a cumulative exam, one covering all the course material, or an exam that just covers the last part of the course? That information can help you plan the likely amount of time you'll need to get ready for it. Putting the exam schedule on your master calendar will keep you from going to your professor during the last week of class to ask if you can take the final early because you booked a nonrefundable airline ticket on a flight that leaves just hours before the scheduled exam. That request may not be met with a sympathetic ear.

If you attend to it, you'll notice that the "rhythm" of exams differs in different types of courses. For example, math and language courses tend to have frequent quizzes, but introductory social science courses such as psychology and economics may have only a couple of hour-long exams or midterms. Naturally:

The fewer the opportunities to show what you know, the more important each one is.

Block out your exam-preparation time accordingly. If you are taking a math class, language class, or any other course that requires frequent homework or reading, add time slots for doing that work.

Class Time, Course Time, and Work Time

It is very easy to underestimate the amount of time that university courses require. Many students get some form of financial aid, and that aid, especially if it comes from the Federal Government, normally requires one to be a full-time student to get the full amount of aid. Full time may be defined as 12 (or more) credit hours, that is, four 3-credit courses. To most people, 12 or 15 hours does not sound anything like full time; it sounds more like a vacation. But this number was not chosen at random. The workload associated with college courses is much greater than for high school courses; you have to allow plenty of time for the out-of-class readings, papers, projects, and so forth.

A commonly stated rule of thumb is that you should plan on 3 hours per week outside of class for every hour in class. Thus, for 12 credits you need to plan for 36 hours outside of class. However, a big problem with this informal formula is that in the early weeks it tends not to hold. The coursework, lab work, paper assignments, projects, etc., simply don't take up that much time. That can lead to overconfidence, overbooking social events, or planning to work more hours at an off-campus job. Later in the term, the time demands go up and may—and usually should—get to the 3:1 ratio people talk about. Thus, while class time may equal 12 hours, the total course time may be over 40 hours, especially later in the semester.

The time you spend in outside work for pay should be added to course time, not to class time. Given that, how much can you "afford" to work? Studies show that, on average, there is a negative effect on college performance when outside work exceeds 20 hours per week. Though not a huge effect, these results lead me to recommend that you work off campus even less during your first semester. We'll discuss this topic more when we talk about finances in Chapter 14, but for now:

Keep your priorities straight—school before work.

If you don't, you may soon find yourself without the chance to have a choice between school and work.

Some students, especially transfer students, have additional high priority items: for example, a spouse or partner and children. Faculty members will be sympathetic to doctor's notes when children get sick; children have to be a priority, of course. Balancing family and school responsibilities along with the demands of work is not easy and must be assessed on an individual basis. In addition to the school-before-work priority, I feel it is better to reduce the number of credits and to make steady successful progress toward a degree rather than to overreach and then have to drop courses you've already paid for.

Your calendar may now be getting a bit crowded—12 or 15 hours of class per week at first seemed like a dream schedule, with tons of free time or time to work at an off-campus job. But the calendar reveals that your free time is not so free. In effect, you are managing all of your courses simultaneously by using this organizational tool. Or, perhaps more accurately and more important, you are managing yourself.

Creative Procrastination?

> Perhaps the most valuable result of all education is the ability to make yourself do the thing you have to do, when it ought to be done, whether you like it or not; it is the first lesson that ought to be learned; and however early a man's training begins, it is probably the last lesson that he learns thoroughly.
>
> —*Thomas Huxley,* Technical Education

I've put it off long enough; we should give some consideration to the procrastinators. It's easy to be critical of them, but perhaps there is such a thing as a *creative procrastinator,* someone who believes that "it doesn't matter when I do the work, just as long as I get it done by the deadline." That seems sensible. The really creative procrastinator may say something stronger: "Working up to the last minute creates motivation and excitement that I can harness to do a good job—I do my most creative work under pressure." "Furthermore," this procrastinator may add, "because I'm more efficient when I work under pressure, overall I get more free time and have less stress."

Alas for our supposedly creative friend, research on this topic definitely does not support this belief. For example, in one project psychologists studied college students who identified themselves on a standard questionnaire as either procrastinators or not. The students then were tested both for performance on exams and assignments (e.g., writing a paper with a deadline) and for symptoms of stress (e.g., visits to the health center and the number of health-related symptoms they experienced in the past week). Early in the semester the procrastinators had somewhat fewer symptoms than the nonprocrastinators, so it looked good for the laid-back types. But it didn't last. Later in the term they had a much larger number of health symptoms, and their performance on the exams and on the paper was much poorer (Tice & Baumeister, 1997). Similarly, another study (Hartwig & Dunlosky, 2012) found that differences exist between the highest and lowest achievers as measured by GPA, "with the lower achievers focusing (a) more on impending deadlines [the procrastinators], (b) more on studying late at night, and (c) almost never on planning their study time" (p. 133).

What is most creative about procrastinators is their ability to make up a good story about why putting things off is beneficial. Those stories are a cover up, though, a bit of self-deception that is also self-defeating.

The time map (your master calendar with lots of subgoals) will be especially useful if you have any tendency toward procrastination.

Time to Get a Life

Finally, you should also use your master calendar for the time-consuming parts of your social life. Don't keep these two calendars separate because they are not separate in your life. Going to the out-of-town game affects your ability to turn in the paper on Monday. Once you're used to making and using the calendar, and disciplined in managing your college time, then perhaps you can realistically plan to finish the assignment early and hit the road. But, to repeat, I recommend against doing that during your first term. That's the time to prove to yourself that you have the self-discipline to manage your time effectively.

It's okay to get a life—you were planning to do that anyway—but get a good one.

If you volunteer to tutor a child learning to read or to help build a Habitat for Humanity house, or if you join a Greek letter organization or any other group with structured social activities, put the expected meetings and other events associated with your extracurricular activities on the master calendar. Also, put on it time for exercise or sports; time for the predictable chores of life (e.g., doing laundry or even eating regularly); and if you need to work, the hours committed to your job. You are just fooling yourself if you don't include these items. However, the clock and the calendar do not fool easily.

Recall that there are two Rules of Time Management: Prepare for the predictable, and allow time for the unpredictable. The master calendar allows you to accomplish the former. How about the latter? One way to deal with the unpredictable is to avoid scheduling yourself so tightly that you can't afford to have something unexpected happen—a case of the flu, for example, or a heartbreak in your love life. Alternatively, you may find that you've hit a wall in your math course and nothing is making sense. To succeed with it, you have to devote additional time to that course. And, honestly, sometimes that one party is more important in the scheme of things than tonight's homework. As the T-shirt (inaccurately) says, "You can always make up a test, but you can't make up a party." (It's inaccurate because not all tests can be made up.) If you haven't totally overbooked yourself, you can afford the occasional unscheduled party, of course recognizing that your actions have consequences for you.

In my administrator jobs I found that the unpredictable easily could take up 10% of my time, and some weeks it was more. Of course, given that we're talking about the unpredictable, I didn't know which weeks those would be. We have to be ready as best we can anyway. The way to do that is to have a few spare hours each week that you can redirect to your priority issues. Sometimes you might have to borrow them from your recreation time. If that happens, don't forget to pay them back—after the final.

Summary

College success requires an understanding of the college culture; a commitment to manage one of your most precious resources—your time; and a way to help ensure that you regularly advance toward success. Gaining an overview of the big picture will help you get the most from college. You will quickly develop an initial mental map of the physical layout of campus (in particular, the locations of your classes), though that representation will be missing some useful information that I'll help you add as we go along. Constructing a time map allows you to see what you need to do each week and each day. It provides a tangible and realistic picture of what you have to accomplish and therefore reduces your stress and the chance you will pass up the splendid opportunities that college brings. Failing to take advantage of those opportunities is one of the biggest sources of regret in people's lives. The key to constructing a useful time map is to be explicit about your assignments and exams, as well as your work and social obligations (the goals), and also to be explicit about the major actions (the subgoals) you must carry out to reach those goals. By constructing a goal and subgoal tree you will boost your chance of successfully completing any project, both in college and after. Setting up goals and plans to reach them is a key aspect of critical thinking, a highly valuable skill both in college and after. Also, these planning tools help prevent procrastination, which has been shown to lead to bad outcomes all around.

TAKE ACTION— NAVIGATE YOUR FUTURE

1. Construct a master calendar for this term using your course syllabuses. Put all your class and lab meetings on the calendar, as well as all exam and assignment due dates. Then enter all regularly scheduled or time-consuming additional commitments (e.g., social club meetings, on- or off-campus work schedule, holiday travel commitments).
2. Add the most important subgoals to your master calendar. For example, if you have a lab report due, enter the day when you will write that report.

3. Pick a major assignment from one of your classes (e.g., a term paper, a laboratory project). Set up a detailed goal and subgoal tree for that assignment; add the dates by which you will meet each of the subgoals.

EXPLORE YOUR CAMPUS

Without looking at a source, try drawing the campus map. Indicate the library, the recreation center, the student union, the location of your classes, the health center, and the career center. Then print out an actual campus map and locate each of these sites on it. Also, is the campus divided into "districts"? For example, is there a science district and an arts district? (Tip: Fine arts facilities often have lovely, out-of-the-way spots that can inspire you to study.)

SELF-TEST ITEMS AND SELF-REFLECTION ITEMS

1. What is the number one regret people list when asked to look back over their lives?
2. What is the difference between class time and course time?
3. State in your own words what we know about the effects of procrastination on college students.
4. What is the difference between a goal and a subgoal?
5. What is a time map?

ACING ACADEMICS ‖

How to Study Effectively

3

I heard from people that the methods of studying, taking notes, and preparing for tests in college are different from high school. I'm kind of scared, since I have to find those methods by myself based on experience.

Studying just blows and takes up too much of my free time.

I really do like the freedom in college. No one tells me where to go, what to do, and when to do it. That is a good thing because now I have to take the responsibility on myself and take care of myself because no one else will do it. So if I screw something up it's my own fault and I can't blame it on anyone but me. But on the other hand, when I accomplish something I know it was all me, and that's a good feeling.

—Students' reflections on starting college

Where Are We Going?

A superb way to become a successful student is to duplicate what experts do to become excellent at their craft. By the end of the chapter, you will be able to describe how experts get that way. You will know the importance of having a concrete goal and why it is critical to know where you are in relation to that goal. You will be able to explain the importance of

http://dx.doi.org/10.1037/14181-003
Your Complete Guide to College Success: How to Study Smart, Achieve Your Goals, and Enjoy Campus Life, by Donald J. Foss

self-assessment and list ways you can carry it out. In addition, you will be able to distinguish between massed versus distributed practice and know which is better, and you will be able to describe the "testing effect" and state its benefits.

The first student quoted above is understandably uneasy. He thinks he has to figure out by himself how best to study and prepare for exams. Also, he probably believes that the more hours he studies, the better grades he'll get, and he is worried that he won't have enough time to do well. Happily, though, research on these topics has yielded clear pointers. There is no need for him—or you—to rely on trial and error to discover what works best. I'll provide those pointers in this chapter and the following ones. The good news is that studying smarter is much better than studying longer.

What Do You Actually Do When You Study?

When he was a young man, one of my professors, Dr. Calder, lost a hand in combat and received what we would now consider a very primitive replacement—a metal device, not so different from the one used by Captain Hook in Peter Pan. When Dr. Calder thought our attention had flagged, or that no one was brave enough to work the problem he was discussing, he would occasionally bang his hook against the blackboard with such force that a student dozing two classrooms down would wake up startled. In other words, he believed we should be attentive and active learners!

Dr. Calder liked to call on people and, to my shock, in the first few days of the course he learned my name. After that, he would call on me. He would do it whether I was sitting tall and looking him in the eye or I was making myself very small and concentrating hard on the name scratched into the desk many years ago.

I couldn't escape unless I stayed away. But it was foolish to stay away because his teaching was much more systematic and clear than the book was. And he was funny—except, of course, for the times he was calling on me. I was often grilled and sometimes cooked. However, I learned a tremendous amount from Professor Calder because I had to do all the homework on time, and I had to pay close attention to what he was saying. Most important, I had to keep track of my progress in the course: Almost every day I had to be aware of what I knew and what I didn't know.

You may not be called on all the time, but you want to be prepared as if you will be. In addition, you'd like to learn in the most efficient way, getting the most out of your study time so you can add more social time to your master calendar. You can.

We know a lot about the most efficient and best ways to learn, though there is still much we don't know. There are some shortcuts, but the truth is that to master material, you have to put in time. This is not a "simple" truth, however, because to learn the material efficiently you have to use the time in particular ways.

Before you read on, it will be instructive if you take a couple of minutes to think about and write down how you currently study (or review what you wrote in response to the Take Action question at the end of Chapter 1). That is, what do you *actually do* when you study? After you've done that, let's see how it compares with what the experts do.

HOW THE EXPERTS GET THAT WAY

If you participate in sports or play a musical instrument or are devoted to a video game, you know that it takes time to develop a skill, whether it's the serve in tennis, playing Chopin on the piano, or shooting down many alien invaders. Experts in sports or music practice for thousands of hours to reach international performance levels. Of course, you don't need to spend that kind of time to get a good grasp of college algebra, chemistry, or world history, but you do have to commit time to learn the subject matter well enough to make good grades in a college course. However, how you use that time makes a huge difference in how much and how fast you learn.

Experts do not just put in the hours of practice. Here is a solid finding, and perhaps a surprising one, from psychological research:

Practice does not make perfect.

And here is another one:

Amount of time spent studying is not a very good predictor of college grades.

When you think about it, though, and remember that many people play a game for years and do not improve much, these results are not so surprising. Quite a few people, probably most, out on the golf driving range or shooting free throws do not improve their actual game by such practice. Doing something over and over does not necessarily make you better at it. Helpful practice has to be attentive or "mindful"; you have to pay attention to what you're doing and to strive explicitly to get better at it. If—and only if—a driving-range golfer or a soccer player has a target and strives to get closer and closer to it, and if the player gets meaningful feedback on what he or she is doing, then that person will improve. Ditto for the pianist and violinist.

All the evidence says that the same is true for learning college algebra, accounting, French, or psychology. Learning college material requires attentive, goal-oriented practice along with constant assessment and proper feedback. You can waste a lot of time "studying" for your courses unless you copy what the experts do. That is one reason why pure "amount of time spent studying" is not a very good predictor of college grades. Diligence—putting in the hours—is necessary, but it is not sufficient. You have to be smart about how you use the time.

WHERE ARE YOU IN RELATION TO YOUR GOAL?

Let's use the idea of a goal again, though in a slightly different way. Your goal in each course is to learn the material to the point where you can display your knowledge and apply it in new situations. One important place where you will apply it is on the next exam. A key idea, perhaps the single most important idea, is to:

> **Be aware of your present knowledge state and know how far it is from the goal.**

When practicing effectively, the "student" of golf or soccer wants to get close to the target. To say it more precisely: As the practice goes along, he or she wants to reduce the average distance between the intended target and the place where the ball actually ends up. To accomplish that, the student must pay careful attention to his or her progress toward that end: Where was I aiming? Where did the ball actually go? What do I need to do to get closer next time? Help me out, Coach!

Similarly, when you are a student of chemistry or French or economics, you want to reduce the distance between your present state of knowledge and where you want to be: your target or goal state. To do that, you must make a realistic assessment of what you currently know and how far it is from what you need to know. This is sometimes called *metaknowledge*—that is, knowledge about your state of knowledge.

You will help yourself enormously if you develop the habit of monitoring (assessing) your current knowledge and paying attention to how far away it is from where you need to be. In other words, of being aware of what you don't yet know but need to learn.

GOAL: Goal-Oriented Active Learning

Let's coin a term to represent this approach to learning. I'll call it the *GOAL* method, which stands for Goal-Oriented Active Learning. The *goal-oriented* part reminds you to be clear about what you have to know (e.g., all those terms in bold print at the end of the chapter) or what you have to be able to do (e.g., play from memory a new piece of music, solve a quadratic equation). It also reminds you to verify and be aware of what you can do now (your current level of knowledge or skill) and how far it is from the goal state. Then you have to mindfully *act* to gain the necessary knowledge and skill so you can get to the goal. Thus:

- *Goal oriented* represents your goal, where you are now, and the current "distance" between them.
- The *active* part prompts you to take concrete action to reduce that distance and to get feedback on how well those action steps are working.
- Genuine *learning* will occur when you study in this mindful way.

A very simple example of the GOAL approach might involve learning a set of French vocabulary items. At the end of the week you'll be quizzed on, say, 20 terms related to cooking. Your goal is to know them all. You test yourself on Tuesday and find that you know four of them. Now you know what you do and do not know (you have good metaknowledge), namely, that you are 16 items away from your goal. You have to take action to learn those 16 items (we'll shortly discuss how best to do that). Of course, you will frequently evaluate how you're doing by seeing whether you've closed the gap to zero. (See below for another simple example from a French lesson.)

GOAL: Goal-Oriented Active Learning

Goal

- For Friday: Know the forms used to construct spoken questions in French (qui, que, pourquoi, etc.).
- Also, know the basic sentence structures for sentences.

Current State

- I know that qui = who, and that que = what.
- I know the sentence pattern when the subject is a pronoun.

Actions

- Memorize the other question forms (pourquoi = why, comment = how, quand = when, où = where, combien = how many, how much).
- Memorize sentence patterns when subject is not a pronoun (see the book).
- Practice by doing exercises from the book.
- TEST myself on English to French question translation.
- TEST myself on French to English question translation.
- Check results against the Goal and fix when necessary.

Many students have a tendency to avoid taking a clear-eyed look at what they actually know. It's not comfortable to realize that you're falling short of the goal. However, without doing an accurate and frequent assessment of your current knowledge state, you can very easily fool yourself into thinking you know more than you do. "I put in the hours," you may say to yourself, "so I'm doing the right thing;" or "I was able to follow along when the prof solved that problem in class; therefore, I've got it." In this way you can, and will if you are not careful, waste a lot of valuable time. To repeat our key study tip in slightly different words:

> **Be completely honest with yourself about what you know and what you don't. Then take steps to close the gap between your current knowledge and the goal state.**

EFFORT AND ACHIEVEMENT

Many students believe that if they work hard, they should get a decent grade, and some of them say that to their professors. These students think they deserve credit for trying, and perhaps that was the case in high school. However, professors find that attitude surprising if not shocking. They assign grades based on performance, not on time spent studying. You've got to reach the goal, not just work toward getting there. Therefore, it's a good idea to get close to the knowledge target in the most efficient way.

Also, many students have said to their instructor after an exam, "I knew the material, but I just couldn't answer the questions you asked; they weren't what I studied for." Or worse, "I know it, but I just can't say it." The latter is what I call the *myth of the ineffable*. Things that are *ineffable* are beyond expression, or indescribable, or literally unspeakable. Thus, these students are saying that they just cannot find a way to express something that they really know when they're asked to do so aloud or on paper. Now that might be acceptable when we're talking about one's feeling for a piece of music or the scent of mint, but I and other professors don't accept it when students have been asked for the definition of a term like *greatest common factor of a polynomial* in algebra or *marginal utility* in economics, or when presented with a problem that asks them to apply those concepts.

When a student says to me that he "knows it but just can't say it," I adopt the role of Dr. Calder: "Here is a piece of paper and a pencil," I say to the student. "Just jot down for me . . . " and then I'll ask something simpler than the original question. Most often the student gets stumped very quickly. By the time he leaves my office we have come to an agreement on what his present knowledge state really amounts to. Only then, when the student has a realistic understanding of his actual knowledge, can he work on moving forward toward the course goal. *My goal on such occasions is to reveal to him, in a somewhat sugarcoated and helpful but nevertheless direct way, the self-delusion that he was living with. In other words, I have to reveal to the student the terrible state of his metaknowledge. When that happens, we can find a way to move from his current knowledge to a more desirable state: one close to the knowledge that he needs to do well in the course.

Visiting your professor or teaching assistant to get a check on your current knowledge can be highly useful, and I recommend doing so. But you will benefit even more if you develop the habit of routinely carrying out an honest self-assessment. In other words, you can become your own Professor Calder by calling on yourself! You need to be as relentless as he was, calling on yourself even when you'd much rather be ignored for the day. If you can't really answer your own questions, you have to admit it. That's often a frustrating moment, but it's an important step to wisdom. Then, of course, you must act on your assessment and put in some additional time mastering the material—getting close to and then reaching your knowledge goal.

THE EFFECTIVE STUDY GROUP

In addition to calling on yourself, it may help a lot if you get together with one or more students from the course and call on each other. There are many advantages to such cooperative work when done well. Let's say you find one or two "study buddies" for the course that most concerns you. If you set up a regular time to meet, say once a week, then the commitment to be ready for that meeting will help keep you motivated and on track. You'll want to keep your end of the agreement just as much as you want them to keep theirs. The group should agree that your meetings will cover work that each of you has accomplished—or tried to accomplish—on his or her own. The weekly meeting is not the place where you begin to do the homework, or begin to work on the questions or problems at the end of the chapter. Preparing in advance means that everyone will have concrete items to ask about or to discuss. (Some students decide to meet much more often, sometimes daily. In that case, it's okay to start the homework together.)

Also, and starting with the second meeting, each member of the group should take time to quiz the others on the week's material. The nature of the quiz will vary depending on the course topic and the type of exam that the professor has promised. It's important that the quizmaster of the moment be realistic in what he or she is asking—everyone should try to pick out material the professor will ask about. In many courses the textbook will have end-of-chapter questions or problems; those are obvious candidates for the quizzing process. Also, the attempt to form a good question is itself a very helpful step to organizing and understanding the material.

It is exceedingly important that every member of the group, especially you, should answer the questions either out loud or in writing. That is how you can get a realistic sense of what you know and determine in all honesty how far away it is from what you need to know. It's likely that one or more of your group members will be able to help you close that gap when you're having a problem, just as you will help them when you can. Everyone benefits when the group acts in this way. It's also great to give each other positive feedback when deserved. An upbeat meeting will help keep everyone coming back. But remember that honesty is the key point. A realistic assessment in a supportive atmosphere is the hallmark of a successful study group. Going out for a bite to eat afterward helps, too.

For now, the take-home message of the GOAL perspective is this: If you (a) know your goal—that is, know what you have to learn or be able to do; (b) realistically know how far you are from that goal—that is, you honestly know what you do and do not know right now; and (c) actively monitor your progress as you strive to get closer to the goal, then you will learn more and—if you follow the tips in the next section—you will learn it more efficiently. Therefore, you'll have more time on your calendar for other things.

How to Learn and Remember Most Efficiently

> To this point college has been the best experience of my life. I am very happy with everything associated with it except the amount of studying.
>
> —*A student's reflection on starting college*

In Chapter 2, I discussed the importance of a time map and a master calendar. Now I'll focus on getting the most out of the time you spend on your courses. Learning how to do that is incredibly important: One of the three best predictors of college success is simply whether you know how to study effectively and then put that knowledge into practice—in other words, your study skills, habits, and attitudes toward your college largely determine how well you will do. The other two top predictors of success are previous grades and standardized test scores, but those are already in your past.

Your study skills, habits, and attitudes are the top predictors of success over which you presently have control.

Of course, you don't want to wait until you feel pressed for time before you start using the best study techniques. The more effective and efficient you are as a learner, the better you will do and the more time you'll have for other things. So let's start now.

I've said that practice does not make perfect and that time spent studying is not a good predictor of amount learned or college grades. Don't misunderstand, though: Practice is important, and so is time spent studying—after all, you can't just breathe in the information and knowledge. But what you do and how you do it are more important than how long you do it. Here I will describe study techniques that are backed by evidence even though they are not all obvious, and in some cases, they may not agree with what you initially think works best. These techniques are related to one another, and you'll notice a couple of underlying themes. When you understand and accept those themes—when you "own" them—you'll be on your way to improved learning and test performance. Let's start with a simple question.

MASSING VERSUS DISTRIBUTING YOUR TIME ON A SUBJECT

Suppose you have 10 hours to devote to the material in a section of a textbook for, say, a biology course. How should you use those 10 hours? It seems reasonable to concentrate your efforts, setting aside 5 hours Saturday and 5 hours Sunday to focus on biology, rather than spreading your "biology time" out over an entire week or longer. Intuition tells you that immersing yourself in the topic will lead to quicker and more thorough understanding, and therefore to better memory. Not only that, when you focus on one topic for many hours you only need to warm up to it once. After a while studying seems to go smoothly— you get a real feeling of familiarity with the material.

On the other hand, when you set a topic aside and then come back to it later, it seems to require additional warm-up time to get back into it. Furthermore, that warm-up period seems to add difficulty to studying; it also feels like time wasted. Thus, the "concentrate-your-forces" strategy is a typical and common sense way to organize your reading and study time. In short, it feels right.

However, a great deal of research has convincingly shown that these common sense beliefs are in fact wrong!

It is much more effective in the long run to spread your learning out, to distribute it over days, rather than to concentrate it. For example, five 2-hour sessions distributed over 5 days is greatly superior to two 5-hour sessions concentrated in 2 days. Ten days of 1-hour sessions is better yet. Indeed, there is evidence that spreading out the study time for a topic over a couple of weeks leads to much better learning and retention than working on it over a concentrated weekend. (There are practical limits, of course: 600 one-minute sessions over a month is unlikely to be a good schedule!)

The "concentrate your forces" technique—known as *massed practice* and often amounting to cramming—can (sort of) work in the short run. But material studied in this way does not get firmly lodged in memory. If the material is needed only once, right now, and never again (not even a week later), then cramming may be able to get you through, but that is rarely the case. Most of the time you're going to need that material later in the course, or in the next course, or in a work setting at some point in the future. If you try cramming it in there by using massed practice, it won't be there when you need it later. Also, massed practice or cramming doesn't save time. In my example the student spent 10 hours on the material in both cases.

Imagine a swimmer preparing for an important swim meet. How should he or she practice? An hour a day for 10 days, or nothing for 9 days and then 10 hours the day before the contest? Here your intuition no doubt differs from what it was in the study example. In sports it seems much more plausible that *distributed practice* leads to greater improvement than massed practice—and it does. The sports analogy carries over to studying. Therefore:

Distribute your learning sessions for a topic over days; do not mass them into 1 or 2 days.

The distributed practice effect is big one; it can make a real difference in your grades. For example, in one experiment (Rohrer & Taylor, 2006), college students were given a set of 10 math problems to solve. Half the students got five problems to solve one day and returned a week later to solve another five (thus, they spaced their practice). The other half did all 10 problems in one sitting (massed practice). The students were then given a test either 1 week or 4 weeks later. Though the effect 1 week later was minimal, at 4 weeks there was a big difference in favor of those who had gotten the distributed or spaced learning. As the graph on the facing page shows, the accuracy in problem solving at the 4-week test was twice as great for those who had the spaced practice compared with those who had solved the same number of practice problems in a massed fashion. Thus, each day you should work on a number of your courses; except on rare occasions, don't spend all day Wednesday and Thursday cramming for one of them.

Your subjective experience of what works best, massed or distributed study, may not agree with what I've just told you. As noted, it's common for people to feel that massed practice makes the material easier. Don't be fooled, though; this is an illusion. Just as your eyes can

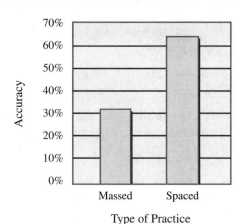

A comparison of massed vs. spaced practice and their effect on performance. Data from Rohrer and Taylor (2006).

be fooled by optical illusions, so your feeling of confidence can be misled by the immediate reward of massed study. It (sort of) works in the short term, but as psychological scientists such as Robert Bjork (1994, 1999) at the University of California, Los Angeles, have convincingly shown, it does not work in the longer term. Let's call this phenomenon *Bjork's illusion*—the impression that massed practice is better than distributed practice. It's not. We now know that making the effort to recall the material from memory as you warm up the next day is similar in one respect to giving yourself a little test. Tests add difficulty, but they also help you recall the material over the longer run. In other words, some difficulties are actually helpful. Let's look at that more closely.

THE TESTING EFFECT

You must honestly assess what you know and what you don't in order to make good progress toward reaching your learning goals. But how much of your study time should you allocate to such self-assessment? Realistically, you are going to spend limited time on your studies, and it may seem that devoting much of it to self-testing, or having a classmate test you in a study group, is robbing from that study time. Is it?

To find out how much time you should dedicate to being tested, or testing yourself, let's imagine three groups of students who spend time studying (S), or being tested (T). Assume that, altogether, the students in each group spend equal amounts of time on the material.

One group, we'll call it the *study condition,* organizes their time like this:

S S S S S S S S. That is, there are eight periods of study time.

Another group, let's call it the *minimal test condition,* organizes their time like this:

S T S S S T S S. This group has six periods of study time and two tests over the material.

The third group, the *many tests condition,* has even fewer study periods and more self-test periods (four of each). They look like this:

S T S T S T S T.

Finally, there is one more test—the one given by the professor—that everyone takes 2 days later. Now we ask: Which group will do better on the professor's test?

Your intuition will probably favor those in the study condition; most people think that's the winning technique. After all, those in the study condition spent twice as much time studying (eight study sessions) as did those in the many tests condition (just four study sessions). Once again, though, and as shown in a study by Zaromb and Roediger (2010), our intuitions are misleading us in a big way. In fact, trying to recall the material, and trying to use it to answer a question or solve a problem, helps you remember that material even *better* than reading over it again, or underlining it. The apparent advantage of study time versus time spent being tested is another illusion. Again, this is a big effect, as shown in the graphs on the following page. What predicts the ability to recall is *not* the number of study periods, but rather the number of prior tests!

It turns out that being tested, or honestly testing yourself, does two really important things. First, it shows you what you know and what you don't know—it's the way to develop your metaknowledge. Second, it helps protect the information in your memory from being lost. In other words:

Testing *is* a form of studying, and a highly effective one.

This outcome is called the *testing effect.* You will increase the amount you learn and remember, and improve your exam performance, if you devote a large fraction of your study time to being tested. Trying to retrieve information from memory, or to produce or generate an answer, has a positive effect on the amount you learn and remember in the long run. Some scientists (e.g., Karpicke & Grimaldi, 2012) prefer to call the testing effect by another name, the *retrieval effect,* in order to emphasize the importance of actively trying to recall information from memory. In short, rather than robbing from your study time when you test yourself, you actually are increasing the effectiveness of that time. You can get a sense of the testing effect yourself by reading the material shown on page 54 and answering the questions posed there.

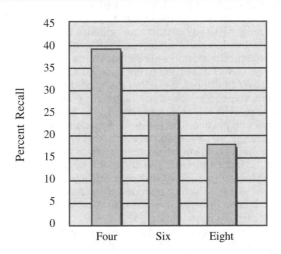

Number of Study Periods

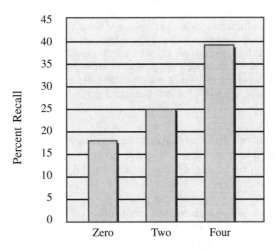

Number of Prior Tests

Relationship between number of study periods, practice tests, and recall. From "The Testing Effect in Free Recall Is Associated With Enhanced Organizational Processes," by F. M. Zaromb and H. L. Roediger, III, 2010, *Memory & Cognition, 38,* p. 998. Copyright 2010 by Springer Science+Business Media B.V. Adapted with permission.

Example of Self-Generated Test Items and the Testing Effect From an Actual Reading

In his classic book *Teaching Tips,* McKeachie (1986) advised beginning college teachers to create classroom environments that maximize student involvement. An advocate of student-centered learning, he cited considerable evidence that class discussion, compared to lectures, increases motivation and facilitates critical thinking. Discussions afford students the opportunity to evaluate their comprehension of course content and apply concepts. Even instructors of large classes are urged to encourage student comments and questions.

Those who take his advice undoubtedly find many of their classes receptive to opportunities for interaction. In others, however, discussions may never occur or become productive. Furthermore, whereas some students profit from increased involvement, others . . . remain silent and passive. This is especially problematic for students who despite being confused take little or no advantage of instructors who not only provide time for discussions and questions in class, but offer other forms of assistance as well. McKeachie (1986) proposed that the lack of interest and knowledge, habitual passivity, fear, and embarrassment are reasons why students do not contribute to class discussions. After all, students do take risks when offering opinions; they can be easily ridiculed as well as rewarded for seeking needed information or clarification in (public) classrooms and even in the privacy of faculty offices (Karabenick, 1990).

Creating effective learning environments means recognizing, and minimizing, such impediments to involvement, which includes increasing students' willingness to seek assistance from others when necessary. Cultural norms that stress independence are part of the problem. More than in most societies "going it alone" is a maxim to which many American parents and undoubtedly many teachers probably subscribe. This is reflected in . . . [approaches] that define the ideal learner as one who accomplishes tasks on his or her own, *without* assistance from others (e.g., Winterbottom, 1958). In their view, seeking assistance from others is antithetical to academic achievement. . . . This chapter reviews evidence suggesting that such a unidimensional approach is too narrow. It fails to distinguish between relying on others as a substitute for involvement and employing them as an important resource in the learning process, that although seeking assistance may manifest dependency, it can also represent an important component of a mature strategic approach to learning (Karabenick & Sharma, 1994, pp. 189–190).

You can try rereading these three paragraphs to be sure you get the main points—or, alternatively, imagine that you or a member of a study group have created some questions based on these paragraphs. Then try to explicitly answer them; write down what you think. For example:

1. What does McKeachie believe about the desirability of classroom discussion? According to him, what can it provide for students?
2. List three reasons given for why some students might not participate even if the instructor encourages it.
3. The article talks about an American view (a cultural norm) of the ideal learner. What is that view?
4. Do the authors of the article agree with that view? What alternative do they suggest?

After you've finished trying to answer the questions, check your responses against the three paragraphs. Note the difference in how engaged you are with the material compared with simply underlining it.

Quote from "Seeking Academic Assistance as a Strategic Learning Resource," by S. A. Karabenick and R. Sharma in *Student Motivation, Cognition, and Learning: Essays in Honor of Wilbert J. McKeachie* (p. 189–190), P. R. Pintrich, D. R. Brown, and C. E. Weinstein (Eds.), 1994, Hillsdale, NJ: Lawrence Erlbaum Associates. Reprinted with permission.

Effective Studying and Desirable Difficulties

Here is a paradox to summarize the main point and to help you remember it. If we take "studying" to mean what most people first think when they hear the term—that is, studying means reading and rereading the book, highlighting or underlining parts of it, plus reading over your notes and highlighting them—then:

"Studying" is not the most effective way to study!

Instead, study effectiveness goes way up if you devote lots of time to self-testing (or testing by a classmate) and giving yourself (or getting) feedback about how you do on that testing. The testing effect is a big one, much bigger than you first expect. Indeed, a recent summary of the research concluded: "The most consistently effective technique seems to be self-testing . . . taking a test on material sometimes more than doubles retention compared to . . . restudy of the material" (Weinstein, McDermott, & Roediger, 2010, p. 308).

I want to emphasize again how much these findings are counter to what most students think and do. For example, one student wrote to me, "I don't think the 'test yourself' idea is realistic." And another said, "I think it is impractical to test yourself as much as the book suggests." These reactions are not surprising. When a large number of college students were asked about their study strategies, rereading was favored as a strategy almost eight times more often than self-testing (84% vs. 11%; Karpicke, Butler, & Roediger, 2009). However, when it comes to the effectiveness of study strategies, the minority rules: The 11% are correct. Not only that, they generally are the students who do well. Other researchers have found that "almost all of the most successful students (GPA > 3.6) reported using this strategy, and its reported use declined with GPA" (Hartwig & Dunlosky, 2012, p. 131). We'll discuss a related topic—tutoring and why it works—in Chapter 9.

The testing effect, on the one hand, and the advantage of distributed practice over massed practice, on the other, have two things in common: First, they work, and second, the winning strategy does not fit with your intuition. The superior strategy is the one that initially does not feel like it's the winner; it feels more difficult: Distributed practice seems harder than massed practice, and testing yourself (or being tested by a classmate) seems much harder than rereading or restudying the material.

These effective study techniques introduce what are called *desirable difficulties* (e.g., Bjork & Linn, 2006; Richland, Linn, & Bjork, 2007). They are desirable because they force you to pay close attention to the material and to connect it with what you've already learned. And as previously mentioned, these winning strategies provide you with up-to-date knowledge about how you are doing as you work to reach your goals—the metaknowledge that helps you stay honest with yourself. The desirable difficulties are desirable not because they are difficult (some difficulties are just annoying), but because they have these useful properties—and therefore because they work! Yes, the desirable difficulties may lead to some discomfort. But so does getting in shape to participate in a sport. The "stretch" is part of it.

WHERE DO GOOD TESTS COME FROM?

Let's assume you're convinced about the value of the testing effect, or at least convinced to give it a solid try. Where, then, do you get the material for the tests you give yourself or your study mates? There are some obvious sources. Many textbooks have back-of-the-chapter questions, and you should explicitly try to answer them (obvious, indeed!). In math and science books there will be plenty of problems given in the books, and the professor may hand out or post additional ones. Also, it is a good idea to use the chapter headings as a guide to developing questions. It's reasonable to assume that the main points will be signaled by something as simple as the size of the print or the number of pages devoted to the topic. You can ask yourself to explain the terms used in those headings or to give a 1-minute summary of what you learned in that section of the book (see, e.g., the four questions at the end of the above sample reading).

Somewhat less obvious, perhaps, you can find problem sets at many Internet sites via a bit of searching. Some of those sites may also post tips on how to solve the problems or show the complete solution along with the steps it took to get there. The answers and hints are nice, of course, but for sure *do not skip over the attempt to solve the problems yourself.* If you do skip trying to actually solve them, you are merely humming the tune and not singing the words; in that case, you will not get the benefit of the testing effect.

Some professors make available copies of old exams. They are a diamond mine of useful information about the exams to come and provide one of the best ways to test yourself. Other professors will hand out sample questions to give you a sense of the type of item that will be on the exam and the level of detail you are responsible for knowing. If your professor does not volunteer to provide sample questions, ask him or her to consider it. Also, if the syllabus is not clear about the type of exam, go ahead and ask about it. The question "Will this be on the test?" is not as helpful as the question "What type of test items will be on the exam?" As we'll see later, your preparation strategy will differ depending on whether the exam is multiple choice, short answer, essay, or problem solving.

Your class notes provide the raw material for other questions you can ask yourself or your classmates. We'll discuss note-taking in Chapter 5; for now, it's sufficient to say that the topics highlighted by the instructor, and the examples or problems discussed in class, make good sources for questions. Can you solve a problem that has the same or similar form to the one discussed in class? If not, you need to learn how.

Before moving on, let's look at one more reason for you to trust and make use of the testing effect. There is evidence from an experiment with college students that those who made up at least three relevant questions per week over the course material significantly improved their exam performance. This effect was particularly strong for students who initially were not doing well in the course. That's a good reason to stick with a commitment to make up questions every week. If you do that, then on the real exam you won't have to make up answers; instead, you'll know them.

WHEN AND WHERE TO STUDY

We've talked about the advantages of distributed rather than massed practice for acquiring knowledge that sticks. Having made that point, I want to caution that you also don't want to be overly choppy in your study habits. You do need time for uninterrupted work. There are mornings, afternoons, and evenings, and you will find time blocks in between classes, labs, etc. Suppose you have 2 hours between classes. "How should the student use this time?" asked Richard Light (2004, p. 92). He listed alternatives ranging from chatting with friends and running errands, to getting some physical exercise, to studying. He then said something wise: "There is no single correct thing to do. Rather, whatever he chooses, the key point is that it should be done with some thought" (p. 92). I'll put it this way: You should be mindful in assigning yourself appropriate amounts of time to meet the subgoals of the week. No one tells you what to do and when to do it. As usual, it's up to you.

You may be advised to find a quiet place to study and to use it regularly for study and not for anything else. This is good advice, but only in part. You do want to find study spots that allow you to concentrate on your work without interruption. However, what you are able to remember is partially associated with where you learn it. If you study in the same place all the time, you will be able to recall the material better when you are in that place than when you are somewhere else—for example, in the classroom where the exam will take place. It will actually help your long-term recall if you study in a few different locations so you get used to recalling the material in a variety of settings, which is, after all, what you need to do.

Furthermore, I advise my students to do some reviewing and recalling right in the classroom, if they can manage it—to sit in the eventual testing room late some afternoon when it no longer is in use as a classroom and to work at recalling the important course material. I recommend, in other words, that they (and you) carry out a self-test in the same setting where the real test will be given.

MULTITASKING WHILE STUDYING

Try this little test on yourself. First, count to 10 out loud as quickly as you can—time how long it takes you (probably a bit over a second). Next, say the letters A through J as fast as you can, again timing how long it takes you. Then, put them together—count from 1 to 10, then switch and say the letters A through J out loud—and time that sequence. I can do it in a little over 3 seconds. Now for the interesting part: Interleave the numbers 1–10 and the letters A–J as quickly as you can out loud (that is, say 1–A–2–B, etc.) and time that. The first time I tried it, it took me more than 10 seconds. There is a big penalty for mentally switching back and forth between these two tasks, each of which is very easy by itself. You can think of that time increase as the penalty for multitasking, and take it to heart when you're tempted to try to do two different things at once (driving while texting, for example).

While studying, you should not frequently interrupt yourself with other tasks such as electronically communicating with friends or "site-seeing" on the Internet. There is often a multitasking penalty for such frequent self-interruptions. However, please don't confuse this advice—that is, to avoid multitasking and frequent interruptions—with the advice to distribute your learning rather than engaging in massed practice. Both are valid. We've already stated that you're better off studying, say, math for an hour or two, then switching to psychology. Such distributed learning is not the same as quickly jumping back and forth between a social network site and your math; only the latter counts as a "frequent interruption." In other words, it's all right to switch when

Attention Switching Difficulty

Time yourself on these four tasks:
- Counting from 1 to 10.
- Saying the alphabet from A to J.
- Counting 1 to 10, followed by saying A through J.
- Saying 1 – A – 2 – B . . . 10 – J.

the time on the topic is measured in, say, a unit as long as 45 minutes or an hour. That kind of interleaving of topics is okay; it allows you to distribute your learning, which is much better than just okay.

Summary

Learning takes time, but time is not the best predictor of how much is learned. Practice does not make perfect. Instead, effective and efficient learning requires mindful practice. In turn, mindful practice requires having a goal (knowing what you need to know), assessing how far you are from that goal, and learning what to do to get closer to the goal. When you know these things, you are said to have good metaknowledge. Honest self-assessment, perhaps with the help of others, is a critical component to making good progress in your college work. Also, the most efficient ways to learn are not always the ones that feel right or are easiest. For example, distributed practice is superior to massed practice, and frequent self-testing is much more effective as a learning strategy than rereading the material. In general, some difficulties are desirable because they require active mental processing and they facilitate an honest look at what you know.

TAKE ACTION

1. Pick the course that you have most concern about. Set up a study group of two or more students. If you are not sure how to begin, consider posting your idea about a study group on the course website, or asking the instructor to help find others who are interested by passing around a sign-up sheet, or asking interested people to stay after class for a few minutes to exchange contact information. Don't forget to put the meeting time on your master calendar.

2. Make up five short-answer questions from the previous chapter. Make up five from this chapter. Find a partner who will do the same, and ask each other the questions. Also, do the same with the study group or study partner you set up in response to Item 1. Each of you should make up five questions from each of the initial chapters in the text for that course. Honestly assess how well you can answer those questions—how far are you from your goal?

3. Review your master calendar with respect to how you've arranged your study time. Also, take a look at what you wrote in response to the question at the end of Chapter 1, "What do

you do when you study? Again, the important word is *do*. Jot down the things you do and the order in which you do them." If necessary, revise your calendar—and your study habits—so that you gain the advantage of distributed practice.

4. Write a personal goal statement for each of your courses. How close are you to reaching those goals? What can you do to increase your chances of meeting all of them?

EXPLORE YOUR CAMPUS

Does your college have a place where you can get help with mathematics if you feel you're hitting a snag? with writing? If so, locate it on your campus map.

SELF-TEST ITEMS

State in your own words:

1. What is metaknowledge? Why is it important?
2. Describe the difference between massed and distributed practice.
3. Evaluate the claim: Practice makes perfect.
4. Explain GOAL.
5. What is the testing effect? How can you take advantage of it?
6. You read in this chapter that studying is not the most effective way to study. Explain this claim.

Strategic Reading | 4

I have *so* much reading to do for my classes . . . I have to read for psych and I haven't even started reading for Biology II.

I am about 3 days behind in all my reading for almost all of my classes. I don't know if I will ever get caught up. I have so much reading to do and I need to start on it but I am afraid I will fall asleep.

I have realized that life can be much more exciting and interesting if I am completely honest with myself as well as those around me. I have also found a new interest in my homework. I have never in my life done any sort of homework, but now I do not only enough to get by but more than I have to, because I have this drive that I have never had in the past.

—*Students' reflections on starting college*

Where Are We Going?

Though you are a good reader, you can be a better one if you become strategic in how you approach your reading assignments. This chapter will provide the basic tools that will allow you to read faster and with better comprehension. By the end of the chapter, you will know how to use the goal-oriented approach to reading, along with your assessment of the reading

http://dx.doi.org/10.1037/14181-004
Your Complete Guide to College Success: How to Study Smart, Achieve Your Goals, and Enjoy Campus Life, by Donald J. Foss

materials and your prior knowledge, to appropriately adjust what you do when you read. You will be able to describe and implement the various action steps that will make you a strategic reader. You also will learn when and how to significantly increase your reading speed. In addition, you will be able to describe the similarities between effective studying and effective reading.

t's common for college students to feel swamped by their reading assignments ("I have *so* much reading to do . . . "). Three things contribute to this feeling. First, it is simply true that the amount of reading per course is much greater than it was in high school. Second, there may be a lot of unfamiliar material, which slows your comprehension speed. And third, the level of understanding that is expected by the professor is likely to be greater than what you are used to. College courses require both attention to detail and a sense of the big picture—for example, how does this material relate to what was said in the lecture, or to what you've been told in another course, or to what was presented in this course 6 weeks ago? Rather than get bogged down, though, we need to avoid this swamped feeling.

Reading is one of the great all-time human inventions, maybe the top one (Huey, 1908/1968). It gives us access to worlds we'll never directly see and to the ideas and feelings of others, including people who lived long before us. But learning to read is not "natural" in the same way that learning to speak is natural. You had to make an effort when you learned to read, and it will take a little effort to get better at it. But without doubt, you can get better.

We've all had the experience of reading for a while, our eyes darting back and forth across the page, and then all of a sudden realizing that we don't have any idea what we've just read. That kind of passive or mindless reading is clearly a waste of time. Effective reading requires us to be mentally active. Exactly how you do that—how you are active and how you approach the material—affects what you get out of the time you spend reading.

You're a good reader, but how good? Students who have spent lots of time reading and have developed large vocabularies tend to be more comfortable with a college textbook than those who spent their earlier years doing other things. Also, readers differ in how much they already know about the material covered in a particular text. Not surprisingly, familiar material goes down more readily than less familiar or new information. That's because what you read has to make "mental contact" with what you already know, and then your knowledge must be adjusted or updated. Reading is relatively easy and quick when the new material smoothly fits in with what you know. In contrast, when there are lots of new ideas or new vocabulary items in a passage, you have to do some time-consuming mental work to connect them to what you already know and to update that knowledge. College reading assignments usually present lots of new material, which slows down reading speed. Happily, persistence yields a big benefit:

The more you know, the easier it is to know more.

Understanding Your Goals and the Author's Goals

You are a good reader, but you can become a more effective one if you are *mindful,* or *strategic,* about how you read. The strategic reader takes a purposeful and thoughtful approach to reading. The strategic approach has a number of components, many of which are completely consistent with the now familiar Goal-Oriented Active Learning (GOAL) approach. It takes some getting used to, but becoming a strategic reader has a big payoff.

Reading is—or should be—affected by your purpose and goals. Are you reading in preparation for a multiple-choice exam, an essay exam, or a term paper? (I'll revisit this topic when I talk about preparing for tests.) Are you reading to learn how to do something, such as carry out a procedure in a chemistry lab? Are you reading to update your knowledge of the latest news crisis or to find out what's happening with your favorite music group? Or are you simply "reading for pleasure"—to be taken out of yourself and into an imagined new world (Mulcahy-Ernt & Caverly, 2009)? To get maximum value out of your reading time, what you do differs somewhat in each of these cases.

When reading to acquire new knowledge or to learn a new procedure, it's important at a minimum that you pick out and understand the basic ideas presented in the reading assignment. Suppose you've decided to underline or highlight the main points in, say, a chapter in a history textbook. When I first got to college I overdid it, highlighting huge amounts of such a book. I joked to a friend that the book weighed more than when I'd bought it because of all the additional yellow ink. Rereading what I'd highlighted didn't help much because it took me almost as long as rereading the whole book. If you don't know what to highlight, or are tempted to highlight too much, that's a sign that an important basic reading skill requires work. In particular, you need to get better at figuring out just what constitutes the main points.

To determine those points, stop and ask yourself what the author is trying to accomplish in that part of the book. In other words, one of your goals is to work out the author's main goal for the section or chapter. Fortunately, the author often will simply tell you. After you get into it, you may also get a sense of the author's subgoals, too. (Yes—thinking in terms of the goal and subgoal approach also helps greatly in reading, just as it did in studying.) In other words:

> **One of your main goals is to determine the author's main goal; another of your goals is to figure out the author's subgoals.**

"READING" AND *READING*

Previewing the chapter before you start reading can help you clarify your goals and subgoals and those of the author. Such previewing is actually an important part of the reading process. In other words, active reading requires more than just scanning your eyes along the print. For the moment, I'll put "reading" in quotes when I'm referring to moving your eyes back and forth across the page. And I'll italicize *reading* when I'm referring to the deeper, strategic, or thoughtful reading processes.

From the wider perspective, then, you are already *reading* when you take a look at the summary at the end of the section or chapter, when you look at the initial material where the author may explicitly state the goals of the chapter, and when you page through the section looking at the main headings and subheadings to get a further idea of the subject matter and how it's organized. You should do all those things before you start "reading." Not only that, you are already *reading* if—after you have done the just-mentioned previewing—you jot down a few questions about what is to come. Then, as you "read" the material, write out the answers to your questions as you come to them. When you do that, you are on your way to being an active, strategic *reader.*

Some students have said that being strategic seems like overkill for something as simple as reading. My response is to ask about something even simpler, for example, running. When you start to run, you usually have some idea of the distance you're trying to cover, and you adjust your pace accordingly. Also, the pace you adopt depends on the shape you're in, how hot it is out, and whether there are some hills ahead. In other words, you assess yourself and the situation, and you respond accordingly. In three other words, *you are strategic.*

FINDING THE MAIN POINTS

Though it's highly useful to be able to detect the author's main points, and that's what we'll return to momentarily, it may be that those points are not the same as yours. As just stated, how you approach the material depends on your purpose. If your goal in reading the chapter is, for example, to see what the contribution of women has been to the topic (and assuming that was not the author's goal), you will highlight different parts of the text than you would have if you were reading to get the author's perspective.

Take a look at the passage below and on the following page. In it I've ruthlessly pared down the first paragraph of this section to show its main points. Then I show the supporting points. The technique used to find the main points was pretty straightforward: I deleted everything I could while trying to leave the most important material that would make sense when read alone. If you're not confident about what to underline or highlight, or what to jot down as a summary of what you've read, practice finding the key points by cutting out everything you can and see if you agree that the result stands by itself and provides the high calorie content of the paragraph. You're not on your own, though, because the text itself provides useful signals. For example, the phrase *in other words* tells you that what follows is redundant with something already presented and therefore is probably not the main point. On the other hand, being told that something is *actually an important part of the reading process* is telling you . . . well, that it actually is important. Note, too, that many of the main and the supporting points are directions for action—instructions on what you should do. With practice, you can get good at picking up these signals and thereby speeding the process of figuring out the important material.

Finding the Important Points While Reading

Main Points

<u>First Main Point:</u> Previe~~wing~~ the chapter before you start reading [That] can help you clarify your goals and sub-goals and those of the author. ~~Such previewing is actually an important part of the reading process. In other words, active reading requires more than just scanning your eyes along the lines of print. For the moment, I'll put "reading" in quotes when I'm referring to moving your eyes back and forth across the page. And I'll italicize~~ *reading* ~~when I'm referring to the deeper, strategic or thoughtful reading processes.~~

~~From the wider perspective, then, you are already~~ *reading* ~~when you take a look at the summary at the end of the section or chapter, when you look at the initial material where the author may explicitly state the goals of the chapter, and when you page through the section looking at the main headings and sub-headings to get a further idea of the subject matter and how it's organized. You should do all those things before you start "reading." Not only that, you are already~~ *reading* ~~if—after you done the just-mentioned previewing—you~~ <u>Second Main Point:</u> jot down a few questions about what is to come. <u>Third Main Point:</u> Then, as you "read" the material, write out the answers to your questions as you come to them. ~~When you do that, you are on your way to being an active, strategic~~ *reader.*

Main Points and Supporting Points

First Main Point: Previe~~wing~~ the chapter before you start reading [That] can help you clarify your goals and sub-goals and those of the author. ~~Such previewing is actually an important part of the reading process. In other words, active reading requires more than just scanning your eyes along the lines of print. For the moment, I'll put "reading" in quotes when I'm referring to moving your eyes back and forth across the page. And I'll italicize~~ *reading* ~~when I'm referring to the deeper, strategic or thoughtful reading processes.~~

~~From the wider perspective, then, you are already~~ *reading* ~~when you take a~~ First Supporting Point: look at the summary at the end of the section or chapter, ~~when you~~ Second Supporting Point: look at the initial material where the author may explicitly state the goals of the chapter, ~~and when you~~ Third Supporting Point: page through the section looking at the main headings and sub-headings to get a further idea of the subject matter and how it's organized. ~~You should do all those things before you start "reading." Not only that, you are already~~ *reading* ~~if—after you done the just-mentioned previewing—you~~ Second Main Point: jot down a few questions about what is to come. Third Main Point: Then, as you "read" the material, write out the answers to your questions as you come to them. ~~When you do that, you are on your way to being an active, strategic~~ *reader.*

It is almost impossible to be a passive reader when you interact with the text in this way. When you ask yourself questions about what is to come, or stop for a moment and ask yourself to state explicitly the main and supporting points, then the material will make mental contact with what you already know and with other things you are learning. Among these few steps, the last one, the little test or quiz you give yourself, is the easiest to skip—but as we've seen before, you must not skip it because once again:

Self-assessment is critically important.

ASKING THE RIGHT QUESTIONS

Asking yourself questions about the reading material helps guarantee that you will actively attend to what you read. But that raises the question: What kinds of questions? Some possible ones would be just silly. You would never ask yourself: How many words in this paragraph start with the letter *t?* In contrast, a factual question about, say, the date of an event described in a history text might be a good one and would be a good one if you know that the instructor will hold you responsible for knowing the dates of key events. More likely, though, a valuable question will start with "why" or "why not" or "how" rather than with "when" or "who." Compare the question "When did World War I start?" with "Why did World War I start in August 1914?" If you can address the "why" question, you certainly will know a lot more about what was going on and why it was happening than if you can only answer the "when" question.

Here are two summaries of some research on the topic of question type: (a) "students in a psychology course who used factual questions in a study guide scored higher on quizzes than those students who did not respond to the questions" (Brothen & Wambach, 2000, as cited in Mulcahy-Ernt & Caverly, 2009, p. 186) and (b) "when students . . . answer 'why' rather than 'what' questions . . . [they] are able to recall more information, identify more accurate inferences, and create more coherent mental representations of the text than students who merely re-read the text for understanding" (Ozgungor & Guthrie, 2004, as cited in Mulcahy-Ernt & Caverly, 2009, p. 186). You might have noticed that the first quote referred to questions from a study guide. Useful questions can come from such a guide, from the end of the chapter, from one of your study buddies, or you can make them up yourself. The important thing is to ask them and to be able to answer them. Of course, it really helps if you know what kinds of questions will be on the exam. That's a good question for the instructor.

When you learn how to address "deep" why questions, you are on your way to actually learning the material and to being really educated. To be blunt, although knowing facts is important, we don't need many college graduates who just know the facts; indeed, we usually can find the needed facts at Wikipedia or in a scholarly source. We do, though, need people who can put information together in new ways, who can figure out how things are connected and why. By becoming a strategic *reader* you also are preparing yourself to be a strategic or critical thinker and therefore getting ready to be a sought-after graduate.

READING TO TEACH: ANOTHER DESIRABLE DIFFICULTY

It's commonly said that the best way to learn something is to teach it. That's because you can't fake it—teaching a concept requires you to be explicit, to spell it out. Preparing to teach a topic requires effort, but it is a "desirably difficult" way to ensure that you've really understood what you've read. Thus, it can help you greatly if you write out a summary or an outline of the material as though you're going to use those notes to teach the topic to someone else. Over the years I've found this to be the best technique for me. To convince myself that I know the material, I've got to produce an outline or perhaps the draft of a presentation on the topic. If you can do that, especially if you can do it without looking back at the book, then you've probably got it. If not, you have more work to do—perhaps including just learning more of the background material needed to be able to make a sensible outline. Either way, you'll know where you stand.

Recall again what we've said about the importance of metaknowledge, of knowing what you presently know and how far away it is from your target. To gain that metaknowledge, you need to test yourself and to "grade" your self-test. Without explicit self-assessment you are just guessing whether you've learned what you need to know. And as we now realize, that guess easily can lead to self-deception rather than to self-knowledge. Also, your current performance on an honest self-assessment reasonably predicts how well you'll recall the material later.

This change in how you read is a bad news/good news story. The bad news is that it initially takes more time to *read* than to "read" (though you'll likely save time in the long run; for one thing, you won't be spending as much time in simple and not very effective rereading), and it takes some getting used to. The good news is that you are in the driver's seat; you determine how much you'll get out of your reading time. The other good news, and it's really good, is that it is known to work. Those who carry out this learner-controlled testing method recall up to twice as much as students who just read and then reread the material. That's huge (see Callender & McDaniel, 2009; McDaniel, Howard, & Einstein, 2009).

SPEED READING

We've mentioned that how you read should be affected by your purpose and your goals. When reading a magazine, a news blog, or a fan update about your favorite band, Nails on the Blackboard, you can instruct yourself to read very quickly—it's not hard to double or triple your "natural" reading rate (which is probably something like 300 words per minute).

There are at least two reasons why you can go fast. First, you already know much of the material. The new stuff easily makes contact with what you know, and you're likely not adding much to your knowledge—or at least the new material is not complex even if it is highly interesting. As a result, comprehension goes fast. Second, there usually isn't a lot at stake if you don't get it all. If you miss the Nails on the Blackboard update today, you'll hear about what's going on from another fan or easily figure it out when you next read about them. You therefore can zoom through the article. On the other hand, missing a key concept in, say, your economics textbook can hobble your understanding of the rest of the material. You can't zip through that chapter.

To summarize, you can modify your reading speed by understanding your purpose in reading the material and by figuring out how much of that material you need to understand. This is another instance of how you can benefit by being strategic or purposeful while studying.

That brings us to the question, Is there such a thing as speed reading? We sometimes hear about people who are said to read many thousands of words per minute. Do they exist? My answer is: Sort of. I can *read* an introductory psychology textbook enormously fast. You might "read" such a book at 300 words per minute, while I *read* it 10 times faster. I've italicized *read* for me, because I don't bother passing my eyes over every word; I actually skim most of the material, looking for what themes are emphasized, what material is covered at what depth, and similar issues. I've "read" enough Intro Psych books so that by now I know the material that most of them cover. As a result, I now can *read* them fast. It would be foolish if I spent the same amount of time "reading" as someone new to the topic must put in. In other words, speed readers can go fast because they already know most of what is in the text; they can skim.

I've already said that you should take advantage of the fact that you can monitor and modify your reading speed in accordance with what you need to get out of the material. And, anyway, it's the recall and recitation time that is most important to your learning, as you now know. I'll return to this topic when I look at how you can best prepare for college tests. The type of test you're preparing for should also affect how you read.

Six Steps to Strategic Reading

Because active reading and self-testing can make such a big difference in what you remember, let's review the process. Studies have shown that this method leads to much better recall than simple reading and rereading. Modifying and updating the excellent advice developed from the pioneering work of Francis Robinson (1946/1970) over 60 years ago, we can break it down into six simple steps:

> *Step 1*. Ask yourself what you expect to get out of the chapter. How will you be different in a couple of hours—what will you know or be able to do? When you carry out that exercise you are, in effect, figuring out what the author's goal(s) were for the chapter. Usually you want to align your understanding with the author's aims.
>
> *Step 2*. Preview the material. Previewing what's coming can help you by letting you know up front what the author considers the important concepts in this part of the book. Previewing is

done by flipping through the chapter or section and looking at the headings, and by reading the summary of the material that is at the beginning, or end, or both, of the section or chapter. The preview also activates the relevant knowledge you already have on the topic, which will make "reading" easier.

Step 3. Jot down some questions about the material. Or if there are questions/problem sets/new vocabulary items at the end of the chapter, look at them.

Step 4. Read through the material, highlighting or otherwise marking the high-level text, especially if that helps you concentrate and keeps you active.

Step 5. Test yourself. Strategic reading involves your assessing whether you understand the key terms and concepts. To do that, you have to close the book, look up, and explicitly state in your own words what you've read. Even better, write down what you think are the important ideas, formulae, or key concepts. Also, answer the questions or work the problems that are at the end of the chapter, and answer the questions you wrote down at Step 3.

Step 6. Compare your statements and your solutions to the information in the text. That's the feedback part of the process. Remember what I said about actually improving when trying to learn in sports or music—namely, that you have to honestly assess how far you are from the desired goal. Same here: How far apart are your statements from what the author wrote? Try grading your self-quiz on a 5-point scale.

I know that this all sounds like overkill, and occasionally it might be. But remember that the time you spend recalling the material, along with the time you take to ask yourself questions and answer them *explicitly,* is time very well spent. If you go back to the book after that, you will fill in many of your knowledge gaps. Simply rereading without self-testing is a poor use of your time. And self-testing, even if you don't

---

Six Steps to Strategic *Reading*

---

1. Ask: What do I expect to get out of this chapter? What will I learn or be able to do when I'm done?
2. Preview the material.
3. Write out some questions about it.
4. "Read" the material, highlighting the high-level text.
5. Test yourself. State in your own words what you've read.
6. Evaluate your test results—get honest feedback.

---

reread, is a good use of your time. I've emphasized the term *explicitly* because some people, I'm one of them, have an initial tendency to "hum" the answer to their question rather than to "sing" it—in other words, to say to themselves, "Oh, sure, I got it," or, "Oh sure, I can recall that stuff," without actually stating what it is that they "got." That is a form of self-delusion. Professor Calder would scoff at you (as he did me) and bang the blackboard.

Reading and Studying: Putting Them Together

Now let's put the ideas of GOAL, distributed practice, and strategic reading together. The GOAL approach asked you to spend much of your time recalling the material, posing questions to yourself, and answering them. So does the strategic reading approach. On Day 2, you should quiz yourself on what you read on Day 1. On Day 6, can you answer the questions you jotted down on Day 4? If so, you are doing very well. For one thing, you are distributing your learning. In addition, you are frequently checking your state of knowledge and therefore are being a highly active learner. The time you spend testing yourself, reciting the main points of what you've read, providing your own summary, etc., is extremely valuable to you. Together, these goal-driven activities will definitely lead to improved retention of what you read.

Even so, the reality is that you still will make mistakes when studying in this active way. On Day 6, you may not get the correct answers to the questions you wrote down on Day 4. As indicated earlier, that may lead you to conclude that this way of reading and studying produces more errors than if you simply massed your reading and active learning and asked yourself the questions at the end of a long study section. Also, it feels more difficult to do all that previewing, questioning, and self-testing and then looking up the right answers. But please don't be a victim of Bjork's illusion. These are desirable difficulties. There is substantial evidence that long-term learning and recall is greatly aided by following the path I've described. You will not only learn more, you'll be more efficient—you will learn more per hour than if you mass your study time and if that time is spent "reading," underlining, and rereading.

Incidentally, while you are making up questions, you can speculate about what quiz questions you would ask if you were the instructor, and of course you'll make sure you can answer them. There is a good chance that you will actually figure out some of the actual exam items. That's a bonus.

Think once again about athletes trying to excel at their sports. They spend some time "reading" the material—for example, studying a book or a playbook, or watching how it's done either on film or in person. But they can watch until the next Olympics and have no chance of doing well unless they become active; in other words, unless they attentively and actively practice—with feedback, of course. The same techniques that work for them will work for you.

I mentioned earlier that raw study time was not a very good predictor of college grades. Now we know some more reasons why. If you read and study using the previously described methods, then overall you are likely to spend less time, and learn more, than equally diligent students who put in the same, or even more, hours in an inefficient way. The key to efficiency and success is being strategic and goal-oriented in both your reading and your studying.

Summary

Effective reading requires you to be strategic—to take into account what you know about the topic, to understand your reading goals, and to monitor your comprehension. At a minimum, you want to pick out the author's main points and the primary supporting points. I've provided tips on how to do that with unfamiliar material. Monitoring your comprehension requires you to ask yourself questions about what you read. In general, the most useful questions require you to process the information deeply; these are questions that require you to give reasons rather than just facts—for example, questions that begin with "why" or "how." The chapter presented a six-step method for strategic reading. There are great similarities between it and the procedures that result in effective studying. Both rely on active assessment of where you stand with respect to the goal of the day.

TAKE ACTION—NAVIGATE YOUR TEXTBOOKS

1. Go back to the section on the testing effect in Chapter 3. Write down that section's main points and the most important supporting points. If you are uncertain, make two copies of the section and, on the first one, cross out everything except what you consider the main points. On the second copy, cross out everything except the main points and the important, second-level support points. Compare your work with that of a classmate and give each other feedback. Alternatively, practice finding the main and second-level points in a section or chapter of a text for another class that you are taking.

2. Make up five questions covering the material in this chapter or from the section or chapter of a book you use in another class. It is important to make sure that two or three of them begin with "why." The aim of this exercise is to make sure you understand the reasons for the points made, not just what those points happen to be. Ask a classmate your questions, and try to answer his or her questions. Provide feedback for each other.

3. Time yourself as you read approximately 1,000 words from a newspaper or magazine. Then time yourself as you read approximately 1,000 words from one of your textbooks. Note the difference in ease of comprehension as well as the time to complete the task. Why does this difference exist? Now jot down the main points from what you read in each case. Any difference in how easy that is? Why?

4. Read another 1,000 words from a newspaper of magazine. This time, push yourself to read very fast. Write out the main points. Note whether there are any speed and comprehension differences from the newspaper/magazine reading you did in number 3.

EXPLORE YOUR CAMPUS

Until they visit it, many beginning college students are not aware that the college library likely subscribes to numerous magazines, newspapers, and other "light" reading material. It also will have audio and video multimedia resources, both related to classes and for more recreational purposes. Visit the reading room to see what's there.

SELF-TEST ITEMS

State in your own words:

1. What is strategic reading?
2. Is there actually such a thing as speed reading? Explain.
3. Describe the difference between "reading" and *reading*.
4. Describe the typical steps involved in strategic *reading*.
5. What do strategic reading and studying have in common?

Going to Class With Class 5

It doesn't matter what your IQ is, or what you made on the SAT, if you don't go to class for a month, you will not do well. They should put that in the next Bulletin.

—A student's response to the dean's letter dismissing him from the university

Eighty percent of success is showing up.

—Woody Allen

Where Are We Going?

You will take three or four dozen college courses, and the majority of them will involve three- or four-dozen lectures. In this chapter, I will explain how to get the most from the approximately 1,500 hours you will spend going to those classes. To get those benefits, you need to capture the most significant information presented by the professor—by paying attention, by successful note-taking, and by effectively using those notes as you review for exams. By the end of the chapter, you will know how to improve your attention, and you will learn the best techniques for spotting and "encoding" the most valuable lecture points

http://dx.doi.org/10.1037/14181-005
Your Complete Guide to College Success: How to Study Smart, Achieve Your Goals, and Enjoy Campus Life, by Donald J. Foss

and the chief supporting material. In addition, you will learn about useful note-taking styles. You will also be able to describe how best to use the notes—possibly with classmates—including how to use them in your program of self-assessment.

Millions of college students spend hundreds of hours taking notes each semester. If we were to convert that note-taking time into the equivalent of full-time, year-round jobs, there would probably be a million of them! Bottom line: You will spend a lot of time listening to lectures and taking notes from them. Let's be sure that you do it effectively and efficiently, and that you get the most from your time in class.

Although college teaching methods differ depending on the course material and the preferences of the professor—for example, science classes typically have a combination of both lecture days and laboratory days, and fine arts performance courses may have a great deal of one-to-one interaction—many of your classes will involve a professor lecturing about the course topics. The style and pace of lectures are quite different from high school. For one thing, the lecture material often supplements rather than duplicates the reading material. Also, the expectation about what you will learn from the lectures is greater than in high school. Given all that, you may share a concern expressed by a student at the beginning of a previous chapter: "I heard from people that the methods of studying, taking notes, and preparing for tests in college are different from high school."

Getting the Most Out of Lectures

The first thing I have to say about lectures is: Go to them. You don't want to be like the student quoted at the beginning of this chapter who just blew off going to classes. He had willfully challenged "the system," and after he got the dean's notice dismissing him from the university, he wrote me a letter filled with immense regret. In one sense, this student was really smart (that is, he had high test scores). However, he did not have a good mental map of university culture; said differently, his level of "street smarts" about college was low. He also wrote, "School was always easy for me growing up, and I quickly got in the habit of relying on my superior intellect instead of developing serviceable study skills . . . I did OK [early in college] and just assumed things would continue on as they had always been. I could not have been more wrong." He blew a big scholarship, his family's respect, and more; he now has a towering challenge to do what's necessary to get back in the university. You can avoid this fate.

There is a getaway car full of published evidence that he is right: If you want to do well, you should go to class. Nevertheless, it's a fact of college life that lots of students skip class. I think there are three reasons why.

One is intoxication with the newfound freedom to determine their schedules. These students feel that cutting class shows their independence and confers on them a cloak of bravado, a hint of the rebel—they can't be bothered with such an ordinary way of dealing with college life as actually going to class, especially after a night of partying. Normally such students are not doing as well as they could be and as they pretend to be; many are at risk for academic trouble.

The second reason is more understandable: Some students have real conflicts. They may have to choose between working extra hours and going to class, they may have child-care responsibilities, or health issues may deter them. Many professors will have empathy for these students and try to work with them, but that is not guaranteed. Virtually all professors believe that students are responsible for prioritizing their time. In Chapter 14, we'll talk more about working, finances, and college, and I'll show how and why the decision to take a short-term financial gain can lead to major long-term losses. The priority issue is a real one, but in general, finishing college and doing so on time is the best option.

The third reason for skipping class is the belief that the instructor is not presenting enough "value-added" material. As a result, students think they can do all right simply by reading the textbook or other materials; they imagine they don't have to attend to do well. Although at times this may be true (it temporarily worked for the student who got dismissed), it's not as common as many students think. As one student wrote while reflecting on college life, "The frequency of skipping most likely increases because the student has no idea what he is missing. It is kind of like a drug to many students."

Some colleges provide electronic access to lectures in selected courses, which allows students to catch a lecture they had to miss for unavoidable reasons. It also allows them to manage more of their time by "attending" the lecture when they choose to do so. In addition, electronic access permits students to review a lecture they attended but found difficult in spots. These are all positives. It is tempting, though, to skip the live lecture with the intention to "look at it later." I believe that is a mistake. It encourages procrastination and allows things to pile up; it also works against the advantages of distributed learning.

Overall, the positive relationship between attendance and grades is a strong and very solid finding from the research on what determines college success (Credé, Roch, & Kieszczynka, 2010).

This story has a very simple moral:

The most obvious way to benefit from the material presented in the class is to be there to hear it.

Though Woody Allen famously said, "Eighty percent of success is showing up," in fact, after he showed up he obviously paid attention and did a lot more. Just as you will.

As mentioned, there are different types of college courses. We'll focus here on the most common type, the "standard" lecture courses offered in such areas as humanities (e.g., history, literature, philosophy); social science and business (e.g., psychology, economics, finance); and many science classes, especially introductory ones (e.g., biology, physics). Other types (e.g., laboratory sections, recitation meetings, and performance classes) involve variations on the basic themes, although the underlying principles are similar.

ATTENTION

What should you do to maximize the benefit you get from a lecture? Psychologists who have studied this topic break your mission into three parts: attention, encoding, and retrieval/review. The first part is *attention*. To learn something, you have to attend to it. Although that's obvious, we know that for many students there is a tremendous amount of class time when their attention is wandering—perhaps peeking at incoming messages or attending to the good-looking person three rows over. That's understandable, especially if the lecturer is speaking in a monotone, the material does not have a lot of intrinsic interest to you, or the material is just plain hard. Nevertheless, because you're there and you want to do well, there are some things you can do to increase the chance that you will be paying attention when the instructor gives that useful nugget of information that ties the topic together. Indeed, it just might be the keystone item that pushes you to the next level of understanding and to the next higher grade.

The first thing to do in controlling your attention is to arrange your life so that you can have a decent level of overall alertness. In other words, don't be exhausted when you enter the classroom. Students in general, and first-semester students in particular, are famous for adopting lifestyles that skimp on the sleep time. As one wrote:

> I am so tired. Not just the normal 'tired.' The stressed out, not really getting a break kind of tired . . . as if I am not really in control of what I'm doing, but rather just watching myself doing things in the 3rd person.

It's completely understandable that your newfound freedom, coupled with the great richness of things to do around most campuses, will tempt you to trade in 7 hours of sleep for 5 or 6 hours. However, a chronic lack of sleep and the dulled thinking that goes along with it is one of the ways to ensure that you will miss important information in the lecture. And you already know that it's hard to read effectively when you're sleep deprived. It is also is risky if you nod off. Your slumping head might crash into and damage a university computer. Who knows, that could subject you to a fine!

A second attention-control technique is to sit in a place that maximizes your chances of staying alert. For most people, that's near the front of the room, or in the center where the professor's gaze tends to focus. Immediately after Professor Calder began calling on me I started to look for out-of-the-way spots in his classroom. But I soon realized that he was not so easily fooled and, more important, that he was good for me. In general, I learned that I should pick a location that guaranteed I could hear the professor—especially if he or she had an accent—and one that ensured I'd really be embarrassed if my head slumped against my chest (okay, I didn't always follow the advice to get plenty of sleep). Even if the instructor does not call on you, it's smart to pick a spot that helps you stay attentive.

NOTE-TAKING—THE ENCODING PROCESS

> The notes are a series of separate entries. I can't see any coherence. . . . The lecture notes are fragmented; a fair number of sentences remain incomplete.
> —*Mike Rose (1989, p. 42), looking back through his freshman year college notes*

A very important way to stay attentive and active is to take notes. If you are writing down information and your reactions during the lecture, that activity itself will help control your attention and your alertness. So taking notes is one tool of self-control. But taking notes is important for three additional reasons: for the *process* of taking them; for the *product* that results—the written record of the lecture and your reaction to it; and finally, and most important, for their role in your *review* and *self-assessment*.

My own college notes were skimpy at first and not very organized—like those initially taken by author Mike Rose (1989), quoted above. Now, however, I know there is considerable evidence that the amount of note-taking is related to academic success (Kiewra, 1983; Kiewra & Benton, 1988). However, this does not mean the student with the fastest pen, or who can write in shorthand and get down every word, will do the best. Your aim is not to make a literal transcription of what you hear. How you take the notes, and what you do with them, are more important than just the sheer number of words captured.

Taking notes is a complicated and even slightly bizarre activity. Attentively listening to a college lecture is itself a complex mental act. And writing down something coherent from that lecture is another complex behavior. One involves language comprehension, and the other involves written language production. When you take notes you are doing both (almost) simultaneously, which requires substantial mental work. It helps that you are writing down something related to what you hear, because it is almost impossible to process two distinct topics at the same time—you can't comprehend the lecture while sending plans for the evening to a friend.

Without training or giving some careful thought to the process of note-taking, the typical college student does not take very good ones. For example, some studies have found that students take down only about one fourth of the critical ideas. A survey of studies on note-taking concluded that "college students probably only record somewhere between 20% and 40% of lecture information" (Armbruster, 2009, p. 225). Furthermore, the evidence suggests that they run out of fuel, recording more of the important material early in the lecture hour and less of it later.

When taking notes, you have to actively process what you hear and make judgments about what to write down. Your goal is to capture the main points of the lecture in an organized way. That's not always easy, but if your notes do that, you are already demonstrating some grasp of the course content. In addition, effective note-takers record the (relatively) important material that supports each main point. By your very decision about what to write down, you are making judgments about the material and how it fits into the big picture. Psychologists say that you are "encoding" it, by which they mean that you recognize the concepts and can relate them to things you have previously heard or read—or that you are building a fresh representation of the important ideas being presented.

Let's again consider a map analogy. The professor has in mind a representation of the day's material, and the lecture is trying to convey that representation to you. Your job is to create or capture that representation for yourself. Said differently, your map of the subject matter needs to become similar to that of the professor's. Your version usually does not have to be as detailed as his or hers is. But unlike the confused tourist in the cartoon on the next page, you have to build a representation of the major landmarks if you are to capture the route that gets you from your present location to your goal. You are encoding the new information in relation to the other information presented that day—or on previous days, or in your prior reading.

A FRIENDLY CIRCLE AND A BRAIN WIDE WEB

You can guess where that comment about "prior reading" is going to take me, and you will be correct. It is extremely valuable to read or

Illustration © The New Yorker Collection 1976 James Stevenson from cartoonbank.com. All Rights Reserved.

carry out whatever assignment has been specified for the day *before* you go to class. Most professors say something like that on the course syllabus, and there is a good reason for this advice.

In most fields of study you have to build up an understanding of the relationships among the concepts—in an economics course you need to figure out whether "marginal cost of goods" relates to "fixed cost," for example, and if so, how they relate. (The idea I introduced in Chapter 4, that you should *read* the material and not just "read" it, makes nearly the same point.) When you are trying to get a handle on new ideas and their interrelationships, there may not be a single, correct order in which to learn those concepts. That is, when you understand Concept A, it helps you to understand Concept B; however, the reverse is also true—you can understand A better if you already know B! So what happens in practice is a kind of "circular learning," but in this case, it is a friendly circle, not a vicious one.

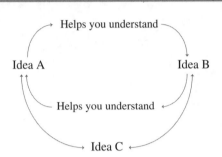

The nonvicious circle of ideas.

To start, you get a partial understanding of Idea A in the figure above; it still feels fuzzy, but you forge ahead and study Idea B. Because you previously got a partial grip on A, you now get a somewhat better understanding of B. Then you go back and think about A again, and you get a better understanding of it because you've learned some of B—though you're not quite there yet. And then you start to learn Concept C, and C helps you with both B and with A, and off you go. You are not building a simple list of ideas, but rather you are creating a knowledge network, a web of ideas for yourself, a "brain wide web." The brain web is one you spin yourself; therefore, you have to be active in creating it.

Students sometimes say that they don't want to read the material before the lecture because hearing the lecture makes the reading easier and more understandable. That's often true, so these students have a point. But it misses the main point. Not doing the reading in advance makes the lecture harder to understand and increases the chance that you will miss (or misinterpret) its main points. Your notes won't be as good because you won't have the proper background to help you encode the lecture material properly. In addition, you are missing a chance to relate the spoken lecture to the written materials just at the moment when you can quickly get some clarification if the relationship is not clear. How would you get such clarification? By asking a question when the instructor says, "Any questions?"! Or, if your instructor or the teaching assistant for the class invites electronic questions, you'll be able to send a good one.

To build an effective web of knowledge and make best use of the time you spend in class:

Read the assigned material before you go to the lecture.

Spotting the Main Points

To repeat: Your goal is to capture the important aspects of the lecture in an organized way. By *organized* I mean that you can make an initial judgment about the major points and the supporting ones and get them down in your notes. Recall our discussion about reading and selectively highlighting what you read. There I said that it takes some skill to decide what to highlight—to pare the written material down to the key issues. You have exactly the same mission when taking notes, except that the time pressure is greater because the lecturer determines how fast the ideas come at you.

Good note-takers learn to listen and watch for clues to what is important. We don't want to overthink this problem because it's not always mysterious. Indeed, it's often easy to tell what's important because the lecturer will be up front about it, saying things like:

- "The important point here is . . . "
- "The take home message is . . . "
- "Mastering this technique is the key to understanding . . . "
- "The four things you should get from this are . . . "

or some other pet phrase that he or she likes to use and that you want to be alert for. Then make sure that what comes next makes it into your notes.

If your instructor does not provide such clear signals, he or she may give others that can help. It's likely that you are about to hear something important right after the professor says things like:

- "As I've said . . . "
- "To repeat . . . "
- "Remember . . . "

or if he or she repeats material without saying that is what is happening. Again, if you pay attention—if you are mindful about it—you can figure out each professor's verbal clues to what is the high-level material.

Even in this electronic age, some instructors will write on an overhead or whiteboard. You want to get most of that into your notes. Not all professors choose to write just the top-level material, though. Sometimes they'll be clear about it, but sometimes you'll have to figure out as you go along—or later—just how important that written material is (top level, supporting level, a relevant example, or sometimes, something just off on a tangent).

Many professors will provide an outline, perhaps as part of a PowerPoint or similar presentation. For example, I often start a lecture by showing a written list of "Goals for the Day." The wise student will get those down in his or her notes. That's pretty obvious. However, research (Kiewra, Benton, & Lewis, 1987) has shown that:

Students who also get down the important supporting information (the second-level material) actually benefit most from taking notes.

In other words, your note-taking goal is to determine the professor's main goals, and your important subgoal is to determine, and get into your notes, the important supporting information. When you do that, your notes are on their way to being organized and helpful.

Taking Notes: Additional Techniques for Success

> Man, I've got way too many messy notes. Damn notes. Got to take care of some of those.
> —*A first-semester student writing about getting his notes organized*

We've gone over some initial tips on how to take good notes. Now let's expand that list with additional concrete suggestions. First, date or number your notes so you can be sure you've got them in order. It doesn't matter whether you put your notes in a loose-leaf file, or use a spiral notebook for each course, or put them in a ring binder, or store them in a computer file. For courses that have many handouts, it's probably better to use a three-ring binder (or scan them into a computer) and to put the notes, handouts, homework assignments, etc., all in the same binder (in that case, invest in a three-hole punch). Being organized helps, and it is useful to have related material stored together for easy reference.

NOTE-TAKING STYLES

Your goal in taking notes is to get down the main points of the lecture, along with the next level of supporting information. Another goal is to be critically engaged with the material. There are various ways to take notes that can help you do that. One common technique is to take "linear" notes, which is basically an attempt to get things down in order, in the same style as the words on this page. Generally that is not a very effective note-taking technique. Another is to divide the page vertically, and on the left one third to one half of the page write the headings, key comments, or thumbnail summaries provided by the instructor. On the right side put the supporting arguments or details.

A more common and very well-known technique was developed by Professor Walter Pauk at Cornell University and is known as the *Cornell Note-Taking System.* The Cornell system embodies the active learning strategies that we've been discussing. In this system, the right 6 inches of the 8.5-inch × 11-inch page (the note-taking column) is used for jotting down the basic ideas, definitions, formulae, and professor's comments during the lecture. The left 2.5 inches (the "cue" column) is used (normally after the lecture) to write down a word or two that captures each point from the note-taking column. You also can write in the cue column a brief summary statement of the main points, or jot down questions that help you see relationships among the points or between the lecture points and the reading. Finally, the bottom 2 inches of the page is used (typically also after class) to write a summary—to "distill a page's worth of notes down to a sentence or two" (Pauk & Owens, 2005, p. 208). You can see various templates for this system by doing a web search for *Cornell notes.*

Another way, and one that I like, is to make judicious use of indentations on a page. Whenever you judge that the instructor is presenting an important or summary point, or a key definition or formula, write that material near the left margin of your note page. Then indent supporting material below it and to the right. That allows you to see at a glance what you consider to be the supporting material for each major theme. It also allows you to have numerous "levels of detail" within each lecture depending on your choice of how far to the right you indent. This is called the *outline,* or skeletal, method of note-taking. I like this method because it helps keep you alert to the organization of the lecture and actively involved in it; you are constantly making judgments about the relative importance of the presented material. You can see in the example that I don't add letters and small numbers in the outline as I go because I don't think it necessary to commit to the number of levels—plus I know that two or three levels usually does the job. Too, I may want to modify the organization later when I review the notes. If you adopt this method, leave some white space between the lines or levels—paper is cheap. That will allow you to add additional material if the instructor remembers something a few minutes later and goes back with a clarifying comment. It also will allow you to write in your thoughts later when you review your notes.

As you take (and review) your notes—using whatever method you adopt—you can control your attention and deepen your understanding by inserting your own comments and questions. Remember, you are not a court reporter just copying down what is being said. You are a participant and a questioner, sometimes even a skeptic, trying to ensure that you are encoding the key points and organizing them in the notes, your "external memory." I believe it helps if you adopt some way of indicating what you think versus what the instructor says.

Outline notes on note-taking styles

3 styles most common
  I.   *Linear or "brute force" style*

     Attempts to get everything down.
     Uses approach of the novel—one sentence after another.

     Users often "run out of gas."
     Too hard to keep it up for whole lecture.
     Does not "naturally" show the organization of the lecture.

  II.   *Cornell System*

     Divides page into 3 sections.

      Largest (right side) tries to capture main points, key terms.

      Left side (done during or after lecture) = cue column.
      Puts down summary remarks. The "main" mainpoints.

      Bottom ¼ of page or so: used to write a summary in my own words. Good to use at review.

  III.   *Outline System*

     Uses indentation or roman numerals/Arabic to show organization of lecture points.

     Supporting points set to the right.

     Leave space for adding comments, evaluation later.
     Forces one to try to see outline as lecture happens.
     [But what if I don't see it??]

An example of class notes in outline format.

I am fond of using square brackets for my own thoughts. In college I decided to use square brackets for my thoughts so I could record in parentheses what might be a side remark from the instructor, a remark whose importance I wasn't too sure about. The brackets and parentheses then showed who was speaking, [me] or (the professor). But any regular scheme will do, and you can experiment with different styles until you find one that flows for you.

No matter what note-taking style you adopt, it's a good idea to do a quick review of the notes as soon after class as you can—while the material has a chance to be retrieved from memory. That's the time to fill in information that you did not get down during the lecture, to check with a classmate about what was said, and to ask yourself initial questions about how well you followed it. A quick e-mail to the professor asking about a concrete point will stand a good chance of being answered. (In contrast, those who foolishly write, "I missed the lecture, did you say anything important? Please send me what I missed," do not stand such a good chance.)

The important thing to remember is that your notes are an important aid to helping you understand the lecture material (your second effort—the first was reading the assignment in advance) and that they help ensure that you are an active participant in the lecture, both at the time it's given and later when you review it.

WHO SHOULD TAKE THE NOTES?

Many instructors present their lecture material via computer-based programs such as PowerPoint or comparable systems. When done well, these presentations add color and zip to the lectures, which helps keep your attention. Importantly, they also help the instructors present the course material in an organized way. Some instructors make these presentations available via the web; some even post their own notes on the web, either before or after the class meeting. Does this mean that the need to take notes (or the desirability of doing so) is going away? There is not a lot of research on this topic, though there are varying opinions. The existing research suggests that there is an advantage to taking your own notes, although at this point the evidence is not conclusive. However, and for sure, there is an advantage to having notes and reviewing them, whether they are your notes or the instructor's. At present, then, I recommend that you take your own notes and compare them with the notes you subsequently get from the instructor's website if they are posted there.

NOTES AS AN AID TO METAKNOWLEDGE

When students do poorly on the first exam, I invite them to make an appointment with me. I might ask if they are willing to show me their notes, and some agree to do so. Often the agreement comes with some embarrassment because we may observe drawings of zombies, or hearts and arrows, or other—how shall I say it?—less-than-directly-relevant jottings in the notebook. But no matter, I tell them, I don't care about the extraneous stuff; what I want to see is what they have been getting down and some indication of its organization (and therefore their level of understanding of the material). This is often a revelation to us both.

Some students don't have a note-taking system but have been trying to be stenographers by writing down whatever they can manage to get—and generally not doing very well at it. More often, though, the notes are very thin. Just a couple of points are written, or a formula that I might have presented is copied down without supporting context or explanation, or the material in the notes does not correspond to the summary points but to some third-level comment that ought to have been indented pretty far to the right on the note page. The notes reflect the mess their comprehension is in. "Honestly," I'm sometimes tempted to tell such a student, "reviewing these notes will probably do you more harm than good."

Why am I telling you about my looking at a student's notes? Because you can take a look at your own notes after a week or so and make an objective judgment whether they reflect the work of a person who has a decent grip on the material or a person who is hanging by his or her fingernails and about to slide downhill. In other words, an honest look at your own notes for their quality is another helpful way of doing a self-assessment. Then, if you pay attention to what you are doing—in other words, if you are mindful about taking notes and consciously trying to get better at it—you will get better. Recall that good notes reflect the main points and one level of supporting points. When appropriate, they will also contain the formulae/equations of the day. Do yours?

If you have a study partner, you can literally compare notes. That can be useful to you both, especially if you agree to give each other honest and constructive feedback about the clarity and completeness of each other's work.

NOTE-TAKING—THE RETRIEVAL AND REVIEW PROCESS

The library is a key to civilization. Without places to store what has already happened and been discovered, and without effective methods to search through and retrieve such information, we could not really build on the discoveries of the past. We would continually have to reinvent and rediscover what already has been accomplished. A library allows knowledge to accumulate. Your notes are part of your personal library.

No one can remember for long much of the content of lectures or textbooks; our "internal" mental storage capabilities are too limited. Your notes, though, provide "external" storage for the important information in the lecture, allowing you to retrieve and review that material—I hope in a distributed rather than a massed fashion—to allow better learning and better test performance. Without notes, your review of the material would have to rely on what you have been able to store internally about the lectures you hear. Research has shown that even if a test is given shortly after you've heard the lecture, and after you've had 10 minutes to review it in your mind, you will do better if you have real notes to look at rather than just a mental review of what you've just heard (Fisher & Harris, 1973). Of course, if the test is delayed, there is a clear advantage to the physical notes above the mental notes. One's mental notes are often written in disappearing ink!

Reviewing Your Notes—Three Ways They Can Help You

Assuming that you've taken solid notes, you want them to help you on the exams. If so, then you have to look at them again. Remember that the evidence is very clear that the most important aspect of your notes is not that you took them but that you properly use them as a study aid.

Active review of your notes is an important key to effective studying.

Your notes can help you in at least three ways. First, they help you engage in distributed learning. That is, you can revisit on numerous occasions the material that was covered in one lecture. As we've already seen, the benefits of distributed learning can be very large, so going over the notes from time to time helps get you those benefits.

Second, your notes make it easier to connect material that spans more than one lecture. Reviewing them can help you see relationships among the lecture topics, or between points in the lecture and material in the textbook, including connections that were not pointed out by the instructor. Searching for and finding such relationships is another mark of an active learner. You are adding additional strands to your knowledge web. Remember my suggestion that you leave some white space in the notes to add things later? Your reactions and the connections you see, your questions, points of agreement and disagreement—these all are good candidates for what to jot down in those spaces.

A third, and perhaps the most important, way your notes help you is that they provide an easy aid to additional self-recitation and self-testing. Recall what we know about how to read and study: You get a larger benefit by spending more time reciting to yourself than you get by simply rereading the material. As recommended earlier: "Close the book for a moment, look up, and state in your own words what you've read. Then check your statement against the text." The same goes for reviewing your notes. You will not make much progress if you simply read them; that's too passive. You should be able to state out loud the key points and the major supporting points.

Recall again our discussion of the GOAL perspective—you retain most when you engage in Goal-Oriented Active Learning. Reviewing your notes is an important occasion to put the GOAL approach into practice. You can ask yourself, "What did the professor want me to know after, say, the three lectures on this topic?" (You can look at the syllabus for reminders about the topics and the number of lectures on each one.) "What were the main points and the important supporting points?" You might want to indicate them in some way by underlining, highlighting, putting one or two stars next to them, or anything that works for you. Next ask yourself, "How far away am I from knowing the main ideas and the important supporting points?" Test yourself, and as usual, be honest in the grade you give. Then review the material that can close the gap between where you are and where you need to be.

As you test yourself, you'll discover that devising and answering good questions that are based on your notes is an excellent use of your time. Appropriate self-testing—or testing with study partners—has been shown to improve performance on exams. And remember that some questions are more helpful than others. The good ones start with "Why," or "Explain how," or "What is the connection between _____ and _____," or "How do you solve a _____ problem," etc. In other words:

Ask questions that force you to understand the material in your notes—questions that require you to do more than parrot back the material.

And, to repeat yet again, you have to be honest with yourself (and your study partners) when you answer such questions and carry out such recitation. Be sure that you really are able to discuss what's in your notes and how those ideas relate to the book, handouts, or other material. Remember, you can't just hum the tune; you must sing the words.

To summarize, you advance your own "civilizing process" by building your own library—that is, by taking good notes and by using them as you study and as you prepare for exams. To the extent that you tie material in the notes together with material from the reading and with other sources of information that are relevant to the course, the more you will learn and retain. And then you will do well on the exams.

Any Questions?

In the ideal college classroom, all students feel free to ask questions when things are not clear. Also, and without hesitation, they might ask how today's example relates to a seemingly contradictory one they heard in a previous lecture, or even in another course, and bring up evidence that appears to go against the professor's point. In the real college classroom, especially large introductory courses, not all students feel such freedom—indeed, most probably do not. What should you do if you have a question? Or suppose the professor asks a question during a lecture and seems to really want someone to answer it. Should you try?

Of course, I believe you should participate freely and actively. For one thing, it keeps you attentive and engaged. Also, when one student jumps in, others are likely to dive in, too. That makes for a livelier hour. I also believe that professors have an obligation to ensure that students feel they can "safely" speak up. Professors set the tone and expectations for participation, and they can help those expectations come to pass.

In every class you should definitely get your questions to the professor one way or another. You may be more comfortable at first by asking something before or after class, and electronic communication is always handy and many students prefer it. I try to be in the classroom a few minutes early and often will stay for a few minutes after the lecture. I like it when students toss me a question or make an observation—which they can do either privately by coming up to me or by lobbing a question or an observation that we can informally banter about before class. Often, the question is of general interest, and I'll then talk about it after the class officially begins.

It's also okay to offer a challenge. Challenges are especially welcome when done in a good spirit. "Hey, Dr. Foss, I'm confused. Last week you said X, but yesterday you said Not X. Which is it?" "Well," I might have to admit, "I didn't make it clear last week that X is true only when . . . " As your college career goes on, you will have smaller classes and more opportunities for lively give and take. It's one of the great advantages of the college classroom and is one way we all grow.

F2F and Hybrid Classes

Perhaps the fastest growing trend in college courses is the large increase in students who take hybrid courses. A hybrid is a course that combines face-to-face (F2F) class meetings with online instruction. The frequency of the traditional F2F meetings varies across hybrids, but one meeting a week for a three-credit course seems typical. To date, most research on hybrids shows that the amount learned is not hampered by this format.

Recall my earlier advice: "The first thing I have to say about lectures is: Go to them." A hybrid course has fewer meetings; if anything, that increases the importance of attending the lectures. There is also a temptation to think that fewer meetings means that less work is required. Needless to say, you should not give in to that temptation; hybrid courses have been designed to be equivalent in work and in the specified learning outcomes.

A hybrid allows you additional freedom to schedule your college hours; you are not as bound to the university's daily clock (and the availability of parking spaces on campus). The flip side of that freedom is, of course, the additional responsibility to schedule your time to ensure that you "attend" the online instruction and carry out the assignments in a timely fashion. Most students who accept that responsibility enjoy hybrid courses once they get used to them. They find that the amount of interaction with the professor and with fellow students actually tends to *increase* in the online portion of the course. If you have good time management skills, you likely will be successful in a hybrid course.

Summary

Evidence shows that students who regularly attend class do better on exams. Attention, encoding, and retrieval are three concepts that, when put into practice, allow you to gain most from lectures. You can control your alertness and your attention by continuing a healthy lifestyle, by sitting in an attention-demanding location, and by taking notes. The chapter reported that the majority of students do not take effective notes, and it provided tips for how to take good ones. Your notes "encode" or capture the important information from the lecture, a process that is helped by reading the assigned material before class. Most instructors provide verbal clues to the important material during the lecture; we've listed some typical ones. There is no single sure-fire format for taking notes, but the Cornell system and the outline system are among the better ones. Research has shown that the most important function of notes is to help you review the material presented in class. Reviewing your notes, and in particular using them as further raw material for honest self-assessment, greatly increases your chance of getting the most from class time.

TAKE ACTION

1. Pick one of the note-taking styles described in this chapter and use it to take notes in your lecture courses this week. In particular, make sure your notes distinguish between the main points and the primary supporting points given during the lecture. At the end of each day, evaluate your notes for how well you believe they capture the main and supporting points. Arrange with a classmate to share and compare your notes, and give each other feedback.

2. In this item, we are referring to classes in which you can choose your own seat (some courses may have assigned seating). Most students choose to sit in pretty much the same location all semester. Break that routine by trying out different locations. In particular, and unless you already sit in an "attention-supporting" location, try sitting near the center toward the front of the class. If you normally sit in the back or another out-of-the-way location, notice how the class feels different—in particular, see whether you feel more engaged with what is going on—when you sit in a preferred spot.

3. Make up five questions covering the material in this chapter (or from the other textbook you've been using as your source for such assignments). Just as we discussed in Chapter 5 on strategic reading, make sure that two or three of them begin with *Why*. The aim of this exercise is to help make sure that you understand the reasons given for some of the recommendations. Ask a classmate your questions, and try to answer his or her questions. Give each other feedback.

4. Put time on your master calendar to read the assigned material before the class meeting.

EXPLORE YOUR CAMPUS

Determine whether there is a study skills center on your campus and whether it offers short courses on topics of importance to you.

SELF-TEST ITEMS

State in your own words:

1. What are three ways to get the most out of lectures?
2. List five signals you can listen for in order to pick out the main points in a professor's lecture.
3. What is the most important function of class notes? Hint: It is not the act of taking them.
4. Describe three ways your notes can help you after you've taken them.
5. True or False: Hybrid courses have been shown to be of less value to learners than courses that are entirely F2F.

Testing, Testing
Will This Be on the Test?

6

Oh, man, I'm so nervous about the test. It's going to be my first official test in college. I just can't imagine me taking a test. I just need to relax, study the best I can, and be optimistic about my academics.

I want to make good grades not only for myself, but also for my parents.

—*Students' reflections on starting college*

Where Are We Going?

If you complete 40 college courses, you'll probably take somewhere between 150 and 200 exams. If we include short quizzes, lab reports, term papers, etc., the number will be much larger. In this chapter, we'll review what is known about how best to prepare for exams. The chapter first defines a test as a sample of your behavior that can be used to predict what you can do in the future. It then points out that being "test wise" can add to your grade no matter what the subject matter.

By the end of the chapter, you will know a variety of test-wise tactics that can improve your test scores. These tactics vary with test type (e.g., essay exam, multiple-choice exam, short-answer exam), so it is very helpful to know in advance the type of

http://dx.doi.org/10.1037/14181-006
Your Complete Guide to College Success: How to Study Smart, Achieve Your Goals, and Enjoy Campus Life, by Donald J. Foss

questions you'll be given. You'll also be able to list some specific clues that help get the right answer in multiple-choice exams, and you will know whether you should change an answer if you have second thoughts about it. Further, you'll learn some concrete aids to improving your score on essay exams. The chapter will also revisit the testing effect to provide further resources that will help you master the most helpful material for the exam. Finally, you will learn about the role of optimism in test performance.

D o the following statements sound familiar?

- "I'm always guessing wrong about what will be on the test!"
- "I know the material, but the test questions throw me so my scores don't really reflect the studying I've done."
- "I'm okay until the test, then I collapse. Tests just make me freeze."

You may have said or felt something similar. By now, though, you know that a lot of test anxiety has been honestly earned. If someone doesn't study properly and enough, then the anxiety is justified; most likely that student won't do well. Of course, it's no surprise to hear that the best way to do well on tests is to know the material and how to apply it. Although it's good advice—actually, it's the best advice—there is much more to say about this topic.

There are specific things you can do to prepare for tests of various types, and there are "tricks of the testing trade" that you should know (and you already do know many of them) before the clock starts on exam day. Also, there is more than one effective way to deal with test anxiety. Before we dig into these topics, let's take a look at one view of what a test actually is and what happens to you as the result of taking one.

In simplest terms, a fundamental belief of psychologists is this:

The best predictor of behavior is behavior.

By which they mean: The best predictor of (future) behavior is (past) behavior. That doesn't mean that people always stick with what they've done, just that there is a reasonably strong tendency to do so.

Not too profound, you may say, but it is a surprisingly powerful observation, and people ignore this insight on a regular basis (famously, "He'll change once we're married"). From this perspective, an exam is simply a small (e.g., 1-hour) sample of your behavior that is used to predict what else you can do in the future. If you do well, the professor concludes that you can also answer related questions; therefore he or she concludes that you have earned a good grade. (By the way, professors believe that students *earn* grades; professors don't *give* grades.) Of course, an exam not only predicts the future, it also reflects the past—if you haven't studied enough, mindfully enough, that will show in the sample of your behavior we call an exam.

When exam day comes, there is a set of useful test-taking tactics that can help you perform better. Together these street-smart tactics help make you test wise. The test-wise techniques don't depend on the topic of the exam, and they apply no matter how much you know or don't know about the subject matter. In fact, some studies have shown that highly test-wise students can do better than chance on multiple-choice tests even if they've never studied the subject matter at all. It follows that you want to be a savvy test taker.

Test-Wise Tips for Multiple-Choice and Essay Exams

Test-wise students know that exam preparation should vary with the type of test they expect. It matters whether you are going to take an essay exam; or one that requires short answers, perhaps of the fill-in-the-blank type; or a multiple-choice exam. In a math course it matters whether you will have to prove theorems or solve new problems, or both. When you prepare, and as part of your weekly study routine, you will do better if you match many of your study questions to the type of item you expect to see on the exam. By *study questions,* I mean the questions you use to test yourself and any classmates you are working with.

I've mentioned before that asking your professor, "Will this be on the test?" is usually not as helpful as the question, "What type of items will be on the test?" Similarly, I said that seeing old exams or sample questions is highly useful. When you know the type of question, you can do the matching—for example, you can make up items that require short answers if that's what will be asked for on the exam. Thus:

Match your practice items to the type of questions that will be on the test.

It's therefore a good idea to ask the instructor whether a previous exam is available. If one is not, ask whether he or she is willing to hand out some sample questions or post them on the class website. Most instructors will agree to do that. Also, if you get a test back, put it in a notebook and use it as a guide to the type of questions that likely will appear on later tests. This advice is particularly useful if the final exam is a comprehensive one.

MULTIPLE-CHOICE TESTS

Suppose I ask you: What happens when you take a multiple-choice test? "Well," you might say, "I do my best to recall the material and figure out the right answer, write it down or bubble it in on the answer sheet, and then I get a grade." Okay, good, anything else? Do you know any tricks? "I know that in multiple-choice tests I should eliminate the obvious wrong answers and then, if I'm really stuck, I should guess at the right one." Okay, I agree with that—unless there is a penalty for wrong answers; in that case, whether you should guess depends on the size of the penalty. Anything else? "One more: I know that I should trust my first reaction and not change answers on multiple-choice tests." Well, no. That's been shown to be a myth (Flippo, Becker, & Wark, 2009). It is not true that your initial intuition is more accurate than what you can come up with after thinking about it—even though some books and websites still recommend going with your initial choice as a test-taking strategy.

Let's take a more careful look at the tricks of the testing trade. Most in-class assessments have a time limit, so you have to manage your time. When the exam is handed out, take a minute to read the instructions before you dive into it. At the front of my multiple-choice exams I include the instruction, "Pick the best answer." I know that test takers can at times find an ambiguity in some of the choices, occasionally even with the correct one. But that choice will still be better than the others, and it is the one that students will get credit for. Next, take a look at how many items are on the exam. Work at a pace such that you will be halfway done before half the time is up. Too, take a moment to jot down in the margin of the test some of the key information that you might have a hard time remembering under the stress of the exam—for example, an important formula or some critical dates.

Make sure you understand each question. If one seems ambiguous or confusing, and if asking a question is allowed, do ask for clarification. That normally means raising your hand and quietly asking your question once the instructor or other exam proctor comes to you. In the meantime, go on to the next item.

When taking a multiple-choice test, or one that requires short answers, it's best to quickly go through the exam first, answering the items you're reasonably confident about. If you skip an item, or don't have confidence that you got it right, put a mark next to that question and come back to it. Quite often a later question will give you further information that may help you on that tricky item, or a later question will bring to mind something that is relevant to it. In that case, don't be afraid to change an earlier answer. As noted previously, the advice to stick with your first choice is not well founded. Indeed, when students believe they have a reason to change an answer on a multiple-choice exam, they are right much more often than they're wrong: The evidence suggests that they gain three points for every point they lose.

When you're not sure about an answer and later information doesn't help you, then eliminate the options you know are wrong and choose one of the remaining ones. Also, don't forget to answer every question unless there is a penalty for guessing. Even then, if you can eliminate one or two of the alternatives it usually pays to guess from among the remaining choices. Meanwhile, watch the clock. Use the time after you've finished to check your answers, and to take a deep breath and think back over the main points of the course. Sometimes that recall attempt will spark additional information that may get you an extra point or two.

HELPFUL CLUES TO THE CORRECT ANSWER

It isn't easy to construct good multiple-choice items—if you're alert, you can find spots where the test maker has accidentally given you a clue to the correct answer, or at least a clue to what is not correct. To take some examples:

- Two of the alternatives contradict one another (e.g., World War I started in 1914; World War I ended in 1914). In that case, it's clear that you shouldn't pick "All of the above" as an answer; either both are wrong, or one of them is the correct choice (or it was an awfully short war, which it wasn't).
- Two of the alternatives mean the same thing (e.g., Alzheimer's disease, senile dementia). Unless one of the other choices is "Both," you can eliminate these two as likely answers.
- One of the alternatives is noticeably longer (or shorter) than the others. That item stands a decent chance of being right.
- The choice does not fit grammatically with the first part of the question. It's probably not the correct answer.
- You know that two choices are both correct but are unsure about a third one. If the fourth choice is "All of the above," pick that one. The test-wise student appeals to this kind of logic as often as possible during the exam in order to deduce the best answer.
- The choice is the only one written in technical language, whereas the others are given in more everyday language. If I were totally in the dark, I'd pick that one.

ESSAY EXAMS

If you know that essay questions are coming, you will, of course, practice answering essay questions. Here are helpful hints on answering those questions on exam day.

1. Time management is again crucial. If there are five questions and 50 minutes, you can do the math. Time yourself when you practice so you learn how much you can get down in an organized way in, say, 10 minutes. You probably won't get that same amount down during an actual exam, but you will develop confidence that you can respond meaningfully and appropriately under such time constraints.

2. Be sure that you understand the question. Are you asked to describe, to compare, to contrast, to explain, or to evaluate or criticize? Are you asked to report what others have said, to give your own opinion, or to speculate about what might have happened next? The grader will notice and mark you down if you don't address the question that was asked.

3. When you get the exam, underline the key words in the question, in particular, the words indicating what your goal is—for example, to explain, describe, evaluate.

4. Next, on a scratch page quickly write down the key words or phrases that come to mind given the topic and the actual question.

5. Then write a sentence that, as best you can, states a conclusion appropriate to the question (e.g., "The United States declared war on Great Britain in 1812 primarily because it wanted to expand its territory on the western frontier").

6. After that, make an abbreviated outline of three or four points that will get you to that conclusion.

7. Then write your essay. Carrying out Steps 5 through 7 is sometimes called *working backwards* and is often an effective problem-solving technique. That is, you come up with a conclusion and then develop the steps that will get you to it. Do the same for each question.

8. If you run out of time, outline what you planned to say and turn that in. You may get substantial credit for knowing where you were going, but you'll get no credit for a blank page.

9. Finally, review your answers to ensure that they actually answer the questions asked—did you describe or explain or evaluate, as requested?

When you prepare for an essay exam it will help greatly if you have example questions that the instructor has previously asked. If you do, use the previously described approach to practice answering those example questions. If you can do it in practice, you are likely to be able to do it on exam day. Recall: The best predictor of behavior is behavior.

DOES BEING TEST WISE HELP?

Sadly, there is evidence that all the great advice I've just reviewed on being test wise may not do you any good! Serious scholars have concluded, "Although the idea of teaching improved test-taking strategies is intuitively acceptable, few researchers have reported success in interventions aimed solely at test-taking strategies" (Flippo et al., 2009, p. 264). Ouch! Have we just wasted our time? (Or more honestly, have I just wasted yours?) Not necessarily. If you just read over the tips and "study" them by, say, underlining the ones that seem most useful to you, I doubt they'll do you much good. If, instead, you put into practice what we know about how to learn and remember, then you can benefit from these hints—actually being test wise does help. To learn about testing, you actually have to *learn* about testing. And as much as anything, you do that *by* testing—testing yourself, that is, on what it means to be test wise. Said another way, use the GOAL (Goal-Oriented Active Learning) approach to help you become test wise.

More on the Testing Effect

I've stressed to the point of nagging the importance of self-assessment. When frequently and honestly carried out, it provides an accurate picture of what you know and what you don't—self-testing is the most important aid to metaknowledge. In addition:

> **The very act of taking a test is an important learning experience.**

That is, taking a test not only assesses your knowledge, it can and often does change that knowledge. Because it's really important that you understand and embrace this view, let's look at it a bit more carefully.

Consider an example from outside the classroom. Imagine you are witness to a crime and later are shown individual pictures of five suspects—a kind of photographic lineup. You're reasonably confident that, say, the fourth one is guilty. A week later you are asked to identify the criminal in a live, in-person lineup. When you actually see the person from the fourth photograph, it's clear they've caught him: That's the guy. However, your certainty may be misplaced. You know you've seen him before, that's true; but one place for sure that you've seen him is in the photo lineup. The very act of being tested (i.e., being shown the pictures and asked about them) can dramatically affect your memory of the crime itself.

This is not just speculation. Errors of memory have sent innocent people to prison for years, with DNA testing later showing they were not guilty. The witnesses were not lying; they were honestly trying their best and were confident in their judgments. They were just wrong. These discoveries, stimulated by the outstanding work of Elizabeth Loftus (1979) and other psychologists (Laney & Loftus, 2009), have influenced how we think about memory and how (some) eyewitness identification tests are carried out. It is possible to reduce the chance of such errors with better testing procedures.

The lineup example illustrates an unfortunate side effect of a prior test on memory—namely, that a test can "contaminate" it. In contrast, testing can have positive effects, sometimes very positive. Testing can increase your success in the classroom by efficiently increasing the amount you learn and retain. An expert summary of this phenomenon concluded that

> testing not only measures knowledge, but also changes it, often greatly improving retention of the tested knowledge. Taking a test on material can have a greater positive effect on future retention of that material than spending an equivalent amount of time restudying the material, even when performance on the test is far from perfect. (Roediger & Karpicke, 2006, p. 181)

As previously discussed in Chapter 3, this phenomenon is known as the *testing effect*.

When you take a test—whether given by the instructor or a classmate or one you give to yourself—you actively try to retrieve information from memory. For reasons we won't go into here, that attempt at memory retrieval substantially protects the tested information from further forgetting. Now that you know that, let's assume you've decided to do self-testing. That raises the question: How often should you do it?

A reasonable rule of thumb is to test yourself on new material soon after you've covered it—later that day, or at most the next day. Then come back and test yourself on it and other, related material a day or two later. A third self-test after another week will help even more. Remember that the amount recalled goes up with the number of such tests. Also, some of the time you should be very inclusive in what you test. That is, testing across a great deal of the material is better than only testing a small slice of it.

Recall, too, that distributed practice or study leads to superior learning compared with massed practice. A test is another example of distributing your practice, and as we've seen, the testing effect states that the consequences of it are as good or better than another practice (study) session. Furthermore, self-testing automatically lets you know how close you are to the course goals and therefore is a defense against self-delusion. In summary, repeated self-testing substantially reduces the amount you forget and makes recall easier in the future—in particular, on the day of the actual exam.

What Did You Expect to Get?
What Did You Earn?

Most college students are optimistic about their future college performance, and that is generally a good thing. Optimistic students, especially when they have good study skills, tend to do better in college than pessimistic ones. On the first day of each class most students are optimistic about how they'll do on the exams and the grade they'll earn in the course. Suppose on the first day I tell students that I've taught this course 10 times and that the percentage of *As* in those classes has ranged from 15% to 20%. Next I ask them to write down the grade they expect. Way more than 20% of the students will predict that they will earn an *A*. Some research has shown that, on average, students predict one full letter grade above what they end up earning. As noted, that's not necessarily bad, and reality tends to replace optimism just before the exam.

However, this optimism can amount to wishful thinking, especially for students who do not have a history of earning strong grades in previous college courses. Such unfounded optimism can put these students at risk for an unwelcome surprise: doing poorly on the first assignments and exam and then having to struggle to catch up during the rest of the term.

It's okay to be optimistic, but you should test that optimism against reality before the professor does it for you.

You want to be accurate in predicting your exam performance, which you can do by trying to answer lots of questions while studying and getting ready for the test. In other words, the likelihood that your prediction will be accurate goes way up if you regularly carry out the needed and honest self-assessment. It is wise to put this advice into practice right away if you haven't already done so. The website at the University of Minnesota–Duluth (2011) has a valuable 10-word summary:

"Start preparing for your exams the first day of class."

Your exam performance provides explicit information about how far you are from your learning goals in the course. A perfect grade signals that you're zero distance from the goal: Yes! But what if you are farther from the goal than you thought; what if your grade is surprisingly low? In that case, it is extraordinarily valuable to get feedback about what you don't know. Like a good doctor, you should first ascertain a diagnosis and then prescribe a cure. Therefore, I strongly suggest to my students that they look over their exam and try to determine the type of items they missed. For example, did they do well on the factual questions, but poorly on those that ask about the underlying concepts? How about the items that ask them to apply what they've learned to a new situation? They can also check whether they did well on questions drawn primarily from the lecture material and not so well on questions from the reading—or vice versa. Or perhaps they do fine on the "objective" items (e.g., the multiple-choice or fill-in-the-blank questions) but poorly on the short-answer or essay items. Once you've diagnosed the types of questions that gave you trouble, then you can prescribe for yourself the concrete actions you need to take to improve on the next exam.

Test Anxiety

Most people get anxious when they are being evaluated. That's a normal reaction, so it's not surprising to hear students say that tests make them nervous. Some students (estimates range up to 20%) claim more, saying that just before the exam they can answer relevant questions and solve problems, but when the exam begins they freeze up. Experienced profs hear this a lot, and some of them think that the student simply is not prepared. Is that all there is to it?

When a student in one of my classes makes the test-anxiety claim, I first ask him to come by my office. I'm aware that such an invitation can itself produce some anxiety, so when the student arrives I spend a few minutes trying to put him at ease. Then in a chatty, give-and-take way I begin to find out what the student actually knows about the material. Quite often he has only a slippery grip on it. Furthermore, I learn that the student has not been doing systematic self-assessment, has not been taking good notes, and has not mindfully been putting in the hours on the course material. In those cases, the test anxiety is well earned and the prescription for the cure is simple: follow the how-to-study guidelines presented here.

Sometimes, though, the student does have a good grasp of the material but still performs poorly on the exam. That person more accurately fits the profile of a truly test-anxious individual. For him the anxiety experience is so intense that it is a genuine barrier to good performance—a case where the test score does not reflect what he knows. This phenomenon is real; there are many high-quality studies published on the topic (Flippo et al., 2009). Highly test-anxious students may show excessive perspiration or accelerated heart rate during exams, they may pick foolish responses and stick with them, or they may spend the test time fixated on thoughts about their shortcomings. Indeed, they may do all of these.

To date there is no single, sure-fire way to "cure" such students. In such cases, a combination of actions is generally called for. Even so, the single best "treatment" is the one we've been discussing: learning how to study effectively, learning good techniques of self-assessment, and putting this knowledge thoroughly into practice. To underscore this point, top experts who study test anxiety have concluded that "the problem of test anxiety would seem to be best addressed . . . by teaching students better ways to study and take tests, and improved methods for exerting active self-control over their own processes of preparing for and taking exams" (Flippo et al., 2009, p. 274).

In addition, there are techniques that can help you deal with the physiological responses (e.g., an elevated heart rate). And there are perhaps even more effective techniques for dealing with and reducing the *worry* component of text anxiety (that's where the student says negative things to himself such as, "I know this is going to be too hard," or, "I'm just too dumb to catch on to this stuff"). In the latter case, students are taught, among other things, how to change the way they talk to themselves in the exam situation. It is beyond the scope of this book and my professional qualifications to "prescribe" or try to teach those techniques. If you believe you are truly test anxious, I urge you to visit the counseling center on your campus to ask for assistance with this problem. It's clearly in your interests to do that because you're not being fair to yourself if your performance does not reflect your knowledge. And as I've noted, evaluations do not stop. Life after college will include many, many of them. If you learn to cope with evaluation anxiety now, you will be better at showing the world—and yourself—what you can do.

Summary

The best way to conquer the worry and concern that comes along with being evaluated is to know your "stuff." Furthermore, one of the best aids to learning that stuff is frequent self-testing. That's fortunate because such testing also provides you with needed metaknowledge, and it presents an opportunity to practice taking a relevant exam. It's quite helpful if you know the type of exam (e.g., essay, multiple choice, problem solving) you'll be given. You should find out and then construct and take such tests as you prepare for evaluation day.

Some test-taking tactics can help exam scores no matter what the course is about. Students who know these tactics are said to be test wise. The chapter provided numerous examples of them. However, because it's been shown that students do not improve after simply telling them about the tricks of the test wise, we urge you actually to learn them—and to do so by using the best learning strategies we've discussed so far.

A certain amount of test anxiety is natural, and a large amount is understandable if you are not well prepared. To repeat, the single best defense against high anxiety is to learn the material. However, some students have more severe anxiety involving physiological reactions (sweating, high heart rate) that can dominate their attention, and they have excessive worry that shows up in the negative things they say to themselves. These reactions can be treated and are best done so with the help of a professional.

TAKE ACTION— NAVIGATE AROUND TEST ANXIETY

1. Once again, pick the course that you have most concern about. I hope you have joined or set up a study group for it. Find out what assessment methods will be used in that class. Has the instructor made a previous exam or exams available? If so, make sure you have one or more. If not, contact the instructor and ask whether he or she will post prior tests or provide you with sample questions. Then take the previous exam or the sample exam. Look up the answers and update your metaknowledge.

2. For the same course, make up additional questions of the type that you expect to be given on the exam. It is preferable to do this with others in the class and then to answer each other's questions—remember, answer them in writing! Again, check your answers (or each other's answers) to make sure you are giving yourself honest feedback.

EXPLORE YOUR CAMPUS

If you are subject to test anxiety that cannot be dealt with adequately by appropriate study (using proper techniques for generous amounts of time), then find the office on your campus where you can go for counseling and make an appointment. Normally this service will be free or very low cost.

SELF-TEST ITEMS

State in your own words:

1. What is metaknowledge? Why is it important? (Yes, you've seen this item before. What is distributed learning?)
2. State the test-wise techniques for dealing with essay questions.
3. True or False? You should be willing to change an answer on a multiple-choice item. Why might you be tempted to do so?
4. What is the testing effect?
5. What does it mean to be test wise?
6. You're stuck on a multiple-choice item. State two test-wise things you will look for to help you narrow down the choices.

MAPPING YOURSELF

Self-Knowledge, Attitudes, and Excellence

7

On high school graduation I was extremely scared to the point that I was angry with the world. I hate change. I wish that I could be irresponsible and young forever.

All of a sudden I'm being expected to do grown-up things for myself and by myself. This doesn't relate to who I am or who I've been in the past, because in the past I've never really been responsible. Who I will be in the future is a complete 180 from who I am now.

College has been a fun experience and an angering experience. I have been enjoying the freedom from my family and parental figures, but there is also a lot of responsibility involved in all of that. I enjoy the social aspects of college, but hate the studying aspects. It is totally up to you to do your work. No one will do it for you or even tell you to do it. If you don't do it, you will suffer. That is a whole new outlook on school for me.

—*Students' reflections on starting college*

Where Are We Going?

College success is affected by your attitude toward college and by your emotional reactions to life events, both academic and personal ones. In this chapter, I'll

http://dx.doi.org/10.1037/14181-007
Your Complete Guide to College Success: How to Study Smart, Achieve Your Goals, and Enjoy Campus Life, by Donald J. Foss

describe some basics about how best to manage your attitudes and feelings. By the end of the chapter, you will understand how your feelings are tied to your academic work and to the goal and subgoal perspective. You will be able to describe how interactions with faculty members and others on campus affect your attitudes, and you will learn how to have positive and friendly meetings with your instructors over any issue. In addition, you will learn how best to interpret and then cope with negative events that come your way.

Both academic and personal issues can lead to restless nights and worse. Even positive emotions—especially affairs of the heart—can result in loss of focus to the point that class work suffers. In this chapter, we'll take a closer look at your feelings and attitudes, and examine how you can make them work for you, even the feelings that start off being unpleasant.

Managing Your Attitudes About College

In addition to good time-management and study skills, there are other factors that predict success in college. One of them is simply your attitude toward your own education and your university. If you feel good about your college, believing that its objectives and practices are worthy and that your instructors are competent and generally have your interests at heart, and if you have reasonably clear educational goals—in other words, if you generally accept that going to college is a good and worthwhile thing—then you are more likely to do well than if you really don't think that it's worth the time, money, and effort to get a college education.

Most readers will have a "Duh!" reaction to this observation, thinking, "Of course, it's a good idea to go to college, and sure, my professors know what they're talking about." But others may be more cynical, thinking that college provides a good reason to get out of the house, that it's primarily an opportunity to get a better party life, or that college is something you just have to put up with to get a decent job. These views won't help you persist when things get bumpy someday. To the extent that you can manage your own attitudes, it's a good idea to stick to the more optimistic perspective—and, in my opinion, a generally more realistic one.

That raises the following question: Can you manage your own attitudes? The answer is, "Yes, but . . . " Yes, but there is no simple and sure-fire way to manage them completely, and even if you work at it you won't be entirely successful. However, just as there are numerous things you can do to optimize the effectiveness of your study time, there are many things you can do to boost your attitude about college. To start:

One of the most important ways you can strengthen your attitude in the positive direction is to do well in your classes.

I'll pause to let that sink in because it might strike you as a very strange comment.

Weren't we talking about how a positive attitude can help you be successful in college? And now am I really turning it around and saying that doing well in your studies can help you have a positive attitude? Yes. However, this circularity is not as silly as it first seems because these two do mutually affect one another—good performance leads to a good attitude, and good attitude helps lead to good performance; it's not a simple one-way street. But even though they affect each other, the stronger relationship is from good performance to good attitude rather than the other way around.

If you've recently taken a test and gotten discouraging feedback, it's likely that the negative result led to bad feelings on your part. For many students—perhaps including you—those feelings do not lead them to redouble their study efforts. Be careful, though. That can lead to a downward spiral: not enough effective studying leading to more bad results leading to bad feelings leading to still less effective studying. What's the best way to avoid or to pull out of such a tailspin?

For a long time there has been a social movement in the United States whose believers think that the way to increase the performance of grade-school children and high school (and even college) students is to ensure that they have high *self-esteem*—a term that refers to their judgment of self-worth. In other words, this approach is built on the assumption that the important influence is from your belief and feelings about yourself to your performance. Many student assistance programs have been developed on the basis of the idea that when they promote self-esteem they also promote learning. However, research has shown that this perspective has its focus in the wrong place. When you accomplish a challenging task, it increases your sense of self-efficacy—that is, your judgment of your own effectiveness and capabilities. It turns out that genuine self-esteem comes from accomplishing something, from being effective, and not just from being told that you are a valuable person.

Feedback and Feelings: The Role of Goals and Subgoals

Therefore, it goes like this: Doing well in college classes leads to a greater sense of self-efficacy, which leads to good feelings, which help motivate you to work, which leads to more accomplishments. So there is a circular process or feedback system at work, but this is a pump you have to prime with the sweat that comes from mindful effort. To repeat, you start by doing something. That's the secret to avoiding or pulling out of a tailspin. When you do something positive, you get a sense of accomplishment or efficacy—you feel good about it and about yourself—and that helps you do more. Good feelings and a good attitude result from being effective.

Some psychologists have found that positive feelings are an automatic reaction to doing well, where "doing well" means that you are making progress from your starting point to your goal state. And they have evidence that the quicker you close that gap, the more intense the good feelings. Therefore, quickly getting off to a good start in college will literally make you feel good—and, of course, it is in your long-term interests to sprint rather than saunter away from the starting gate. That's another reason to put the evidence-based reading and study techniques into practice right away. Furthermore, this research suggests that if you've had a setback, you need to get back on track as soon as possible by adopting the proven techniques for effective study and honest self-assessment. You'll then perform better and feel better, too (Carver, 2004).

Let's examine how you can make sure you benefit from closing the gap toward your goal. Suppose you want to transfer to a university from a community college, or graduate by some particular date, or go to a professional school (e.g., an MBA program or a pharmacy school) after college. From your current status, say as a first- or second-semester

Studying Motivates Studying

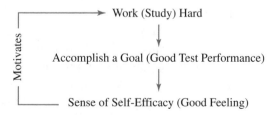

The circular (feedback) relationship between studying, goal accomplishment, and motivation.

freshman, that goal is a long way off. Doing your math assignment this evening will not move you one tenth of 1% from where you are now to being a pharmacy graduate. That goal is too big and too far away to have much impact on you today.

However, if you've registered for the proper courses, set up your time map, and explicitly put down on your master calendar a set of goals and subgoals for this term, then you can get lots of feedback that you are making progress. The example about learning some French, shown here, gives an expanded picture of this process. Your subgoals allow you to see that by doing today's work you are, right now, closing a gap and therefore that you are being effective at something you care about. That will make you feel good and will help keep you going. This feedback is helpful as you become enmeshed in college life. Later you may not need it as often, but you do yourself a service by arranging for it early.

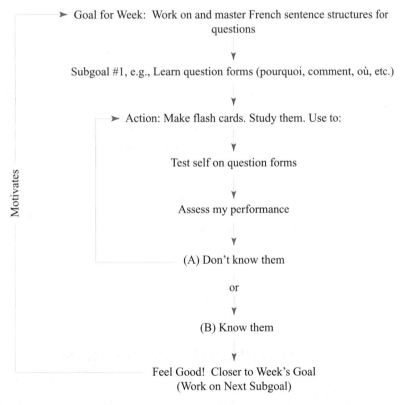

Top Goal: Learn French 501; make an *A* or *B*

➤ Goal for Week: Work on and master French sentence structures for questions

Subgoal #1, e.g., Learn question forms (pourquoi, comment, où, etc.)

➤ Action: Make flash cards. Study them. Use to:

Test self on question forms

Assess my performance

(A) Don't know them

or

(B) Know them

Feel Good! Closer to Week's Goal
(Work on Next Subgoal)

Motivates

An example of the relationship between motivation, goals, and subgoals.

We now see that constructing the master calendar and the goal and subgoal map are important for many reasons: They have a positive impact not only on meeting deadlines, but also on your feelings of self-efficacy and, therefore, on your attitude and on the likelihood of sticking with the work that will lead to your big goal. The same initial (and easy) task—setting up and sticking with the calendar and subgoal system—will lead to multiple payoffs for you. Also, if you've already gotten some discouraging results, it's not too late to get with this program. Positive payoffs are within your reach.

Managing Your Social Interactions

> I wish I had some kind of medicine to make me stop caring what people think about me so much.
> —*A student's reflection on starting college*

Not surprisingly, your attitude and your feelings about college can also be influenced by the interactions you have with others. To take one example, there is evidence that your dealings with faculty members can lead to positive feelings of involvement or engagement. However, and as you've probably heard, most college and university faculty members don't routinely seek out freshmen or new transfer students to offer them help. There are many exceptions, especially at small liberal arts colleges, but it's not typical. Students overinterpret that fact; one national sample found that nearly 30% of them admitted to being intimidated by their professors. But don't confuse being busy with being coldhearted.

Just as you found a big difference between the 12 or 15 hours of class time and the actual time required to do well on your courses, faculty members also have many obligations other than the hours they are in the classroom—including the obligation to keep up-to-date in their fields so their lectures stay current. They are busy people. Nevertheless, the vast majority of faculty members genuinely like students and are happy to help them, especially those who are truly interested in their own education.

MEETING THE INSTRUCTORS: NEED A DIAGNOSIS AND CURE?

With very little effort you can initiate interactions with faculty members that will have a good outcome for you. One way to start, of course, is to make use of the faculty member's office hour. You can and should go to the office hour if you need help or a "tune-up" on the material. I know that many students find it somewhat intimidating to go to a professor's office to confess that they are lost or that part of a lecture went straight over their heads. They don't want to look stupid, and they may be afraid that the professor will say something like, "What do you want me to do, give the lecture again just to you?" But that won't happen; in particular, it won't happen if you are ready for the visit.

Some brief preparation will allow you to be comfortable about knocking on the instructor's door, even if you are getting lost in the lectures, readings, or homework. The most important thing for you to do is to try your best to describe your own problem, even going so far as to try writing it out. Consider this like describing your symptoms when you're sick. Imagine that your doctor (finally) enters the examination room. You won't simply say, "I'm sick; I don't know what to do." Instead you spend a minute or two describing your symptoms, how you feel, and where it hurts. Plus, a few minutes earlier an assistant would have taken your temperature and blood pressure, thereby providing more information to help the doctor come up with a diagnosis. Next, he or she will usually ask you some questions. The better the information you provide, the more likely the diagnosis will be correct.

Your professor also needs to "diagnose" your problem to help you. If you are lost in, say, a college algebra class, it's not enough to just say you're lost or that you don't get it. Instead, bring some problems that you've tried to work and let the instructor see what you've tried to do. Also, before you go to the office hour, spend time trying to take notes on the explanations given in the book and bring them with you. The more you demonstrate a commitment to working on the course, and the more you show that you've been trying to help yourself, the better the instructor can figure out what your problem is and the more help you will get. Also, bring your lecture notes. If they are a mess, review the note-taking section in Chapter 5. Many students are embarrassed to show their notes, but remember how we improve: We coolly determine the difference between where we are and where we want to be and then get help learning how to close that gap.

Let's consider another reason why you might visit with the instructor (or the teaching assistant): You think there is an error in how your assignment, paper, or exam has been graded, or you don't understand the basis for the grade. It's okay to question these things, but again the best way to increase your chances of success is to come prepared. For example, you may have found a statement in the book that supports the answer you gave or the point you made, but the item was graded as incorrect. If you bring the book and politely show how it supports your answer, and if there isn't an even "more correct" choice, you'll likely get credit. (Unless, of course, the instructor spent time—in the lecture you missed—telling the class why the book is in error on that point. Nothing to do but gulp in that case.)

Finally, please know the instructor's name and use it when you introduce yourself ("Hi, Dr. Hernandez, I'm Nick Smith from your CALC II class"). Thank him or her in advance for seeing you and then describe your "symptoms" or your issues as clearly as you can. It's a good idea at the end of the visit to ask whether it will be okay for you to return in a week or so—well before the exam, if possible—to get feedback on how well you've been able to take the advice that the professor or teaching assistant has given. If you follow these simple recommendations, you'll usually find that you've had a positive experience and have begun to get to know one of the faculty members. Then when you see that person on the campus, say hello.

MEETING THE INSTRUCTORS: GIVE YOURSELF AN EDGE

A wise faculty advisor reported that he gives this advice to many students each year: "Your job is to get to know one faculty member reasonably well this semester, and also to have that faculty member get to know you reasonably well" (Light, 2004, p. 86).

The advice is excellent. Almost no one follows it.

It's great advice because getting to know a faculty member will connect you with your college, making you feel more a part of it. Such interactions lead to a positive attitude in the vast majority of cases. And as we've seen, a positive attitude can help keep you engaged in your studies; it provides an attitude booster shot to help protect you if things start to go wrong.

Almost no one follows the advice because either they are embarrassed to try or they don't know how. I think a lot of students would like to get to know a faculty member, but they don't know how to do it without feeling that they'll look stupid. Here's how.

First, let's start with a little nonsecret: Most people like to talk about themselves. Faculty members are no exception. Pick a time in the semester when neither an exam nor a paper is due in the next few days. Take a couple of minutes to look up one of your instructors, one whose class interests you, on the departmental website and read about his or her professional interests. Most departments will list their faculty and provide some information about each one (though this is less common for instructors who are graduate students or adjunct professors and for those who teach at community colleges). You may not understand all or even most of what is stated on the website, but that's okay—drop by during the faculty member's office hour and say you are simply curious to know more about his or her special topic, whatever it is. (If you can't find the instructor on the website, don't let that stop you. Just say that you're interested in the class and would like to know more about his or her interests in it (e.g., "What do you specialize in?").

As noted, almost no one does this—comes by to ask a faculty member about his or her professional interests—so right away you will stand out as a curious student (which is a very good thing in the college culture). Furthermore, because in fact you are a curious person, you will probably learn something interesting and unusual. For example, you may be surprised to find that your professor studies some aspect of global warming or has been to Antarctica to collect and study meteorites. If so, you'll leave the office feeling that you are in a cool place, even if it's not Antarctica.

Just now, and more or less at random, I picked a professor (Professor Dorothee Dietrich) who teaches psychology at the school I attended my freshman year, Hamline University. The Psychology Department's website states that her "primary research interests are in the areas of social rejection and aggression, domestic violence, and self-handicapping." First, I'd zip over to a search engine to see if there is a handy site or two for *self-handicapping;* there is. After spending a few minutes getting a grasp of the basic idea, I'd go to Professor Dietrich's office hour and ask whether she agrees with the definition of self-handicapping I found on the Internet. I'd then ask how she studies it and also ask how she studies domestic violence. I bet students who make inquiries like these will come away impressed and feeling good about their school.

Here are two additional advantages of getting to know your professor during his or her office hours. First, suppose later in the term your paper is borderline between a *B* and an *A,* and the professor is sitting there trying to decide which way to go with the grade. If he or she has a face to put with your name and remembers the earlier interest you showed, then—honestly—I think you have a better chance of snagging the higher grade. It likely won't be a conscious decision on the part of the professor, and a clear *B* paper won't receive an *A.* In borderline cases, though, the human interaction will tend to tilt things your way. Second, you now have a person who you can more comfortably ask for advice about your plans for next term or for next decade.

INTERACTIONS WITH OTHER STUDENTS

The only problem I have been having is with my roommate. She is into drugs, although not heavily. She's not very courteous and doesn't think about how her actions affect others, especially me.
—*A student's reflection on starting college*

Your attitude and moods can also be shaped by the interactions you have with other students, of course. Psychologists have observed something quite obvious, namely that your *positive affect* (a $5.00 term for "feeling good") will be stronger and more frequent if you spend enjoyable time with others. The clear implication is that you should manage your associations—by which I mean that spending too much time with the unhappy, the cynical, and the angry will not make you feel better. (I'll describe in Chapter 13 how to deal with roommate problems.) Instead, find others who share some positive interest of yours, who like to have a good laugh, and who enjoy the give and take of late night discussions. This time the data fit with common sense and with what you've been told many times: Pick your friends wisely.

As with many of the tips in this book, following the advice about learning to manage your attitudes and emotions will help you after college as well as while you're enrolled. Psychologists have evidence that self-control and the ability to regulate emotions predicts career outcomes in the wider world. Consider the title of this article by respected psychological scientists (Tangney, Baumeister, & Boone, 2004): "High Self-Control Predicts Good Adjustment, Less Pathology, Better Grades, and Interpersonal Success." Can't beat that.

Coping With Negative Attitudes

None of us can stay upbeat all the time, of course. Bad things and sad things and simply annoying things happen. And sometimes you can get in a bad mood without an easily identifiable cause. What happens then, and what should you do to help get over the "negative affect" (bad feelings)?

You won't be surprised to hear that some ways of coping are better than others. I'll describe a couple of the most valuable ones, and also let you know about common, tempting, but much less helpful ones. The sad, bad, annoying events I'm referring to are such things as doing very poorly on a midterm exam, or bending a fender on your car, or having a new romance go in the direction of thorns rather than flowers. Generally we'll focus on negative events over which you have or can get some control. I'm not going to discuss here major events such as a death in the family or a serious illness over which you have little or no control.

What happens when the news is bad and you feel sad, or guilty, or ashamed, or angry? Well, of course, those feelings are first. But even that—experiencing the feelings themselves—is not just a simple reaction. The particular negative emotion you experience is not always automatic; it is influenced by how you interpret or "frame" the event.

The same event can lead to different reactions depending on how you see it.

FRAMING THE PROBLEM AND ATTRIBUTING ITS CAUSE

No doubt you've had the experience of arguing with someone about the "proper" way to interpret something; often those disagreements depend on your assessment of who or what was responsible for causing a bad thing to happen. Did little Josie break the vase on purpose, or did she do it by accident, or because she was overly tired because her mother didn't put her down for a nap—in which case, the mother may deserve more blame than Josie? Your reaction depends on which explanation you adopt, not simply on the fact that the vase is broken and that little Josie was involved.

Not only that, you, me, all of us, are subject to systematic errors when we make such judgments or attributions. When others misbehave we tend to think they do so in accordance with their predispositions or their "true nature"; it's easy to see them as naturally mean or thoughtless. We don't give much credit to the circumstances that affected them—for example, that the person we see as mean was on this occasion forced to choose between two undesirable alternatives. In that case, when the decision maker was caught between two evils, he or she was destined to appear nasty. This phenomenon—focusing on other people's dispositions rather than on their circumstances—is tremendously well documented in psychology.

There is a flip side, too. Namely, when we are the ones making the decision, then we directly experience and are aware of many of the factors that constrain what we can do; we're sensitive to the fact that we have limited options. For example, we may feel directly and clearly that we only have two terrible alternatives to choose between. In those cases, then, we believe that the environment causes us to (mis)behave the way we do. We feel we are victims of the circumstances in which we find ourselves. When we are mean and nasty it's not because we *are* mean and nasty but because we were forced by events to be that way, just this time. To summarize this in one oversimplified compound sentence:

You behave badly because it's the way you are; I behave badly because circumstances made me do it.

Falling prey to this systematic error (which we all do) can lead you to misdiagnose what you need to do to climb out of academic trouble. It can lead you to look someplace other than the mirror. More accurately, when you are doing poorly in your work, this error can lead you away

Four Common Coping Strategies (Two Are Effective)

▪ Rumination: Turning over and over in your mind a negative event and what it means for you.
▪ Venting Your Anger: Expressing your feelings (especially anger) in an open and perhaps uncontrolled way.
▪ Analyzing the Source of the Problem: Carefully analyzing what happened, in particular, what you did—or did not do—that led to the poor outcome? What might you have done differently?
▪ Distracting Yourself: Doing things incompatible with feeling bad.

from a truthful assessment of the reading habits, note-taking practices, self-testing efforts, etc., that could help you improve if only you would fix them. And, of course, occasionally being mindful of this error can help you understand aspects of your friendships and other relationships.

Let's return to our discussion of what you can do when something goes wrong. Somehow, you've got to cope.

We've seen that our immediate reaction to a negative event is determined in part by how we frame it. How we feel after that can also be influenced by coping mechanisms over which we have some degree of control. I'll mention four common strategies: (a) repeatedly thinking about the negative event (that is, turning it over in your mind or ruminating on it until you see it from all angles); (b) directly expressing your anger to get it out of your system; (c) analyzing and engaging directly with the problem; and (d) engaging in diversions that take you away from the problem. Two of these strategies can help, depending on the circumstances, and two do not help. Do you know which is which?

RUMINATING OVER THE PROBLEM

Let's begin with a common—and unhelpful—way of handling a problem: ruminating over it. No doubt you have spent time turning over in your mind some negative event and what it means for you. You think about the different ways it could have turned out and spend time wishing the other person had turned left instead of right, etc. You've also had the experience where something in your daily life, perhaps seeing a particular person, reminded you of that negative event and thereby drew your attention back to it. If your attention stays there, the negative associations and feelings may be reinstated; that leads your thoughts back to alternative ways you wish matters had turned out. And so on, over and over—it is possible to devote enormous numbers of hours to such ruminations, returning to these thoughts and feelings over literally years. Do this enough and you can send yourself into a mental tailspin. It might be worth it if such rumination led to a later, highly positive outcome, but that does not happen.

Remember that to *ruminate* means merely to ponder, or to chew over again (the word is related to *ruminant,* the cud-chewing, four-footed animals such as cattle or sheep). Ruminating doesn't get you anywhere, except perhaps to grind down your mental teeth. You prolong the negative feelings with no payoff. In summary, this way of directly engaging the negative event—just thinking about its bad outcomes or about what might have been—is a poor way of coping with it. In shorthand:

Rumination can lead to ruination.

VENTING YOUR ANGER

A second common way to deal with negative events is to blow off steam, to vent, to roar, or to carry out other behaviors that suit the analogy to a volcano. You will hear it said that expressing anger is useful or even *cathartic* (a term meaning an emotional cleansing). It's healthy, according to this point of view, to get these feelings out. You should vent your anger and not "bottle up" your feelings. This is a myth.

There is virtually no evidence that people feel better or do better after an emotional outburst of anger. Nor is there evidence that uncorking anger protects you from ill health because you no longer are soaking your insides in negative feelings. On the contrary, the evidence shows that the penalty for frequently expressing anger is more health problems later, not fewer. That is, there is no health penalty for controlling your anger—you are not bottling up inside yourself some psychological or health poison when you develop such self-control.

Of course, it is often difficult to deal with anger's strong feelings. No one can avoid the occasional outburst. However, the best advice is to either (a) go off by yourself for a brisk walk (and focus on the things you see on the walk; don't ruminate and play over in your mind the event that caused your anger) or (b) distract yourself with things you like to do and that are as far away from anger as you can get (e.g., going to a witty movie).

The one time when anger may make you feel better is when it is expressed in a situation that might lead others to modify their behavior. In that case, you are knowingly expressing anger for the effect it has on others. But, caution, that's for the advanced class, not this one. My simple point here is this: Don't be fooled by the "common sense" advice to express anger when things don't go your way. That advice is likely to be counterproductive to your eventual health and your interpersonal relationships; venting gets in the way of using better techniques to deal with negative events. In shorthand:

Anger just leads to more angst.

ANALYZE THE SOURCE OF THE PROBLEM

The third strategy is a constructive and helpful way of coping with a bad event: namely, to carefully analyze what happened. In particular, what did you do—or not do—that led to the poor outcome? What might you have done differently? If the answer to this question is "Nothing," then you safely can conclude that you should stop thinking about this matter (see below for how to do it). It was out of your hands; don't ruminate over it. However, if there is an answer, then you can use your analysis to *make an improved plan* for dealing with an upcoming task that is similar to the one that led to your misery.

For example, suppose your analysis reveals that the exam in your psychology class was based on the lectures much more than you expected. You got flattened on the midterm in part because you studied from the book but hardly at all from the lectures (perhaps because you skipped quite a few of them). In that case, you can shift the balance of your study time toward attending class, taking good lecture notes, and actively testing yourself over those notes. Then you busy yourself with those actions, ones that will lead to a better outcome. This is not the same as rumination, which amounts to wallowing in thoughts about what happened and how bad it was. Active engagement with the problem will help you avoid rumination because, now, thoughts about the previous exam can trigger useful actions—ones, incidentally, you should put on your calendar as a set of subgoals for the course (e.g., go over lecture notes, summarize the lecture notes in your own words, make up your own practice questions). Just this act of planning has been linked to improvements in mood.

This third strategy, directly analyzing the disappointing event, can be facilitated if you write to yourself about it, describing how it came about, what it meant to you, and—this is important—how you will deal with it. Early in this book you wrote about your feelings as you start college life and how you might deal with some of the issues that concern you. I pointed out then that such a writing exercise has been shown to have long-term benefits. This is another time—when you've hit a bad patch—that you can make use of that private writing technique. You can construct an autobiographical story or narrative about the event and what you can do about it. This exercise can help you understand yourself better and will lead to the positive planning acts mentioned above. In shorthand:

Analysis and planning can lead to actions and progress.

DISTRACTING YOURSELF

The fourth coping strategy is another helpful one, at least for a while. College students (well, probably most people) tend to avoid analyzing the bad events that befall them. It's not easy to directly and constructively confront such events and the accompanying negative feelings. Instead, they distract themselves; they do things that are simply incompatible with feeling bad. They go to a witty movie, or play video games, or attend a sports event; they take a look at what's most popular today on YouTube, or go out for a beer, or generally do whatever it takes to get their minds off the problem. In effect, they are making sure that the negative event can't command their attention and thereby prolong the bad feelings. This can be a helpful strategy. We all need some down time, and using that time to help avoid the pitfalls of rumination is healthy.

Some ways of distracting yourself are better than others, of course. According to one pair of experts on this topic, moderate exercise is "a reliable method for the average person to change a bad mood and boost felt energy" (Larsen & Prizmic, 2004, p. 48). Between ruminating and distracting yourself, the latter is preferable. And proper distractions (e.g., moderate exercise vs. taking drugs or drinking alcohol, going to a movie with friends vs. venting to them about your bad luck) can help get you past the strong negative feelings. Briefly put:

Distractions can provide some distance.

The benefits of distractions are short-lived, though. Carrying out actions incompatible with bad feelings is a useful strategy for the short term. In the long run, the best coping strategy comes from positively engaging with the event, understanding what happened and your reactions to it, and making and carrying out a plan to do things that will reduce the chances of "it" happening again.

Combining distraction and direct engagement in reasonable proportions will help you to manage yourself out from under the bad feelings and reduce the chances of making the same mistake. Soon you'll again be the person who your friends want to be with—and the person you want to be.

Summary

To some extent you can affect your own attitudes and emotions. To do that effectively, it helps to understand the proper relationship between actions and feelings. In particular, increasing your self-esteem results from actually accomplishing something. You can start by simply accomplishing one of your subgoals on time—that is, complete one of the required steps on the way to a goal. That will lead to a good feeling, which can motivate further work. Note that this is another way the goal and subgoal perspective, along with good time management, will help you.

Your attitude can also be positively affected by developing good interactions with faculty members and fellow students. For many students, the thought of meeting an instructor is an intimidating prospect. If difficulty in a class leads you to visit a faculty member for the first time, you should prepare for that meeting by being explicit about your "symptoms"—the parts of the course you are not following. If you are doing all right in class, the visit can focus on the positive. This chapter has supplied concrete suggestions on how to prepare for the visit and to get the most out of it.

Unfortunately, bad things happen during college, and you have to deal with them. Four reactions (ruminating over them, anger or venting, analyzing what happened, distracting yourself) are common. The first two are counterproductive, but the second two can help you get through the difficult time and back to being an effective student.

TAKE ACTION— EXPLORE YOUR COMFORT LEVEL

1. Remember Professor Light's wise advice: "Your job is to get to know one faculty member reasonably well this semester, and also to have that faculty member get to know you reasonably well." I believe it's great advice but that almost no one follows it. You will be glad if you do. For many students, taking this step involves getting out of their comfort level. In truth, though, there is almost no risk to you, but there are benefits. Therefore, pick out the professor that, so far, you find most interesting. Go to his or her office hour, or make an appointment. Prepare for the visit as described in this chapter. Ask for advice about something to read that is related to what he or she works on or teaches about. When you later see this person on campus, be sure to say hi. Someday, especially after a couple of more visits over the years, this may lead to a great letter of recommendation for you!

2. If you are having difficulty understanding the material in any of your classes, take the important step of letting the instructor know as soon as you can. Go to the office hour, or make an appointment. Before you go, review the section of this chapter on helping the professor make a proper diagnosis of your difficulty.

EXPLORE YOUR CAMPUS

Find the health center and the student counseling center on your campus. If you ever feel that a visit to a counselor might help you, give in to that feeling; don't resist it. Resisting the need for such assistance is a 19th-century attitude, not a modern one.

SELF-TEST ITEMS

State in your own words:

1. What are the four common coping strategies people use when things go wrong?
2. Only two of the common coping strategies are good ones. Which two?
3. Describe the feedback loop between class performance on the one hand, and your attitudes and feelings on the other.
4. State two benefits of reaching a subgoal.
5. Describe what it means to "frame" a problem.

Your Interests, Your Major, Your Career | 8

I don't know what I want at all. As a child I thought I wanted to become an astronaut. Now, years from then, I, "older and wiser," haven't got a clue.

I was very close to graduating, but I decided to change majors because I was so unhappy . . . I am very motivated now and extremely happy because I am doing what I want.

—Students' reflections on starting college

You don't build your life around a major and a career; you build a major and career around your life.

—Joe Cuseo (n.d.)

I always wanted to be somebody, but I should have been more specific.

—Lily Tomlin

Where Are We Going?

If you haven't already done so, you will soon select a major field of study. It's also likely that you are in the process of clarifying your long-term career goals. It turns out, though, that many

http://dx.doi.org/10.1037/14181-008
Your Complete Guide to College Success: How to Study Smart, Achieve Your Goals, and Enjoy Campus Life, by Donald J. Foss

students are uncertain about their major and where it can take them. In this chapter, we will discuss the relationship between your major and your career, and I'll provide multiple tools that can help clear up uncertainties you may have about them. The chapter first shows that selecting a major is not the same as selecting a career. It then discusses how you can learn more about both the realities of careers and how well you're likely to fit with one you are considering. By the end of the chapter, you will know how to improve your knowledge about your own real interests. That will help you to select a major and to narrow down career choices to those that fit your interests and values. You will also know how to take appropriate steps that will increase your chances of successfully entering the career path you choose.

've mentioned that I had a tough time figuring out a major and deciding on a career. Alarm bells were going off in my head because I was approaching my junior year and had not settled on a major. Worse, I didn't know how to go about deciding on one. I was narrowing things down by taking courses and concluding that the topic wasn't for me. But that strategy can't work; there were more than 50 majors on campus (some schools have more than 100), and no one has time to try them all. The problem was getting serious. As we would now recognize, though, I was ruminating on the topic rather than dealing with it. My finger was inching closer to the panic button.

Research at Penn State and other universities has shown that my reaction is a common one (e.g., Leonard, 2010). Up to three fourths of students entering college are unsure of their major field of study, even if they have declared one. And many, many students (up to half) change their major at least once, and some change a number of times. There is nothing wrong with being uncertain nor, if done wisely, with changing your major—indeed, there is evidence that a thoughtful change can be beneficial. You presently may be at the point in your life where exploration and investigation about your future are quite appropriate. As time goes by, though, the uncertainty can become troubling. One day you've got to choose.

If you've made a choice and are confident about it, that's great. Many students choose a major while in high school or very early in college and continue to be both happy and secure in that choice. Some of the topics and tips we'll cover in this chapter may not apply to you. However, that confidence could waver—it happens to nearly half the students—so the relevance of this subject may increase. And whether or not you are secure in your choice of major, we're also going to talk about career planning; that's a topic of interest to nearly everyone.

Choosing a Major:
Your Major ≠ Your Career

There is a variety of issues related to the two questions "What's your major?" and "What's your career goal?" Here's the first one:

A major is not a career choice.

Your choice of major is an important one. But whether it is easy or difficult for you to make that decision, it's not the same as deciding what you want to do on a daily basis after you graduate or in what type of setting you will work (e.g., large company, government agency, small start-up business). Some biology majors go to medical school, others work outdoors in an environmentally related occupation, and still others work for pharmaceutical companies. And those are just a few of their possibilities. Simply put, the major does not determine which of these career paths a particular student will follow.

Let's take what seems like a clear case: What do you imagine you would do on a daily basis if you finished medical school? How would you spend your time? There is no single answer to this question. It depends greatly on which specialty you choose—the life of a surgeon is different from that of a radiologist, which is different again from that of a family practice physician. For example, radiologists (specialists who use X-ray and other imaging techniques to diagnose and treat disease) don't see sick children in person on a daily basis and rarely get the late-night phone call, but many family practitioners do. In addition, there are more options than you might first imagine. A bright young physician I know, one who finished his training in family practice medicine, plans eventually to work in the area of health care policy. His family practice training provides him with one set of tools, but it is not the only set he'll need for the position he eventually sees himself in. The lesson is: The variety of career options is still quite large even for such a specialized "major." I'll have much more to say about selecting a career goal, but first here is another tip about choosing a major.

MAJORS ≠ DEPARTMENTS

When prospecting for a golden major, you should know that:

An academic department is not the same as a major.

In many colleges there are more majors than there are departments. Although this runs the risk of adding to your confusion—having more choices is not always better—you might find a very good fit between your interests and a major that is provided within a department but named something different. Alternatively, your interests and career goals might be well served by a major that is offered across a number of departments.

For example, many undergraduates are fascinated by neuroscience, the study of how the brain works and how it affects learning, action, feelings, etc. This major is a good one for those interested in medical school, pharmacy, and many other health-related careers. If such a major exists on your campus, it may be housed in a department with that name—for example, the Neuroscience Department—or it may be an "interdisciplinary" major (sometimes called a concentration). In that case, the courses that make up the major will be offered by a number of departments. To take just one instance, at Carleton College, a highly regarded liberal arts school, the required courses in the neuroscience concentration are taken from the Biology and Psychology Departments, and the elective courses come from those two as well as from the Philosophy and Linguistics Departments. Other interdisciplinary majors have a similar, multidepartmental structure.

In contrast, sometimes multiple majors will be offered inside a single department. This is particularly common in language departments, especially in smaller universities and colleges. For instance, at Hamline University, another fine liberal arts college, we find that the Spanish, French, and German majors are embedded inside the Department of Modern Languages and Literatures, as are programs in Chinese and Italian. Similarly, you might find a major in statistics housed inside a Math Department. Your campus website (and certainly the university catalog—usually posted on the website) will have a list of majors that is separate from the list of departments.

Finally, some colleges allow students, with permission, to create a tailor-made concentration that is not part of the official catalog of majors; it's sometimes labeled as an *interdisciplinary studies major.* You'll find such an opportunity at the University of California at Berkeley, for example. The individualized major described on its website is not just a collection of courses, though. It must have a unifying issue, theme, or topic; at Berkeley the courses normally need to be selected from three or more disciplines. If you are interested in creating such a tailored, individual major, it is important that you have a reasonably clear idea what your theme is and that you discuss your idea and goal with an advisor as soon as possible.

PREPARING YOURSELF FOR ADAPTIVE CHANGE

Although it is true that your major does not determine your career, it's also true that your major does narrow your initial career options.

Putting it more positively, your major helps you prepare for some career opportunities better than others. This is especially true in fields in which the undergraduate degree includes substantial professional training. Engineers, nurses, and piano majors cannot swap initial career prospects on graduation day.

Professor Joe Cuseo (n.d.) captured nicely the relationship between a major and career opportunities. He wrote:

> The trip from your college experience to your eventual career(s) is more like climbing a tree. You begin with the tree's trunk—the foundation of liberal arts (general education), which grows into separate limbs—choices for college majors (academic specializations), which in turn, lead to different branches—different career paths or options.
>
> Branches (careers) do grow from the same limb (major), so typically a particular major will lead to a group or "family" of related careers. For example, an English major will often lead to careers that involve use of the written language (e.g., editing, journalism, publishing), while a major in Art will often lead to careers that involve use of visual media (e.g., illustration, graphic design, art therapy). The website, MyMajors.com, provides useful information on what groups or families of jobs tend to be related to different majors. (pp. 3–4)

Students frequently question the usefulness of the initial requirements, those Professor Cuseo called the "foundation of liberal arts (general education)" courses. Because they are so important, I'll return to this topic twice, once later in this chapter and again in the next one. For now I'll simply mention that these "tree trunk" courses may be among the most valuable you take, not only for your personal development, but also as part of your career preparation. Consider this comment from Thomas L. Friedman (2011), a columnist for *The New York Times* and a multiple winner of the Pulitzer Prize for journalism. He is talking about what modern employers seek:

> And while many of them [Silicon Valley firms] are hiring, they are increasingly picky. They are all looking for the same kind of people—people who not only have the critical thinking skills to do the value-adding jobs that technology can't, but also people who can invent, adapt and reinvent their jobs every day, in a market that changes faster than ever. (p. A27)

In other words, desirable hires have the ability to embrace adaptive change. They can recognize, analyze, and solve new problems. Those foundation courses help provide you the knowledge tools to adapt in this way.

A related point is that modern career paths are winding rather than straight; preparing yourself to walk down such a meandering path is wise. These days the typical person changes employers and jobs multiple times during his or her career. According to the U.S. Department of Labor's Bureau of Labor Statistics ("Lifetime 'Career' Changes," 2006), the average is about 10 jobs for workers between the ages of 18 and 38 (though many, but not necessarily all, of those jobs may be related to one another and on the same or similar career path). In college I did not fully understand the implications of the fact that nearly everyone changes jobs and even careers over his or her working life—even though members of my family did! Thus, while you want to pick a major that will prepare you to be competitive for the entry positions that interest you, you also are well advised to take courses that will help you adapt to the changing world.

Your Career Planning Strategy

Thinking back on it, I was reluctant to pick a major because my career goal was hazy. Although I finally was able to select a major, I had not yet really resolved the deeper concern: What was my goal when I entered the world of work after college? That uncertainty arose from four gigantic and common sources of ignorance. You may have them, too. Let's take a look at them and turn them into sources of knowledge. One is the belief that a major determines your career. We've hit that one already.

OCCUPATIONAL OUTLOOK: WHAT WILL YOUR DEGREE PREPARE YOU FOR?

A second source of ignorance arises from the uncertainty about the entry-level positions you will be ready for after you graduate. It's important to have a realistic assessment of the initial opportunities open to graduates with your prospective major. As we've already noted, those opportunities are wider than you may first think, but they are not boundless. For example, a psychology major cannot become a professional psychologist right out of college. He or she must have at least a master's degree to be qualified for an entry position as an industrial or organizational psychologist; a doctoral degree (PhD) is required to become a full-fledged clinical psychologist (though there are opportunities for doing certain types of therapy with a master's degree). Other specialty areas have their own requirements; you can usually find out about them via a web search. For example, for school psychology, you can look at the website of the National Association of School Psychologists (http://www.nasponline.org/about_sp/careerfaq.aspx#education).

The undergraduate degree in psychology is a fine liberal arts degree, and it prepares students to join many businesses (about two thirds of psych grads do that), to work in many service fields, or to be competitive for law school or other professional degree programs, including medical school if the proper science courses are taken. Analogous opportunities are available for history, English, sociology, and many other majors.

Relevant information is available on your campus. You can ask the appropriate departmental or college advisor to point out resources that describe the occupations commonly held by graduates with that major. Off-campus information sources can also help. Many professional organizations publish useful information in books, brochures, or on the web. For instance, the American Sociological Association has a "careers and jobs" link on its website (http://www.asanet.org); the National Society of Professional Engineers provides much useful information on its website (http://www.nspe.org/index.html); and the book by R. Eric Landrum (2009), *Finding Jobs With a Psychology Bachelor's Degree*, published by the American Psychological Association, is a useful resource for psych majors. (I have a bias toward looking at sites and materials from either professional organizations or universities; they aren't trying to sell you anything.) And, as Professor Cuseo noted, the MyMajors website (http://www.MyMajors.com) can help guide a search for materials that describe career possibilities for other majors.

Federal and state governments have also produced excellent publications and websites that can serve as a guide while you explore possible occupations and the qualifications you need to enter them. One remarkable site allows you to delve into the Occupational Outlook Handbook (http://www.bls.gov/OCO/), a product of the U.S. Department of Labor's Bureau of Labor Statistics. This handbook presents a gold mine of information about literally hundreds of occupations, including the training needed for each, typical earnings, what people do on the job, the working conditions, and even the expected job prospects over the next decade. For example, you can learn that the number of registered nurses is about 2.6 million and is estimated to increase by over 20% in the next few years, that the average salary is well above the national average for all occupations, and that "most RNs work in well-lit, comfortable healthcare facilities."

Another website from the Department of Labor is called CareerOne-Stop (http://www.careeronestop.org/). Among other things, it has a link to government internships available to students, a tutorial on preparing a résumé, and a career exploration section. You can also find occupational information that your home state has provided. Try typing into a search engine your state's name and the words *workforce* or *labor*. That will likely get you to a page that provides information and resources available to you.

INFORMATIONAL INTERVIEWS: CHECKING YOUR DREAMS AGAINST REALITY

A third potential source of confusion about one's career goal is ignorance about the realities of the actual world of professional work, not the imagined one. You can begin to reduce this uncertainty by writing down what you consider to be your ideal job or jobs—though I recommend that you not jump right away to the one-in-ten-million job (e.g., "I want to host a late night, national TV talk show"), but rather stay a little closer to reality ("I want to work in communications, preferably in TV or in a web-based position"). Yes, you should "go for it"—by which I mean you should aim for a career that fits your interests and that allows you to do things consistent with your goals and values. But there should be a decent chance of actually being able to get there. It's hard enough to get into medical school, or to get a first job with a name-brand consulting firm, or to find a paying position at a local TV station; having a dream substantially more difficult than that to fulfill ("From New York, it's the *Dead of the Night Show* starring [insert *Your Name* here]") will require the equivalent of winning the lottery. You can take a statistics course to see how likely that is.

When you've picked an ideal occupation or two, ask yourself whether you understand what the people who work in those occupations actually do. It's easy to have an idealized or romantic view, one that does not capture the day-to-day life of those doing that job. Then do some detective work. Look on the web, but also look past the web. There may be biographies or autobiographies of people who've worked in that world. Reading them provides one person's detailed snapshot of what goes on there.

Try to arrange a visit with someone who works in your desired field. Remember our secret: People like to talk about themselves. Most people will be flattered by a request to give you an informal "informational interview" about what they do. You'll be trying to arrange a visit with a busy person, though, so you may have to make a "pitch" to get them to say yes. But if you get the meeting, he or she will probably buy you lunch. This is a way to expand your people network. Ask family and friends if they know someone, or know someone who knows someone, who works in your dream occupation and, if so, ask them to introduce you to that person—an introduction that can be done electronically or via phone is often sufficient. You can also meet with people who don't quite make the dream job list, but do make the "A" list of occupations that attract you.

There are two things you can do to get, and then to get ready for, an informational interview. First, make a little outline of what you are going to say to the person on the phone when you ask for the interview: Introduce yourself as a student at Excellent U., say you are calling at the suggestion of Ms. Family Friend, state that you know the person you're talking to is an expert in your occupation of interest, and ask for a brief meeting to learn more about it. Imagine you have 1 minute to make your case, and rehearse making it before you call.

Second, prepare a list of questions to ask during your meeting. You will want to know how the person spends a typical day, about the biggest challenges (and frustrations) of the position, about the person's own educational background, and about how one breaks into the field. You will also want to ask your interviewee what courses or college experiences provide the most helpful preparation for the profession. You can also ask if he or she can recommend some things to read that will give you additional on-the-ground information. And, of course, you'll ask what other advice he or she has for you. It's good to end such a meeting by asking permission to contact the person again later. That allows you to come back when you're ready to enter the job market or are looking for a position as an intern. In effect, you are looking both for information and for an informal mentor.

Ask your source person if it is okay to take some notes during your conversation. After you've returned from the meeting, type up a summary and your reflections on what you learned and your plans to follow up by getting more information. You can also write down your assessment of whether you are now more (or less) attracted to the career—and why. And, of course, send a handwritten thank-you note.

ASSESSING YOUR ACCOMPLISHMENTS

The fourth source of ignorance, and in some ways the most difficult one to face, is uncertainty about the realities of who you are and who you want to be—in other words, uncertainty about your real aptitudes and goals. Nevertheless, these must be dealt with in order to make smart choices.

Authentic self-knowledge about your accomplishments—those in the past and those likely in the near future—is an invaluable aid to smart decision making about your career goals. I've talked with students who vowed that they intended to go to medical school, but whose GPAs were well below *B* and who did poorly in science classes. They are not going to be admitted to a medical school and are well advised to find a different path to a fulfilling, health-related career. Similarly, I recently spoke with a student who thinks that he's going to be finance major at my university but who doesn't have the grades to qualify for the College of Business. Worse, his GPA wouldn't make him eligible even if he got 15 hours of *A*s next semester. For these students, a direct and difficult conversation is called for. They are faced with a tough decision, but one they need to confront.

Professors really want students to aim high and to be successful. But there comes a time when a reality check is needed. It does no good to hold on to unrealistic beliefs about what one will reasonably accomplish. (And remember, one of the best predictors of future behavior is past behavior.) Students who could not reconcile their accomplishments with their aspirations have wasted years, along with armored cars full of money. The tricky part, of course, is to determine when the moment has arrived to make a change.

Three markers signal that the time for change has arrived. One is the "waiting game" with respect to taking courses. That is, if you find yourself taking courses for more than one semester in the hope that you can qualify next semester for the major or college you aspire to enter, you should reevaluate. Second, if you have hesitated to take the "killer" courses required for the major or the profession, you're likely telling yourself something you should listen to—that's a signal of a mismatch. Third, if you've taken those courses and simply not done well in them, then you ought to take a close look at yourself and your aspirations.

One student wrote to me, "I just need an introduction to the right person over in College H__. If I can get that introduction, he will see that I am committed to [that career]; really, I'm passionate about it." This student thinks that enthusiasm or simple persistence will get him where he wants to be. Although enthusiasm and persistence are definitely important, what is (or more accurately in his case, what was) needed was studying and mastering the prerequisites to get into College H__. These are sad cases that will only get sadder if time continues to slide away. This student is in denial about his situation and needs to formulate Plan B and then act on it.

If an objective look at your transcript suggests that you are not progressing toward a degree, seek advising help right away. Facing up to a difficult decision has its benefits. You may, for example, come to appreciate that there are many wonderful majors and many wonderful occupations in the health professions other than being an MD. Recall, too, that many successful businessmen and women did not get a degree from the Business School. Moving on can lead to moving up.

ASSESSING YOUR INTERESTS AND PRIORITIES

It is essential that you accurately determine your own interest pattern. "Wait," you may be thinking, "don't be stupid; of course, I know what I'm interested in! I even wrote down the careers of interest to me when you talked about setting up informational interviews." But although at first glance knowing your own interests may seem easy, straightforward, and even self-evident, for many students it isn't quite so obvious. For example, they may feel that they're interested in so many different things that nothing stands out—that's pretty common. Or they may be avoiding this topic because they're scared to approach the point at which they have to make a decision; they fear the bad consequences of making a mistake. Furthermore, for some individuals—I was one—the initial self-assessment turns out not to be highly accurate. They don't know themselves as well as they first thought they did. When first asked about their ideal career, they might say something that is socially acceptable or that reflects their parents' desires more than their own.

Also, and strange as it may seem, we frequently are not accurate about what motivates us, nor are we even very good at predicting how we would feel if our heart's desire came to pass (e.g., T. D. Wilson, 2002; T. D. Wilson & Dunn, 2004). People who win the lottery are ecstatic at first, just as you and I would be. Surprisingly, as time passes, they are no more happy—and quite often less happy—than they would have been had they not won. I know this sounds ridiculous; you are sure that you would be different (me, too), and that you would stay very, very happy. But the evidence strongly suggests that we wouldn't, that we are simply wrong about this prediction of our future feelings. Thus, it is worthwhile to spend some time making sure that you "know thyself." Here, of all places, you want to be as authentic as possible.

There are things you can do to clarify your interest pattern, and therefore to narrow down your career goals, and therefore to help you select a major. A good first step is simply to write down what you like to do. What classes, either in college or in high school, have you found most interesting? What did you like about them? Write out your answers to these questions to force yourself to be clear.

You can travel another road to self-discovery by asking your good friends and family members—people who know you best—what they think you would be good at doing. Listen carefully to the answers because their opinions come from observing you—sometimes a little more objectively than you observe yourself. (You may have had the experience of friends telling you that "he—or she—is no good for you" and wishing later that you had listened to their advice.) You might have to work at getting your friends to take this request seriously, but you can do that. If their opinions are consistent with your own, that helps confirm your self-assessment. If they differ, ask why they see you in that occupation (and no fair getting hurt feelings if they say something unexpected). This can be a moment of learning and is a sign that this topic—that is, *you*—needs more study. Perhaps you think of yourself as conscientious, but your friend points out that you are nearly always late. Late won't work for a TV host.

In addition to your likes and dislikes, you should review your values as they apply to your prospective career. How important is money to you? How important is prestige, helping others, or a work environment in which the duties and responsibilities are clearly defined? Write down, in order, the values you believe are most important to you in the career you hope to follow. Remember, writing things down helps you clarify what you think. This is a test you grade yourself; you don't have to show it to anyone. Which occupations do you think best reflect your values? Here's a good question to consider while comparing your values to those you will find in the work environment: What do you imagine would lead you to quit a job? When you carry out these exercises, you are actively engaged in creating your future.

TESTING TO FIND YOUR INTERESTS

Which is closer to the truth? (a) Opposites attract. (b) Birds of a feather flock together. Please pick one.

When it comes to predicting who will be friends, or how successful a marriage will be, the answer is clear: People who have common interests, common abilities, and common core values tend to have longer and better relationships than those who are opposites. This finding can be extended to help you increase your chance of finding a rewarding career.

Behavioral scientists interested in predicting workplace success have developed tests that measure the interests of successful people in a large number of occupations. One relatively straightforward way to assess a particular individual—for example, you—is to compare your interests with those of people in the various professions or occupational categories. If your interests are similar to those of, say, accountants, but not at all like those of graphic designers, then you are likely to be more successful in the former occupation or occupations that are similar to it. Said differently, such an "interest test" allows you to see which groups you are like and which you aren't. The idea is that you'll more likely be happy and successful if you "flock" with similar "birds." (This is an old idea—Parsons, 1909, wrote about it over 100 years ago—but still a powerful one.)

Some of those interests may not be related in any obvious way to the work itself (e.g., the test may ask: Which do you prefer doing on a spare afternoon? (a) Hiking in the countryside, or (b) Doing a crossword puzzle). Nevertheless, the interest patterns reasonably—though not perfectly—classify people into meaningful and useful groups. In short, one way to get some evidence about whether you'll like an occupation is to see how your interests compare with the interests of those who work in it.

The Campus Career Center

During college, when I was in my near panic state about picking a major, I was fortunate that a friend in one of my classes pointed me to the campus career center. After hesitating for a few days, I made an appointment with a counselor there. It was one of the best things I ever did. After talking with me for a while, the counselor asked me to take an interest test and to come back in a couple of days to discuss the results.

When we met again, the counselor compared my scores, my *interest profile* he called it, to those made by people in various occupations. The upshot was that I was given additional information about myself and a nudge to further explore a topic that I really did find interesting—scientific psychology. By the next term I was getting course credit for working in a professor's lab. I didn't understand all of what I was doing, but it was interesting, challenging, and fun. I had found my major.

The point of this story is to let you know how much help the career counseling and the testing were—how important it was to get these additional, objective sources of information about myself. These days, happily, there are many more resources, including web-based ones, to help determine one's interests. But most important:

Your campus will have dedicated people whose goal is to help you find yours.

Do not hesitate to let them help you. If you have any uncertainty over career goals or the choice of a major, definitely make use of the campus resources. You've already helped pay for them via your fees; the reason they exist is to give you a hand.

Universities vary in how they organize these offices. Smaller universities may have a single, centralized career counseling and placement office, whereas larger ones may also have placement offices associated with various colleges (e.g., Business, Engineering, Education, and Liberal Arts may each have a separate one). Once you've determined the organization on your campus, then visit the one most relevant to you.

Well-constructed tests can help as you explore yourself and your career options. Before you take one, though, you should know that the results will be presented to you in broad occupational or career categories. You will not get results saying, for example, that you should be an elementary teacher rather than a secondary school teacher. As a matter of fact, someone with a particular set of interests can be happy and successful in a wide variety of related occupations—many jobs might fit your interests. Simply said, there is not one magic occupation any more than there is just one person who can be your great love. The details of your particular occupational conditions (e.g., the nature of your supervisor, the overall success of the organization, the physical working conditions) are important in how it works out for you, and no one can predict those details from a test.

Let's examine further how (and when) you can take an interest test. As already stated, I strongly recommend that you visit your college career or counseling office; you can find it either by asking an advisor or by doing a web search on your campus. Second:

Visit the career office early in your college career, preferably during the first year.

Many students think that a career office is simply a placement center, meant to help them find a job during the spring term of the senior year. That is a mistake. John Kniering (2010), writing as career services director at the University of Hartford, put it this way: "If we see them on the cusp of graduation, often it's too late to make a significant difference." The sooner you make use of their services, the more you will benefit from the career office. In particular, it pays to get the feedback from an interest test as soon as possible.

The professionals in the career office will be glad to see you and will direct you to the assessment resources your institution has available, most of which will be free to you or available at low cost. Later the counselor may go over the test results with you and offer additional, tailored information or advice. But, of course, the counselor will not tell you what you should do. You choose.

In addition, websites are available that provide interest testing at low cost and in a responsible way. (You may have used such a website, or a printed version of it, in high school. If so, your current results will probably be similar to what they were then because interest patterns do not change very rapidly.) I've waited to mention the online option because I believe that making use of the counseling or career office is, by miles, the better place to start. However, if you want to get a head start by doing some self-testing before you go off to college, one useful website (http://www.self-directed-search.com) provides an opportunity to carry out a "self-directed search" for your interest pattern at low cost. I am not endorsing this site over other responsible ones, but I am referring to it because of its modest cost and because it uses the most common set of interest scales, those developed by psychologist John Holland (1985).

One Approach to Career Assessment

According to Holland's approach to career assessment, it is useful to classify people into six broad types or categories. In addition, Holland proposed that work environments and occupations can meaningfully be divided into the same six categories. The categories or "types" are known as RIASEC: Realistic, Investigative, Artistic, Social, Enterprising, and Conventional. The table on page 143 provides a summary of the

RIASEC Categories and Their Typical Traits

Realistic (R) people like realistic careers such as auto mechanic, aircraft controller, surveyor, electrician, and farmer. The **R** type usually has mechanical and athletic abilities, and likes to work outdoors and with tools and machines.

The **R** type generally likes to work with things more than with people. The **R** type is described as conforming, frank, genuine, hardheaded, honest, humble, materialistic, modest, natural, normal, persistent, practical, shy, and thrifty.

Investigative (I) people like investigative careers such as biologist, chemist, physicist, geologist, anthropologist, laboratory assistant, and medical technician. The **I** type usually has math and science abilities, and likes to work alone and to solve problems.

The **I** type generally likes to explore and understand things or events, rather than persuade others or sell them things. The **I** type is described as analytical, cautious, complex, critical, curious, independent, intellectual, introverted, methodical, modest, pessimistic, precise, rational, and reserved.

Artistic (A) people like artistic careers such as composer, musician, stage director, dancer, interior decorator, actor, and writer. The **A** type usually has artistic skills, enjoys creating original work, and has a good imagination.

The **A** type generally likes to work with creative ideas and self-expression more than routines and rules. The **A** type is described as complicated, disorderly, emotional, expressive, idealistic, imaginative, impractical, impulsive, independent, introspective, intuitive, nonconforming, open, and original.

Social (S) people like social careers such as teacher, speech therapist, religious worker, counselor, clinical psychologist, and nurse. The **S** type usually likes to be around other people, is interested in how people get along, and likes to help other people with their problems.

The **S** type generally likes to help, teach, and counsel people more than engage in mechanical or technical activity. The **S** type is described as convincing, cooperative, friendly, generous, helpful, idealistic, kind, patient, responsible, social, sympathetic, tactful, understanding, and warm.

Enterprising (E) people like enterprising careers such as buyer, sports promoter, television producer, business executive, salesperson, travel agent, supervisor, and manager. The **E** type usually has leadership and public speaking abilities, is interested in money and politics, and likes to influence people.

The **E** type generally likes to persuade or direct others more than work on scientific or complicated topics. The **E** type is described as acquisitive, adventurous, agreeable, ambitious, attention-getting, domineering, energetic, extroverted, impulsive, optimistic, pleasure-seeking, popular, self-confident, and sociable.

Conventional (C) people like conventional careers such as bookkeeper, financial analyst, banker, tax expert, secretary, and radio dispatcher. The **C** type has clerical and math abilities, likes to work indoors and to organize things.

The **C** type generally likes to follow orderly routines and meet clear standards, avoiding work that does not have clear directions. The **C** type is described as conforming, conscientious, careful, efficient, inhibited, obedient, orderly, persistent, practical, thrifty, and unimaginative.

six types. The table below lists the types along with some typical majors that are associated with each of them. The sample departments shown in the table provide an idea of the breadth of majors associated with each RIASEC category. To repeat, neither this test nor any other can tell you which major or career surely would be best for you. But if you are very high in, say, the Investigative category, and very low in the Social category, that's a signal that you might take some additional science or social science courses. (It's important to know that social science is not the same as social work; the former can be a good fit for students with Investigative interests, and the latter is likely a good fit for those with Social interests.) Reading the course descriptions available in the catalog/website can also help you see what is emphasized in the majors you are considering.

From Major to Career

Let's return once more to the matter of determining the realistic career prospects that come with your major. In some cases, in particular, those majors with a significant professional component, the choice of initial career is presupposed—an electrical engineering degree leads in the vast majority of cases to an entry occupation that makes use of that technical education. Engineering programs tend to be very good in providing career advice, relevant intern opportunities, and placement help for their students. That's true of many business programs, too.

However, students in the liberal arts, including humanities, social sciences, communication, and fine arts majors, have less well-defined

RIASEC Categories and Typical Related Majors

RIASEC category	Sample departments
Realistic	Physical Education, Mechanical Engineering
Investigative	Physics, Biological Sciences, Geology, History
Artistic	Art, Music, Journalism, English, Theatre
Social	Social Work, Nursing, Counseling, Education
Enterprising	Business Administration, Law, Management
Conventional	Accounting, Criminal Justice, Economics, Library Science

Note. Reprinted from "Established Career Theories" by P. J. Hartung and S. G. Niles in *Career Counseling of College Students: An Empirical Guide to Strategies That Work* (p. 9), by D. A. Luzzo (Ed.), 2000, Washington, DC: American Psychological Association.

initial career paths. From one point of view, that's okay because occupations and career paths are changing in the current world, and a rigorous liberal arts education—one that helps students critically analyze problems and evaluate solutions to them—should equip them to cope with such change. Having said that, though, an early visit to the career center is, if anything, most important for those who major in liberal arts disciplines where the initial occupational placements are less certain—or to put it positively, where there are the broadest opportunities. Students who use these offices early in their college years get a head start on finding pertinent summer jobs and intern placements, and they may get other useful tips and connections that will increase the probability of finding a "just right" initial career placement.

Remember that you live in a world where the ability to adapt to change is highly beneficial. In the early 90s there were no jobs whatsoever for website developers because the web as we know it did not yet exist. Only after 1995 did web-based jobs begin to be feasible. Thus, it was not possible for someone to prepare specifically for such a career prior to that time. Your college education can prepare you to adapt to such change so that you can continue to be productive. Indeed, it can prepare you to create such change. Within a decade of graduation most people are working in positions that are not directly related to the undergraduate degree they earned, even if the title of the occupation is the same. The labels outlast the contents.

Next, you can get additional information about career directions from some of the interest tests we mentioned earlier. The RIASEC report, for example, gives both a primary area of interest and two secondary areas. Professor Holland created a figure, shown on page 146, that can help you understand the benefit of knowing your secondary interests. The categories next to one another in this figure are more closely related than the categories farther apart, whereas those directly across from one other in the hexagon are the least related. There is a set of "good fit" occupations for those who are, say, primarily Investigative, and somewhat Realistic. That is true for other likely combinations as well.

The good fit occupations will still be numerous—though some of them may seem completely odd to you. I've heard students just laugh at some of the occupations labeled as a *good fit* for them. But others will seem better and will give you fresh thoughts about career opportunities. The test has been shown to be useful in real life, so it is worth thinking about the possibilities that it (or other valid tests) present to you.

Career counselors will tell you that most actual jobs are found via personal contacts, not via web searches. You should take every opportunity to expand your contacts with people who can put you in touch with decision makers in your areas of interest. One way to do that is via the informational interview, as we've already discussed. These days,

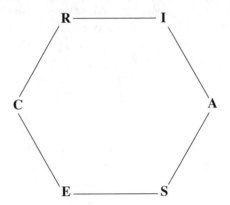

R: Realistic   I: Investigative   A: Artistic

S: Social   E: Enterprising   C: Conventional

The Holland diagram. From http://www.self-directed-search. com/sdsreprt.html. Reproduced by special permission of the Publisher, Psychological Assessment Resources, Inc., 16204 North Florida Avenue, Lutz, Florida 33549, from the Self-Directed Search® Software Portfolio With SDS® Form R Software Module (SDS®-SP) by Robert C. Reardon, PhD, and PAR Staff, Copyright 1985, 1987, 1989, 1994, 1996, 1997, 2001. Further Reproduction is prohibited without permission from PAR, Inc.

working as an intern is another good way to get relevant experience onto your résumé. The career center can also give you advice about how to find an appropriate intern position.

Your Résumé: Start Now

The typical résumé includes a statement of your objective, along with your education, work experience, and contact information. Many websites provide more detailed tips on constructing an effective résumé. I've already mentioned CareerOneStop (http://www.careeronestop.org/) as such a site. Another excellent one exists at Purdue University's Online

Writing Lab (http://owl.english.purdue.edu/owl/resource/564/01/). I will not repeat those tips here except to note that many students feel that their experience is thin and worry that they will not have much to put on their initial résumé. To help combat that, you should keep detailed records of

- your employment history,
- volunteer activities and community service,
- offices held in campus (or other) organizations,
- internships you've held,
- computer skills,
- honors or awards,
- memberships in professional organizations (see Chapter 14), and
- hobbies or interests that might be relevant to a prospective employer.

The Purdue website provides an even more extensive list.

It is good practice to start making a master résumé as soon as now. It will eventually contain more than you will put on an actual résumé that you send to a particular prospective employer, but the master résumé will save you time and anxiety as you construct that document. In every case, the actual résumé should be tailored to the particular employer you are approaching, showing them why it is to their advantage to interview you. To quote the Purdue website:

> The purpose of a résumé (along with your cover letter) is to get an interview. Research has shown that it takes an average of ten (10) interviews to receive one (1) job offer, so your résumé needs to be persuasive and perfect.

A Career Planning Timetable

Here is a brief outline of what you can gain from the career center over your college career and some of the important steps you should take for yourself each year.

First year: Visit the center and make an appointment with a counselor. If available on your campus, enroll in a college/career exploration and success course; many universities now offer such courses (it may be a 1-hour course; if so, take it in addition to your other courses).

Second year (up to about 60 credit hours): Do things that will give you experience relevant to your career goal. Join organizations or clubs on campus. Do some of the work in that group to prepare for and earn a leadership role next year. Volunteer in a relevant setting. Look for summer jobs/internship opportunities that fit with your goals.

Third year (up to about 90 credit hours): Dive into your major. Work with counselors and advisors to further clarify your career goals. Continue to gain pertinent experience in work, volunteer, or intern settings. Meet faculty members in your major and work with one of them on a project (nothing works better when looking for letters of recommendation). Seek a mentor in the professional world of interest. Draft a résumé. Learn about the campus recruitment process and how to be eligible to participate in it. Take on a leadership role in a campus organization related to your interest.

Fourth year (up to 120 hours): Develop a list of potential employers. Use the college or campus interview/recruitment services. Deepen your interactions with faculty and professionals so that you will get excellent letters. Network both on and off campus. Keep in touch with counselors. Outline your job search strategy in detail.

The time and attention you devote to gaining objective knowledge about yourself is time exceedingly well spent. Similarly, time spent exploring various professional and occupational environments is also worthwhile. Take a look at your master calendar and set aside some hours that will enlighten you and brighten up your future.

Summary

Most colleges offer a large number of majors, and you will pick one—not always an easy choice. On many campuses the number of majors is larger than the number of academic departments. Although selecting a major is a major decision, it is not the same as selecting a career. Many career possibilities exist for almost all majors. However, the choice of a college major does set you on a path that narrows the initial professional and occupational options you will have upon graduation. Thus, selecting a major should be informed by your career aspirations, and these can change during the college years.

In turn, your career aspirations should be consistent with your interests, abilities, and values. Although it seems sensible to assume that you have solid knowledge about your own interests and how they fit with various occupations, that is not always the case. It is possible to expand your knowledge about your core interests by the use of certain valid tests. They can help provide you with authentic self-knowledge. Such tests do not tell you the precise occupation or profession that will lead you to maximal happiness and success. No test can do that. However, they do point in general directions and may provide lists of representative jobs that fit with your interests.

Career aspirations also have to be consistent with your accomplishments. From time to time you help yourself if you make an objective assessment of the likelihood of reaching your college goals with respect to your major field of study. The chapter presented various signals you can monitor to help do that.

In addition to determining your interests, it is highly beneficial to investigate the realities of the occupations that interest you. Tips for obtaining and carrying out an informational interview are provided. Throughout, I have emphasized the importance of making use of the career counseling resources on your campus—early and often.

TAKE ACTION— EXPLORE YOUR INTERESTS/ NAVIGATE YOUR CAMPUS AND BEYOND

1. Make an appointment at the career center on your campus. Arrange to take an interest test or other tests that they recommend. Normally this service will be free.
2. What classes, either in college or in high school, have you found most interesting? What did you like about them? Write out your answers to these questions to make sure you are being clear.
3. Write out the values that are most important to you in the career you hope to follow. Which occupations best reflect those values?
4. Arrange an informational interview with a person who works in an area of interest to you. Immediately afterward, write out the individual's responses to the questions you ask and save them.
5. For the same area of interest, go to the Occupational Outlook Handbook (http://www.bls.gov/OCO/) and summarize what you learn; in particular, describe the job prospects for the next few years.
6. Find a website that discusses the qualifications for entering one of your desired occupations.
7. For those who may be interested in a career in the health professions: Many campuses have a separate office that advises students with such interests. Check with your advisor and/or on the campus website to see if your institution has such an office.

SELF-TEST ITEMS

State in your own words:

1. What are the six categories on the RIASEC classification?
2. Evaluate this claim: In the long run, most people enjoy it best when they work with others who have very different interests and values.
3. State why it makes sense to visit the campus career office during your first year in college.
4. List three to five occupations that currently interest you. How much do they have in common? Hint: The commonalities can be determined by seeing where each fits within the RIASEC system.

MASTERING THE UNIVERSITY'S RESOURCES | IV

How to Choose Courses and Get Free Tutoring

9

It was really hard choosing classes for the first time. I was so nervous. I didn't know what to take. I called my dad crying. He was no help. All he did was ask me why I was taking the classes I was taking . . . I have no idea! I'm just taking classes I think I might be interested in. We will see where that leads. I hope it leads me to a good job that will earn me lots of money. Money is good!

I have always known that I want to study medicine, and be a doctor someday. Going to college has given me the opportunity to study so many things outside the field of medicine; this is a wonderful opportunity that I will only be given once in my life.

—Students' reflections on starting college

Why do they make an engineer take an art history course? It makes no sense.

—Nick

Who's the easiest history prof?

—Thousands of students

Where Are We Going?

Some of your courses will be *electives*, meaning you make a free choice to take them. Other courses will

http://dx.doi.org/10.1037/14181-009
Your Complete Guide to College Success: How to Study Smart, Achieve Your Goals, and Enjoy Campus Life, by Donald J. Foss

be part of the university or college core requirements, meaning that you must take them. In this chapter, we'll discuss both types, with an emphasis on the latter. By the end of the chapter, you will know about the types of required courses, and you will understand why the university obliges you to take them. You will also learn how to maximize your chance of getting into a popular course that is already full. You will be able to describe useful techniques for getting into small enrollment courses, especially those at the junior and senior levels, and systematic ways to find out about the star teachers on campus. We will review what students think about the quality of teaching—opinions are surprisingly high—and what to do if you run across one of the exceptions. You will also discover why tutoring is such an effective way to learn, and you will know how to find free tutoring on your campus.

Courses and How to Select Them

Depending on your major, you may have more or less flexibility in course selection. Students in professional schools such as engineering and business tend to have less flexibility than students in liberal arts colleges. In any case, your university will have a set of requirements that must be met to get a degree. Let's start with them. They come in two general categories: first, the overall university or college requirements, which include both the total number of credits needed for the degree and what is called the *core curriculum* or *distributional requirements;* and second, the courses required by your major. As you select your courses, you are well advised to

- make constant progress toward satisfying the distributional requirements,
- sample wisely such that the introductory courses may help you select or confirm your choice of major,
- take electives that truly expand your intellectual and personal horizons, and
- take courses from exciting and inspirational faculty members.

The overall university requirements start with a quantity: the number of college credits needed to receive a degree. For universities on the semester system, a typical minimum number is 120 semester credit hours (SCH); that's about 40 courses. Some programs (e.g., architecture and engineering) require more than 120 SCH. You will find information about the number of needed SCH in the online catalog for the college. Many colleges and departments provide web-based work sheets listing the degree requirements. I recommend that you copy or print out this

Four Guiding Principles for Course Selection

- Meet the core requirements. Make constant progress toward meeting your university's "distributional requirements."
- Use introductory courses to help select or confirm a major. You can "try out" your possible interest in a major. If it doesn't work, the course may still count toward a distributional requirement.
- Choose electives that expand your horizons. This is a good way to learn about a topic (from neuroscience to music) that interests you even if it is not a possible major for you.
- Take courses from exciting professors. They can inspire you.

sheet and put it in a "home binder" so you can update your progress as you meet those requirements. This is important:

You are responsible for knowing the graduation requirements of the university and of your major field of study, and for keeping track of your progress toward meeting them.

You may be bringing some college credits with you, either because you are transferring from another university, because you've earned credit via Advanced Placement (AP) courses, or because you tested out of a particular course (perhaps via the College Level Examination Program or CLEP test). It's important for you to ensure that the credits you think you bring with you, or that you earn via testing, will in fact count toward the graduation requirements of your university. That is not always the case, and you don't want to make assumptions about such an important matter. Some transfer credits may count toward the core or distributional requirements, discussed next. These are numbers you need to be sure about because they affect when you can graduate—so check with an advisor to see what the university officially gives you credit for.

The Core: Obstacle or Opportunity?

Your university and college will have a set of distribution or core requirements that you must satisfy to graduate and that typically you are asked to complete during your first 2 years. In many states the core requirements are (largely) the same for all public colleges, including community colleges and universities—this is done to help facilitate transferring between schools.

The core curriculum usually includes courses on writing and literature, fine arts and humanities (perhaps including history), social science (e.g., psychology, economics), mathematics, and natural science (e.g., physics, chemistry, biology). Acquiring proficiency in a foreign language is also a requirement for students who will receive a bachelor of arts degree. Many colleges also have a multicultural requirement—one that asks students to study a cultural group other than their own.

Though the term *core* is often used, most universities have many options for how each of the requirements can be met. That is, they take a "menu" approach such that you can choose among numerous courses, in some cases dozens, to fulfill each of the core or distributional requirements.

It is common for students to react negatively to the distributional requirements, thinking that they just get in the way of progress toward getting a degree and a good job. To take one example, my friend Nick planned to be an engineer, and initially he resented having to take courses he thought were going to slow him down. Nick wasn't strictly a "Money is good!" guy, but he was in a hurry to begin his career. And so he asked, "Why do they make an engineer take an art history course? It makes no sense."

Later on, though, he worked with designers as well as with engineers. Because he knew something about the history and styles of art, he found it easy to communicate with them. Later still, Nick discovered that he enjoyed visiting museums as he traveled the country and the world—and, as a bonus, he was better able to connect with his international clients. Thus, long past his college years he benefited from the foundation that this single course provided. He's now glad the university required him to expand his horizons.

REASONS FOR THE CORE

There are at least three major reasons for the core courses. Because you will devote substantial time to them, you deserve to know these reasons.

The first goal of the core curriculum is to provide you with a variety of different ways of thinking about the world and how to make your way in it. To return to my earlier metaphor, the distributional requirements provide different types of maps of the world around you. Just as a globe gives you a different picture of the world than does a flat map, so too the typical way an economist thinks about some organizational unit—a household or a nation—is different from the way a sociologist or a political scientist thinks about those units. Learning a new approach can add to your supply of problem-solving skills. Thus, some courses outside your major will be both intrinsically interesting and practical later in life.

Although they have a lot in common—each approach involves gathering information, evaluating it, putting ideas together, and creative thinking—the differences are important and valuable. After a while you will recognize the economist's or the historian's method of representing and discussing important events, and you will be able to listen critically to what they have to say. The most influential economist of the 20th century, John Maynard Keynes (1936/1964), famously said:

> The ideas of economists and political philosophers, both when they are right and when they are wrong, are more powerful than is commonly understood. Indeed the world is ruled by little else. Practical men, who believe themselves to be quite exempt from any intellectual influence, are usually the slaves of some defunct economist. (p. 383)

The distributional requirements are meant, in part, to make you aware of such influences and thereby to keep you from becoming such a "slave."

The second important reason why colleges adopt a distributional requirement is that the various courses give you a foundation for continued learning and therefore improve your ability to adapt in a changing world. Much of the technical material you learn during college will become obsolete during your working years. Continued learning is therefore crucial for your ongoing success. Colleges recognize the need to prepare students to be flexible and adaptive, and believe that the core courses provide a basis for that flexibility. They are an aid to the adaptive changes you will make.

A few years ago I visited the United States Military Academy (West Point) and discussed the academic program with its then commander, Brigadier General Daniel Kaufman. He said:

> Our most important task is to kindle within cadets a lifelong love of learning. The only certainty of 21st-century life is rapid change—social, political, economic, technological. Those who learn quickest and best will lead and shape this change to build the future of our Army, our country, and our world.

Some civilian students may be surprised to learn that the college responsible for educating Army officers—a goal that at first glance might seem narrow and technical—is in fact committed to distribution requirements and for exactly the same reasons I'm giving here. The core requirements at West Point include history, English, philosophy/ethics, foreign languages, math, etc.—a list quite similar to the one mentioned previously. There are similar requirements at the Naval and Air Force Academies.

A third reason for the distributional requirement is that it provides an opportunity to sample among the disciplines for students who are undecided about their major. Though I said in Chapter 8 that you don't have time to take courses from lots of departments, it's nevertheless true that the core requirements permit a "free peek" at a few prospective majors by allowing you to take the introductory course in that discipline. It's free in the sense that the course meets a university core requirement; taking it therefore moves you toward your graduation goal even if the course turns out not to be part of your eventual major.

I should raise two little caution flags, though. The first one warns that introductory courses should not be the sole or even the primary basis on which you should decide on a major. You can be somewhat misled by the quality of the instructor and even by the content of an introductory course. But you already know that further investigation is in order before selecting a major; peeking isn't enough. The second caution flag pops up if the course is a winner for you and, after further consideration, becomes part of your major. Most universities will not let you "double count" that course; that is, you won't be able to count it toward both the major and the distributional requirements. The rule against double counting might say something like this: "You are required to take 9 hours in social sciences from courses outside the major." In that case, majors in economics cannot use the Introduction to Economics course to satisfy the social science distributional requirement. The rule varies from college to college, however, so understanding your particular requirements is, well, required.

GETTING INTO THE BASIC COURSES

Though finding interesting courses that satisfy a core requirement is not difficult, getting into them might be. Popular courses *close;* that is, they reach their student capacity and enrollment is cut off. The class may be popular because of its subject matter, because of the time it's offered, or because the instructor has developed a reputation as a great teacher. Here is how to increase your chances of getting into one of these courses:

1. Before registering, make sure you know which are your first-choice courses for each requirement you plan to satisfy that term—but also have a backup option ready for each course.
2. Register as early as possible. If you register via the web, make sure you log on and select your courses as soon as you are eligible to do so. Delay may cause you to lose your place in line. If one or more of your first-choice courses are closed, do not stop the registration process. Go to your backup plan and complete your registration (again, this assumes you are registering online). You want to be sure that you leave the session with a full course load that allows you to make good progress toward your degree, even if the classes are not the ones you initially wanted.
3. If there is a waiting list, be sure you are on that list for your first-choice courses. (This assumes, of course, that the desired courses will fit into your now-modified class schedule.)

4. If you did not get the classes you wanted, then as soon as you can, make a personal visit to an advisor. The course instructors may have the authority, within limits, to override the computer and let you in the course, and at larger schools they may delegate this authority to the departmental or college advisor. (Though at some schools the waiting list may be the final stop; in that case, the advisor can only wish you well.)

5. Remember my earlier recommendation about getting to know the advisors? If you followed that advice, you can now enjoy a benefit—someone who is motivated to help you. When you walk in, be ready to state your reason for needing the desired course at the desired time. It won't do just to have a strong preference for a 10 a.m. class; everyone has that. You need something better. (Of course, don't make up a false reason such as having a course conflict such as another course at the same time; any advisor can check that out in 5 seconds. If you're caught stretching the truth, your reputation is gone.) You may find yourself on a waiting list kept by the advisor. That's normally a good sign; you're still in the game.

6. If classes start before you've been admitted to the course you want, then for the first meeting or two attend both the course you're officially signed up for as well as the desired one. Mention to the instructor after the first class that you're on the waiting list for his or her course and are attending it in the hope of officially getting in. Ask the instructor whether he or she will admit you. Be ready in case you get a positive answer; have in your hand the form that has to be signed to allow you to add the course. (If you do get into the desired class, don't forget to drop the other one.) If asking the instructor after class doesn't get you in, you have one more shot at it; someone might drop the course later that day, opening up a seat. Check with the advisor one last time before you accept the second-choice class—which, of course, might just turn out to be a great one.

Upper Level Courses:
Three Ways to Shrink Them

The halfway point—for most students it's at about 60 SCH—is a milestone worth celebrating. In many places you are then known as an *upper division* student. After that you will take many more courses in your major—the number varies, but about one half (or more) of the remaining classes will be taken in that discipline, and others will be in a related field of study, perhaps in a minor. It is relatively easy to discuss the core or distributional requirements because they are similar for most majors and institutions. However, in a book such as this it's not even practical to list, let alone cover, the opportunities at the upper level because the variation among universities and fields is so great. There are, though, some commonalities, and I'll mention a few of them.

For majors in the performance disciplines such as music and dance, much university education is similar to that in specialized fine arts conservatories—small classes and one-to-one instruction is the norm. That is not typical for business majors, even when they become juniors and seniors. Class sizes tend to be large in business schools, even at the upper levels. For those majoring in the physical and life sciences, social sciences, and to some extent the humanities and engineering, there is a path from large classes to smaller ones and even to conservatory-like experiences. Thus, even in large universities, many students who try for it can arrange to have one-to-one, or very few-to-one, sessions with professors. Here are three ways to do it.

First, sign up for courses on *special topics;* these are undergraduate courses that focus on a specialized area within your major. The special-topics course may have as few as 10 students in it, and sometimes fewer. Search the course listing for such classes, and try to find one on a topic of possible interest. Students in such courses get to know the professor quite well during the semester, but be sure you are ready to work in such a class. A small enrollment means that the professor will get to know you, too.

Second, participate as an assistant to an advanced student or to a professor. Many universities offer credit (and sometimes pay) to assist on a research project. Doing so brings you in very close contact with a professor. Not every department will offer such courses, but those that do provide a chance to have an unforgettable experience as an undergraduate student. (By the way, if you're thinking of going to graduate school, serving as a research assistant is one of the best things you can do. It gives you a glimpse into the life of a graduate student, and it results in your having a faculty member who can write a knowledgeable, detailed letter of recommendation for you. Also, graduate programs look for, and are impressed by, evidence of your having had such an experience.)

A third way to have a human-sized experience at even the largest university is to participate in an intern program sponsored by the department of your major. This opportunity is more often available to students in engineering and other professional fields than it is for those in social science or humanities disciplines. But even in those fields imaginative intern programs may exist. They are a way for upper division students to get hands-on experience in a practical setting. There are both paid and unpaid internships. Obviously one is better than the other, but even unpaid ones provide both experience and a way into the job market. Intern supervisors are another terrific source for letters of recommendation; they can provide a detailed assessment of your work ethic and contributions to the intern site. The campus career center may help you find an appropriate internship—another reason to visit that office early in your college career.

To summarize, you must meet both the overall university requirements and those of your major field. The latter vary widely, from practice teaching in education to "capstone" courses in some science disciplines. The needed information is in the departmental advisor's office and on the web, and you are responsible for knowing it. Surprises in this part of college life are rarely pleasant ones, so keep good records. Choose courses that allow you to make steady progress toward your degree and in your major.

Teaching Stars

Should you also choose classes by who is teaching them? Of course! It pays to be with knowledgeable and inspiring people. Every campus I've ever been on has had its famous instructors—teaching stars whose classes are always packed. Such special individuals add immensely to your college experience; they even help keep you motivated. The campus grapevine will let you know who these people are. Normally these superstar teachers are not the easiest graders—but that's not the mark of greatness in the classroom, as you will see when you get there.

In addition to the well-known, campus-wide superstars, there will be many other star teachers; when one of them is offering a course that you can or should take, seek it out. The grapevine is not so highly efficient in recognizing these "mere" stars, especially on larger campuses. In addition, there will always be people who confuse grading reputation with greatness and therefore do not put the inspiring but demanding professor on the list you hear about in the hallways.

There are two good ways to find out about these excellent teachers. First, look for the award winners. Every campus gives teaching awards. Some are conferred at the university level (very prestigious), and others at the college or departmental level (still important). There also may be teaching excellence awards strictly for graduate students or instructors. Those winners are terrific lab instructors, composition teachers, recitation leaders, etc. You can find out who has won such awards by searching the campus/college/department websites. Try entering "teaching award" or some variant of it as you search the campus websites. Every place I've tried doing that led, within very few clicks, to lists of winners. However, if names of recent teaching award winners don't show up on the website, or if it is not up-to-date, asking in the department is also a good strategy.

And that's the second way to find the outstanding teachers: Ask other faculty members and the advisors. But here some diplomacy is required. Never ask a professor or an advisor whose course you should *not* take. They can't (or shouldn't) answer that question because the answer might depend on the type of course (e.g., some faculty members are excellent in small classes but not as good in large ones). Also, for a staff member to answer such a question is foolish because you may be asking the person to speak ill of his or her boss (good advice to remember for later in your career); beware the judgment of the advisor who does so. If a student asks me such a question, I turn it around to questions he should have asked in the first place: Who is teaching course X this semester? What are his or her good points? Who do you recommend? Asking with a positive spin rather than a negative one will get you the information you want.

The Quality of Teaching and Class Policies

While we're on the subject of teachers, let's detour a moment to see more about what they are like and what other students think of them. I've mentioned the "superstars" and the "stars," but what do students think about the average college professor's teaching? And what do professors really think about you?

WHAT PROFESSORS EXPECT OF YOU

College professors expect you to be a self-starter, to complete work on time, and generally to act like a responsible adult when it comes to assignments. Like nearly everyone, they are not fond of whiners. Within that framework, the vast majority of them have a lot of empathy for students. Did you have a death in the family, or a car accident, or a bad case of the flu? If so, you will find that most of your professors will make accommodations for you—if you can document your reasons for missing an exam or not turning in a paper. You must get a receipt from the health service or from your doctor if you are sick, for example.

Some excuses won't work even if they are truthful. Most professors are unlikely to be sympathetic if the car accident is a fender bender, it happens the day before the paper is due, and you don't even have a draft you can produce to show that you were almost done with the paper when the fender crumpled. In general, to the extent that you can demonstrate good-faith effort (which means having something to show for the effort other than the sentence, "I've worked hard on this"), that's the extent to which you will get an understanding ear.

Instructors sometimes allow students to discard their lowest test score, using the others to determine the course grade. It's tempting to skip an early exam if you don't feel ready. Doing so is a mistake. My strong advice is to take all the exams. That maximizes your chances for a good grade, and it also allows you to miss late in the semester if you do get ill.

HOW DO PROFESSORS RATE ON STUDENT EVALUATIONS?

These days the faculty members not only grade the students, but in most universities and colleges the students also "grade" the faculty. Typically this is done by use of a questionnaire at the end of the course. On most such questionnaires you will be asked to assess how much you've learned, whether the assignments were clear, and a variety of other matters, usually ending with a question that asks, overall, how you rate the instructor.

These feedback forms are taken seriously. For example, as dean I received a report each semester summarizing the student evaluations of all instructors in the college—approximately 700 of them. I looked at the report every time, especially for new faculty members. If there was an unusual number of low scores for one of them, I asked the instructor's department chair to look into it and to work with that person the next term. We then kept watch for further signs of difficulty. Most universities have help available for both rookie and veteran faculty members, and the student evaluations can indicate need for that help.

You should know, however, that the number of faculty and graduate instructors who get poor evaluations is very small. The vast majority of students say that the vast majority of professors and other instructors do an excellent or a very good job. In my experience, on the basis of data collected at three major universities, the total number of responses pointing to "poor" and "very poor" teaching performance (both categories together) is usually under 10% to 15%, whereas nearly 75% of the responses are in the "excellent" and "very good" categories. These results may surprise you, given the statements in the popular press that college and university professors are not dedicated teachers. It is a happy fact that those statements simply are not supported by student ratings. That's good—it means that your professors will do a very good job of, well, professing.

IF BAD LUCK STRIKES

Of course, there is always an exception to that generalization, and you may be unlucky enough to be put into a class taught by an exceptionally poor teacher. What can you do in such a case? First, take a moment to figure out what the problem is.

One problem that occasionally occurs, though less now than in years past, is that the instructor may have an accent that makes his or her English difficult to follow. If this happens it is likely to be in math, engineering, and computer science courses or in science laboratories. Our country is not developing enough students who are math majors, for example, so many colleges and universities rely on international teaching assistants and faculty to teach such courses. Happily, the problem often corrects itself. For example, you will find that accents tend to fade after a couple of hours of listening. It isn't that the speaker changes in that short time, but that your ear adjusts to the accent and, for example, the R sound being confused with the L sound pretty soon doesn't matter anymore.

If you are having difficulty understanding your instructor, you can talk after the first class and ask the person please to speak slower until you get used to listening to him. You won't even have to mention the accent; he or she will know what you're talking about. Also, you can go to the advisor in the department that offers the course—the math advisor if it's a math course—and see whether there is another section of the course that fits your schedule. Work with the advisor to arrange for a transfer to that section if you are still having a problem by the end of the next class meeting. You should have some patience, give your ear a chance, but do not get more than two days into the course before you and the advisor make a decision about how to handle this matter.

A second possible problem will arise if the instructor assumes that you know more than you do, and you are quickly lost. This problem has two versions. In one version you've forgotten the material that was a prerequisite for the course, or that you did not originally master to the expected level. This can cause trouble in math courses, for example, where some students who have had high school calculus find that they did not really master algebra, or that calculus has disappeared from memory (perhaps because the principles of distributed learning were not used when it was originally studied).

A college course can be unforgiving in these circumstances because it will zoom along at a faster pace than you are used to. In that case, you have to make a quick assessment, and I urge you to go right away to the instructor's office hour and to the advisor's office to get help as you make that assessment. If a dozen hours of refresher work can get you up to speed, you probably can find that time and stay in the course. If not, you should drop back and take a course lower in the sequence, even if it means falling one course behind. (However, students receiving financial aid do have to keep in mind that the amount of aid they get may vary with the number of semester credit hours; they should check with a financial aid advisor before dropping a course.) One purpose of summer school is to allow you to catch up from such glitches. Staying lost or getting further and further behind as the course goes along is a recipe for trouble. Better to retreat from a battle than to begin to lose the war in the first term. In any event, you should make your decision before you are trapped in the course.

Nearly every school allows you to drop a course without penalty before some date, often called the *drop/add date*. Pay attention to this deadline.

When you make your master calendar, look up the drop/add date on the college website or in the catalog and put it in **bold letters** on your calendar. Make sure that on the drop/add date you are prepared to finish all the courses you are registered for. If not, contact an advisor at least a couple of days before that date. Occasionally, something will happen such that you have a valid reason for dropping after the drop date—a documented illness, for example. In that case, contact the instructor and the departmental advisor as soon as possible. You can also visit your college's associate dean for Student Affairs; that person can be quite helpful. In some universities you will have to pay for the course even if you drop it, but that may be worthwhile because it keeps your GPA record clean. Keep in mind, though, that "I'm hopelessly behind," or "I'm failing the course," or "The instructor is terrible" are not valid reasons for dropping a course after the deadline.

Recall that we are talking about what steps to take when an instructor assumes you know more than you do. As noted, the problem has two versions; in the first, the one we just talked about, the problem is with you. In the second version, the instructor does presuppose too much; he or she thinks that students know more than most of them actually do, and therefore many students get lost right away. I like to say that such instructors have "a 10-foot rope" problem: They have now climbed up a 20-foot cliff of knowledge and then, in class, they drop the students a 10-foot rope and ask them to climb up. It doesn't work.

Effective teaching requires the instructor to take into account what the students know and to go from there. College professors can't do that for all students in large classes, but they have to make a reasonable stab at finding a good starting point for the typical student. If you discover that a considerable number of students in the class are struggling—and if both you and they are putting in the required hours in mindful study—then we might have a 10-foot rope problem. It may help a lot if you can get two or three of them to join you in an office visit during which you all say that you are not following the material. A sensible instructor will take this feedback into account.

There is also the rare instructor who does not follow what I call the "Golden Rule of Teaching"—namely, to treat each student the same way he wants his own son or daughter to be treated in college. Unfortunately, every profession has its share of people who do not live up to its ideals, and college teaching is no exception. If you run into such a person and can tell that you are going to need help in the course (or if the luck of the draw gets you the disorganized mumbler), my obvious advice is to try as soon as possible to get into another section with a different instructor. That is not always possible, so short of dropping the course, the best you may be able to do is to provide feedback to the department chair by telling him or her what is going on. Again, it may help if you can recruit two or three other students to go with you. That gives you and your concerns more credibility and, of course, the support of others will make the visit easier for you.

However, given the positive data on teaching evaluations, you are very unlikely to face such a situation. Nearly all your professors will be highly competent and even memorable in a good way.

When Your Notes (and Your Head) Are a Mess—You Need a Tutor!

From the ancient Greeks and Romans through the Age of Enlightenment, the children of the rich and powerful . . . were educated by professional tutors. Today, as we enter the 21st century, tutoring remains the ideal, the gold standard as it were, of education.
—*Scientists who study tutoring*
(Lepper & Woolverton, 2002, pp. 135–136)

I have heard of tutoring somewhere on campus and I think it's time to check that out. Why are these subjects so hard since I have taken them in previous years?
—*A student's reflection on starting college*

You take a look at your notes from your physics course and find that you can't really decipher them. You've been given some homework problems, perhaps computer based, and are struggling with them; you don't know which principle covered in class applies to which problem. You can't really "give the lecture back" to the notebook (i.e., you can't recite the notes rather than just reading them) the way you can in, say, your biology course. It's time to get help.

Here is a wonderful fact: Free tutoring is available in nearly every college and university. But before I tell you how to get such free tutoring, I want to tell you how important tutoring can be and something about how it should be practiced so you'll know how to get the best out of it. Many studies have examined the effects of college class size on the amount that students learn. The results are surprising. At least for lecture courses, class size has very little effect, if any, on learning. A quality instructor can do such an excellent job of teaching in a class of 50, or even 250, that it is difficult to find better results if the (lecture) class size is shrunk to 20, or even to 10. There is, however, one place where class size really does make a difference—that is when the size of the class is one. If there is just one student, then the amount learned is usually substantially more than in other settings; major gains can occur. When class size is one, we call it tutoring.

WHY CHOOSE TUTORING?

One reason why a class size of one is so important is that it allows the tutor to interact directly and repeatedly with you. An important component of that interaction is the back-and-forth, question-and-answer nature of it. The tutor asks a question and—because there is no one else in the room—he or she is clearly calling on you. Just as when Professor Calder knew my name, there is no making yourself invisible. Your answer can then be evaluated immediately to see whether you know the material. That is, the tutor can do a quick and effective assessment of your knowledge. It won't do for you to say, "I know it but I just can't say it"; you both know how lame that is. Also, the tutor can figure out what misunderstanding you have: what you believe that, in fact, is false or inaccurate.

A psychologist and computer scientist once made the analogy between a computer programmer finding the errors (bugs) in a computer program and finding the mistaken beliefs held by a student, or the mistaken techniques that he or she may use when trying to solve a problem (Brown & Burton, 1978). The clever tutor can be thought of, then, as a detector of "mental bugs." If your misunderstandings can be "diagnosed," then appropriate steps can be taken to "debug" you and to get you back on track.

A good tutor will select a question or a problem, or a set of them, and diagnose your state of knowledge by what you say or write. Then he or she will select the right level at which you should be working and move progressively toward more advanced problems as you improve. A good tutor will not give you the answers but will make you work toward them, encouraging you and helping you improve what you know as you go. You'll get hints, not solutions, and that is better for you (Lepper & Woolverton, 2002).

Another advantage of tutoring, and a major one, is that it can make a big contribution to keeping up your motivation. A good tutor will encourage you when you are serious about learning, and this will help keep you going. A very positive chain of events is the result: Tutoring keeps your motivation up, which improves the amount of time you spend in (mindful) learning, which increases what you know, which (yes!) improves your grade.

WHERE TO GET FREE TUTORING

If you are now convinced that tutoring is a superior way to be taught, then you're ready to learn how to get the highly valuable free tutoring I've mentioned. Here's the secret: Free tutoring is available every day on the campus in at least two, and often three, main places. One is the faculty member's office, and the second is the teaching assistant's office, which you can visit during their office hours, or by appointment.

Are you disappointed? Does this seem too easy or too obvious? Many find it so. And yet I know for a fact that a huge fraction of faculty office hours go unused or underused (this is particularly true on large campuses). Oh, sure, students come by just before the midterm, or a few days before the papers are due. You might even find a line outside the professor's office on those occasions, and therefore the time spent with you is rationed such that you can't get all the help you need during the office hour. But at other times professors and teaching assistants know to have other work with them; if they relied on students in the course to take up the office hour they would be lonely. So take advantage of the tutoring opportunities by doing just a tiny bit of planning.

Each fall during orientation I give my "free tutoring" advice to a lot of students. Though I'm sorry to report that the vast majority of them ignore it, in a way that is good for you. If everyone took my advice the lines would get long, the time for each student would get short, and it wouldn't be as much help to you. So do yourself a super-sized favor and be the exception; make the honest self-assessments as you go along and "turn yourself in" during the next office hour as soon as you even suspect that you are getting behind, or getting confused, or just want a "tune-up" to ensure that your understanding squares with what the professor is trying to get across. If your schedule conflicts with the professor's or assistant's office hour, contact her or him to ask for an appointment at your mutual convenience. Occasionally you may need more time than the office hour. My experience is that most professors will set up additional time for the student who asks for it under two conditions: as long as it is not during the crunch time when all those who have put off coming for help are finally showing up, and as long as you make a good faith effort to prepare and to study the material in the ways described in this book.

Incidentally, bring your notes to the office hour and ask the professor or the teaching assistant to take a look at them. That is also a good way of getting a reading on whether your representation of the material will support building the correct knowledge structure.

Finally, it's worth just a minute to ask why students generally don't go to the office hours. Why wouldn't you go? I think the answer is easy, though it may have two or three related parts. First, you don't want to reveal your ignorance. That's understandable; it's uncomfortable to be the ignorant one. Second, you don't want to "bother" the professor; you may feel that he or she has more important things to do. Third, you fear that the professor might think you are not worthy of his or her attention and treat you poorly. These all come down to your sensing a power difference between the two of you, where "knowledge is power" has a more literal meaning than usual.

You should go anyway. First, professors already know that they know more than the students. Why else would they be the teachers? So that's not an issue. Importantly, there is no problem on a college campus with admitting ignorance, assuming that you genuinely want to replace it with knowledge. Professors know that ignorant does not equal stupid; you shouldn't equate them either.

With respect to the possible concern about bothering the professor, don't give that a thought, either. Again, the vast majority of professors genuinely like students and are very willing to help them—especially the students who show an interest in their own education. Indeed, and this is an important point, they will think more of you, not less, if you ask for (the right amount of) help. It's good to be seen as a dedicated student. You do have to demonstrate that you are serious, though. You must have tried to understand the material, read the assignments, tried the homework problems, etc. Professors are interested in helping those who try to help themselves.

Finally, there is a third source of tutoring: Many departments and colleges have help centers to assist you if you get stuck. This is particularly true of mathematics departments, but if you are having trouble in any course, you can inquire whether there is a help center or a tutoring center for that course. Also, many campuses offer Supplemental Instruction (SI), a program built on peer support. Students who have done well in traditionally tough courses are recruited to work with current students on many of the things we've recommended in this book—for example, going over readings and notes and predicting test items. SI programs usually focus on the "killer" courses offered in the first 2 years. Finally, there are websites that provide help for many topics, especially technical ones. These change all the time, so ask your instructor if he or she can recommend such a site.

Summary

Depending on your major, you may have more or less flexibility in course selection. Even so, everyone has to meet overall university requirements, both in (a) the minimum number of SCH needed to receive a degree and in (b) the core or distributional requirements. The core requirements are there to provide you with a variety of tools to help you understand and analyze the world. The typical university has core courses that focus on the physical world; the social, political, and economic world; the fine arts; quantitative and writing skills; the humanities; and perhaps other perspectives. Because these courses are required, it is not always easy to get into them. You can increase your chances by registering on time, of course, and by going to the initial class meetings and talking personally with the instructor and a departmental advisor.

The vast majority of college students rate the teaching of the vast majority of professors very highly. Still, when possible, you should take courses from the teaching stars and award winners. Searching the college website will likely reveal current and past award-winning instructors. In contrast, if you get an instructor who seems particularly unrewarding, you should deal with the problem very early in the term, seeking help from the advisors.

Upper level courses generally have smaller enrollments, but especially at large universities, you may have to search for small enrollment classes. Special-topics courses usually fit this bill, as do for-credit courses in which you participate in research projects. The latter are particularly valuable for students interested in attending graduate or professional schools.

We know that tutoring is a particularly effective teaching technique. It is fortunate that free tutoring is available at even the largest universities. With a small amount of planning, you can get tutoring even from your busy professors.

TAKE ACTION   Once again, pick the course that you have most concern about. Make a visit during the office hour to the instructor or the teaching assistant for the course. Ask whether you have the correct understanding of the issue or problem that most concerns you. If the answer is no, ask for help. Try to arrange the meeting so that you are being tutored. A good way to start is to ask the instructor to ask you questions, starting with an easy one, and to give you hints rather than answers.

EXPLORE YOUR CAMPUS

1. Look at the course offerings for your prospective major or majors. Your goal is to find out whether there are "special topics" courses that are offered—and, if so, to list the special topics being offered in the current term. (Note: the topics likely will change over time.) Also, find out whether there are for-credit opportunities to work with professors on a one-to-one basis as you get closer to graduation, and whether there are internship opportunities provided. If so, make it part of your planning to explore these opportunities when you become eligible. Discuss them with an advisor next time you see him or her.
2. Find the list of award-winning teachers for the department of most interest to you.
3. Locate (your campus website will probably help) and make a list of the tutorial and other student learning help centers on your campus.

SELF-TEST ITEMS

1. Imagine you are in a debate with another student. Your assignment is to defend the core requirements of the university. Write an outline of your debate points.
2. What can you do to increase the chance that you will take courses from the best teachers?
3. True or False: College teachers generally get high teacher ratings from their students.
4. State three ways you can increase the chance of being in small classes.
5. State in your own words why tutoring is a highly effective way of learning new material.

Who's Who—and Who Helps You Be Successful

10

Have you ever noticed how the university just has too many divisions? I mean, there isn't one facility that can handle more than one thing at a time without some other department there to hold their hand. If they can't help you, they send you on a wild goose chase to other places just to get something signed, a question answered, or simple things like that. Kind of pathetic, don't you think?

College is very stressful, but the problems blindside you.
—*Students' reflections on starting college*

The world of human culture is not a mere aggregate of loose and detached facts. [We] seek to understand these facts as a system, as an organic whole.
—*Ernst Cassirer*, An Essay on Man: An Introduction to a Philosophy

Where Are We Going?

Your college or university is composed of many parts, not just the various buildings, but the people, departments, and other units housed in those buildings. It pays to understand these parts, and in this chapter you will get an overview of them. You will learn how the academic side of the university is structured, and

http://dx.doi.org/10.1037/14181-010
Your Complete Guide to College Success: How to Study Smart, Achieve Your Goals, and Enjoy Campus Life, by Donald J. Foss

who's who within it. This knowledge will allow you to quickly find the appropriate person who can help you with any problem or concern that comes up. You'll also learn where to turn next to get advice or help if your first attempt does not work out—in effect, where to make an appeal. In addition, you will understand something about the culture of your professors and the staff people you'll come in contact with. Finally, we will revisit the notion of "success," and you will understand the difference between a narrow and a wide definition of that term.

A few weeks into the fall semester, a student sent her dean (at that time it was me) a request to drop a class after the official deadline:

> Hi, my name is Susan Lopez and I am a freshman. I realize that the last day to drop courses was this past Friday, but I just found out today that I failed my first test in Child Psychology, which we took last Thursday. I am in an upper division class, and it is way over my head. I tried to give it a try but it isn't looking good. I would like to drop my Child Psychology course from my schedule. I really want to get started off on a strong footing and have a great college career. I thank you for your time and hope that you can help me to avoid the penalty of a bad grade. Sorry for such late notice, I realize you are an extremely busy person.

Susan's request reflected some bad judgment at work even before the start of school. I suspected that she had managed to get into that course in spite of her advisor's recommendation to the contrary. Her heart was in the right place, she had a can-do spirit, but her judgment wasn't quite there yet. I'll tell you in a minute what happened to her.

The View From the Blimp: Understanding the University's Organization and Culture

The organization and culture of universities will be somewhat strange to you; it is strange to most people, even to most college graduates (and sometimes even to deans!). To maximize your chance of college success, it helps to understand how it all fits together. At this point I'm referring to the "official" part of the university: the professors, advisors, financial aid people, and, yes, even the parking office—the place you go to pay the ticket you got because you ignored the advice about getting to campus early. We'll get to the student culture later. (Incidentally, pay those tickets. Universities may put "holds" on registration and graduation until you make them good, and it's no fun to discover at the last minute that you can't register or graduate until you come up with money to pay the accumulated fines.)

When you arrived (or will arrive) on campus, some of the first "official" people you met and interacted with were the orientation advisors and course advisors, and a bit later the instructors and teaching assistants—and if you are living on campus, the resident hall assistants. Also, you may have interacted with staff members who arrange for parking permits, financial aid, meal plans, work–study programs, use of the campus recreation facilities, and others. Each of these individuals plays a role in the overall campus network. Each can help smooth your way around.

Before we talk more about them, though, let's take a vertical sightseeing trip—let's float up and give you a view from the blimp so you get a quick idea how these puzzle pieces fit together. When I was a student I had no clue about the big picture; it took me years to learn it. I want you to have it because such knowledge can help your comfort level as you adjust to this complex new world. And, importantly, having an accurate overview has a practical benefit; it will point you to the people who can help you both avoid and solve problems—knowledge that can empower you.

Colleges and universities are like towns or cities much more than they are like high schools. Most likely your college will have a police force, some form of health center (or even a major hospital), a set of people who collect the "taxes" (tuition), a set of hotel-like structures called residence halls or dorms that also involve food service, a personnel office to deal with the employees, a set of maintenance workers who repair and keep up the buildings and grounds, and people who run a recreation facility and perhaps a major sports complex. Plus there will be advisors, office workers, computer technicians and web developers, librarians, and many others. Even relatively small colleges are complex places with numerous people carrying out many different jobs. Learning how to navigate within your institution is good practice for later life; you need to develop these navigational skills to be effective in whatever you decide to do.

Lifting Off: Initial Advising

As we drift up on our blimp tour, one of the first people we see—and among the first you interacted with on campus—is an advisor who helped and will continue to help you select your courses. Nearly all colleges have required advising for their new students; that advising normally takes place during orientation sessions. Orientation may be required or it may be voluntary. If it is voluntary, I hope you attended (or will). You'll save time in the long run, and orientation is a good place to begin making new friends and to learn about the culture of your college. Orientation sessions throw a lot of information at you, and it won't all stick. But orientation can give you a good start on building a systematic understanding out of the many new facts you hear. You'll likely be handed a lot of written material. Save it in a notebook; some of it will come in handy.

A primary goal of the initial advising session is to get you registered for courses. The advisor is there to ensure that you register for work that is appropriate for your prospective major and that the courses you take include some of the required ones: courses that you need to make progress toward getting your degree. You should come to the initial advising session prepared. If that session has already taken place, then what follows is still relevant for the next term. There are three key items to have ready.

First, before you go to the advising session, you should review the requirements for first-year students (or, if relevant in your case, for transfer students). For example, some colleges require students to take a composition course their first year, whereas others allow students to test out of the composition course or to substitute a high school Advanced Placement (AP) course for it. Previewing the requirements will speed up the advising session.

Even though there are numerous requirements, there likely will be choices within each of those requirements as we discussed in the previous chapter. For example, you may be required to take a social science course, but you can choose among anthropology, economics, psychology, sociology, and others. You should definitely have a look at the choices in advance. One way to do that is to look at the websites of the departments or the professors who teach the courses that satisfy the requirements. Many departments and professors will have information about those courses posted on their websites, and in that way you can get an advance idea about the course. Another way to get a feel for what is covered in the courses is to visit the campus bookstore or an online bookstore and browse through the required textbooks.

Second, make sure you've taken any required assessment tests. Many universities give a test or conduct some other assessment to see, for example, which college math class you should start with or what level foreign language course you are prepared for. At some colleges these assessments are given during orientation days, whereas at others you are expected to take them in advance (perhaps via a secure website). These assessments, along with appropriate scores on AP tests or the College Level Examination Program (CLEP) tests, may also earn you college credit toward your degree. The advisors can help you understand the assessment tests and the AP rules for your university and therefore can save you time and money.

Third, you should discuss with the advisor any constraints you may have on your schedule, including a work schedule. Working off campus may limit the number of credits you realistically should take, and it can lead to scheduling conflicts. Advisors are good at helping you get a reasonable schedule. We'll return later to the question of setting priorities between courses and work.

If you are living on campus, another person we'll spot right away is a residence hall assistant or advisor. Some of them will likely be undergraduates who have lived in the residence hall and then received training on how to help new residents like you. They help you settle in to your new living arrangements and brief you on its ground rules. The university requires you to sign a contract specifying the fees you'll pay and, additionally, asks you to commit to those ground rules. We'll talk more about campus living later, but for now I'll simply mention that I've never met a residence hall assistant who did not want to be helpful.

Going Up: Departments and Their Faculty

The next things we see as we gain altitude and scan the university are the professors and their academic homes: the "departments." For example, there may be a Mathematics Department, an Electrical Engineering Department, an English Department, and many others. The academic department is the main educational unit in most colleges; you will have lots of interactions with people at the departmental level. The department members are the faculty who will be your professors when you take courses—so an individual will be a professor of mathematics, or electrical engineering, or English, or accounting, etc.

The departmental faculty members determine the requirements for each major field of study. These are the individuals responsible for proposing and teaching the curriculum: the set of courses that will allow you to become a college-educated person. They are the scholars and scientists, artists and musicians, abstract thinkers and concrete doers—most of all, the teachers—who make the university hum with interest. Their talent and dedication is why you want to be on your campus.

Each department has a department chair or department head who is the faculty member responsible for its operation. This is a very important job, and the chair is an important person. You will probably get to know, or at least learn about, the chair of the department that offers your major.

Faculty members come in three (sometimes four) ranks: Usually the initial rank is that of assistant professor. That is, a new professor gets hired with that title. Typically a person is in that rank for 5 or 6 years. If and when an assistant professor gets promoted, it is to the rank of associate professor. And finally, after some additional years, the individual may be promoted to professor (sometimes called full professor). Some universities start by hiring people as instructors and then possibly promoting them to assistant professor.

The academic ranks are instructor, assistant professor, associate professor, and (full) professor.

In every case, it is fine to call a person at any of these ranks by the title *professor*. Because most professors, including assistant professors, have the PhD degree, they also can be called *doctor*. (By the way, the term *doctor* originally meant *teacher*.) A few universities have the tradition of using *Mr.* or *Ms.* instead of *doctor* as the form of address; you'll quickly note if that is the case.

Some of your teachers, especially in the first year or two, and especially in larger universities, may be graduate students who themselves are studying for the PhD or some other advanced degree. They will probably list their names on the course syllabus as Mr. or Ms. If so, that's the proper way to address them. And, of course, we are pretty informal in this country in how we address each other, so some of your instructors may ask you to call them by their first names. That's okay, but my advice is to use the more formal mode anyway unless the instructor insists on the informal mode—most people respond well if you use the title they worked hard to get.

As I've noted, the department is the core educational unit in most colleges and universities. Universities are fabulous places largely because of all the ideas and activities that are started by the faculty members. They teach classes, of course, and that is a major part of their responsibilities; but they do a lot more than that. Most are real experts on a topic and spend time learning more about it; many contribute new knowledge to their field of interest. Part of the fun of being a student is meeting some faculty members and learning what they do (see Meeting the Instructors, p. 118). Though it may be intimidating at first, getting to know some faculty members can help you grow and mature both intellectually and socially; later on it can help you get a great letter of recommendation. Remember, your professors were once students in the college classroom as you now are. Most enjoy some lighthearted banter and a comment on the day's news, though they assume that you are visiting them with a real question or comment. Here is a simple way to make a good first impression:

When sending e-mail or other communications to a professor, put your best foot forward: Begin with a proper

salutation (e.g., Dear Prof. Hernandez) and write in complete sentences with correct spelling.

I know this will sound terribly old-fashioned to some readers, but anything less will impress many professors as sloppy work and therefore the product of a student who does not care. That is not the image you want to project.

GRADUATE STUDENTS AND ADJUNCT FACULTY

I mentioned that some of your instructors may be graduate students—individuals who are studying for an advanced degree such as a PhD. This is especially likely in first-year labs or recitation sections of courses in large universities. Grad students may also be the instructors in basic writing courses, beginning language courses, college algebra sections, and a few others. A large number of colleges and universities today have many basic courses taught by graduate students (under the supervision of a professor) or other teaching specialists, although this is not as common at community colleges and smaller liberal arts colleges.

Having a graduate student as instructor does not mean that you have someone of shaky competence in front of you. Graduate students are a very bright and highly educated group of individuals: On average they spend more than 7 years getting the PhD degree. Most universities have training programs for their graduate student instructors (sometimes called teaching fellows or teaching assistants), and by far most of them are very fine in the classroom. The graduate students have the advantage of being closer to you in recent experience; as a result, they often are excellent in being able to relate to you and your current state of knowledge (or confusion!). Of course, they do not have as much teaching experience as do the seasoned professors. However, there will always be a professor in some kind of supervisory role behind the graduate student teachers, so both they and you can get the proper advice and guidance if problems come up. Though it's unlikely you'll have occasion to use the following, you should know that:

If you have a concern about a graduate assistant who is teaching a course, you can ask to speak with that person's supervising professor or to the chair of the department that is offering the course.

There is one more category of faculty member to mention. You may also have as one of your instructors an *adjunct professor* or *adjunct instructor*. People with these or similar titles are most commonly found in community colleges and the larger universities. Adjunct professors are temporary faculty members, hired by the institution to teach one or more courses. They may or may not do this on a continuing basis, term after term.

Colleges hire adjunct professors for one of two reasons. First, an adjunct may be a professional in the community who can bring a wealth of practical knowledge and experience to bear on the material being covered. Second, colleges hire adjuncts when they do not have, or cannot afford to have, enough regular, full-time faculty members to meet the teaching needs of the students. Adjuncts, too, are usually very fine teachers. Indeed, they likely have considerable devotion to their teaching role and to their students.

Because of their temporary status, adjunct professors may not be around the following semester to help you make up work or take an exam you missed because of, say, an illness during the previous term. In that case, you need to contact the advisor or the chair in the department that offered the course. One of them will be able to help make the needed arrangements for you.

THE DEPARTMENTAL STAFF—
THE PROBLEM SOLVERS

I said that the department members are the faculty. They are, but in reality the faculty are part of a larger team, and the additional team members can help make your college days a success. These include the staff members who greet you when you go to the departmental office and, in many colleges and universities, a person or persons in the department who serve as academic advisor to students. You want to make use of the knowledge and help you can get from these key people.

In particular, the departmental advisors are very important because they know the requirements for getting a degree and can help make sure that you register for the right courses at the right time—even if you actually do the registering at a website. They may also help with career planning or internships, or direct you to the most qualified people on campus who can advise you on those topics. Too, the advisor is usually the first person aside from the professor whom you will seek out if some form of academic trouble finds your doorstep.

Here is a quiz item: "This presidential hopeful carried a box of thank-you cards with him on the campaign trail and after an event immediately penned thank-you notes to volunteers and event workers. Many believe this helped him win the presidency. Who was this?"

The answer is President George H. W. Bush, the first President Bush. The point is not about him, but about the effect that getting even a very brief note has on the person who gets it. Ninety percent of my paper mail consists of bills or junk; I always open a "real" letter first, and I bet you do, too. If I get a handwritten thank you note, wow! I do not forget it. Therefore, consider sending a brief note of thanks to the advisor who helped you. Sending it electronically is fine, but a card makes a much more memorable impression. Almost no one ever does that, which is fine because it will make you stand out in a really good way. Some students think they'll be perceived as "kissing up" if they take the time to carry out this simple act, and maybe some of their less mature friends will see it that way. But consider this: If it's good enough for a president of the United States . . .

> **After you are registered, and after school starts, make an appointment with the departmental advising office, even if you are not required to. Do this before the next advising "rush."**

When you arrive, ask the advisor whom he or she recommends as instructor for a course you are thinking about taking next term. Your goal is not to find the "easy" professor—it's considered terrible manners to ask an advisor whom he or she thinks is an easy *A;* that's not the reputation you want to get. Instead, ask if any of the instructors for the required courses you need would be better for someone with your interests (for example, pre-med, or business, or engineering). That way you'll get to know one of the advisors if you later have an issue that requires some real help. This will be part of your networking on campus (and it helps you build these networking skills—they get more important as time goes on). Then, of course, send a thank-you note or e-mail.

The other staff members also have key jobs that help make the university run and hum. More often than not they, sometimes even more than the professors, know how to accomplish many of the things you need done: "finding" space for you in a closed class, unlocking the classroom door when you've left your laptop under your chair, getting in touch with an instructor who is nowhere to be found, etc. One way to get help from these people is simply to remember that they are people. A surprising number of students forget this simple life lesson. Of course, it's the right thing to do. Also, from the staff member's point of view, it's only human to want to put yourself out to help those who are respectful. That's one reason for my recommendation to send a brief thanks when someone does help you, even when it is part of the person's job to do so.

The Higher Administration: What's a Dean?

Let's gain some more altitude on our blimp flight. Suppose you end up meeting a dean, or, scarily, you are told to go see one. You should know that they come in two main varieties—as shown on the next page. One

Academic Dean	Dean of Students
• Is responsible for academic programs, degree requirements, academic deadlines for a college (e.g., College of Business, Engineering). • Handles academic problems including plagiarism, dropping classes after deadlines, etc. • Academic departments in a college report to this dean.	• Supports student programs such as student government, clubs, Greek life, etc. • Investigates nonacademic issues such as underage drinking, sexual harassment, etc.

Typical responsibilities of the two types of deans.

type of dean focuses on "student life" more than on academics. This dean works in the student affairs part of the university—such individuals are typically called the *dean of students,* or the *assistant dean of students,* or some similar title. These deans act in a student-support role or in the area of student discipline. The dean of students is the person who may, on the one hand, be in charge of investigating accusations of sexual harassment, or underage drinking, or other nonacademic violations. On the other hand, this dean helps plan many positive campus events such as walks for charities, or building a Habitat for Humanity house. Such a dean will also work with (not for) student government and Greek letter organizations. He or she generally focuses on developing good programs that happen outside the classroom.

The other type of dean is an *academic dean.* Before we can clearly see him or her, we need to know about colleges. An important organizational fact to keep in mind is that large universities are themselves composed of colleges. For example, Michigan State University is made up of its Colleges of Education, Engineering, Arts and Letters, Social Science, Natural Science, Music, Nursing, and others. In contrast, smaller liberal arts schools usually consist of a single college; that is the case, for example, at Williams College, Macalester College, and many others.

Each academic department belongs to a college (sometimes called a *school*—as in the Business School—these days the terms are generally interchangeable). For example, at Michigan State University the Departments of Chemistry, Mathematics, Biochemistry and Molecular Biology, and some others are part of the College of Natural Science. That college, and each of the others, will be headed by a dean: the Business School will be headed by the dean of business, the College of Engineering by the dean of engineering, etc. Universities vary in the number of colleges they have and therefore in the number of academic deans.

The colleges have many key functions in a university. Among other things, they approve the graduation requirements for students in the college, and they determine the overall curriculum and the amount of the college's money available to each of its departments. Because departments belong to a college, the chairs of departments report to the dean of their college. Thus, the academic deans are at the next level up in the university.

An academic dean usually has the authority to hire faculty and staff, to enforce (and to make exceptions to) the college's policies about graduation requirements, grades, and many other items of keen interest to students. The dean is responsible for making sure that classes are available and for doing all these things and more within the budget he or she is provided—deans, too, worry about money. In larger universities some deans may oversee colleges with budgets in the many tens of millions of dollars, or more.

Academic deans delegate certain responsibilities to others. One of the most important from your point of view will be the person in charge of undergraduate student matters in the college—often officially called the *associate* (or *assistant*) *dean* for *student affairs*, or the *associate dean for academic affairs*, or some similar title. Alternatively, your college might have a person in charge of student advising, perhaps with a title like senior academic coordinator. Remember, this is not the same as the dean of students, who deals with nonacademic issues; rather, it is someone in charge of undergraduate academic matters. Usually the students and staff just call him or her the dean, as in "Go see Dean Jones about this; she will decide whether you can drop the course even though the official deadline for dropping courses has past." In most cases, this is the key person for interpreting rules and regulations about academic issues. The academic dean for undergraduates can be a real problem solver when other possible helpers are not able to do so. If you need this kind of academic help, it's worth a few minutes to figure out whom to see in your college.

Remember Susan Lopez? She wrote the e-mail I quoted at the start of the chapter. When we last heard from her she had failed the first exam in Child Psychology and had written to me as her academic dean with a request to drop the course even though the deadline for dropping courses had passed. Susan was a new student and, as she admitted, was in over her head. In her case, I simply forwarded her message to the right person—whose title in the college was associate dean for student affairs. He had the responsibility to deal with student matters, and in the vast majority of cases he did so without discussing them with me. He knew the student policies and rules down to the last detail, and he had the experience and good judgment to know how to apply them. He called Susan in so that she could meet with him or with one of the experienced college advisors. After that, he made an exception to the policy and let her drop the course. As I said earlier, he decided that she was well-intentioned and that her heart was in the right place, but that her judgment had a ways to go. He strongly suggested to her that she learn from the experience and that she should pay better attention to the advisors in the future.

Please note that this card could not be played again unless the student has a serious illness or a similar documented reason. Susan would not be given another late drop if she ignored the prerequisites for a course or ignored the advice of an advisor to wait before signing up for one. In summary, this academic dean can be very helpful; going to see the dean is not always a bad thing!

The Even Higher Administration: President and Vice Presidents

Our blimp ride has taken us almost to the clouds now; we can see the top of the university's organization. Before we talk very briefly about the vice presidents (VPs), let's give a friendly wave to the president. The college or university president is ultimately in charge of all facets of the institution. All of it. Furthermore, he or she has to balance a budget that involves many millions of dollars each year. Indeed, quite a few major universities now have overall budgets involving billions of dollars. It's a huge responsibility.

Even so, and especially in recent years, the president always needs more money to support the university and to make it better, so fund-raising in one form or another is a big part of the job. Sometimes that means meeting with state legislators or even the governor, or with federal officials; or sometimes it means meeting with foundations or private individuals who can contribute the money that supports student scholarships and other worthy projects. The president also has a

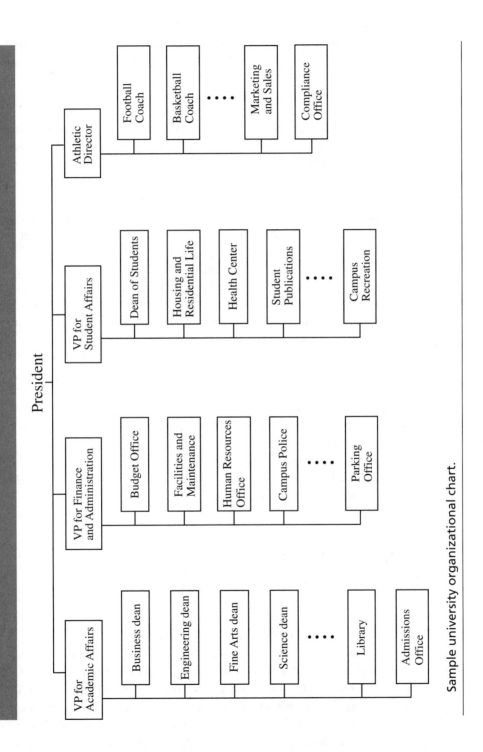

Sample university organizational chart.

major role in setting the overall priorities and vision of the institution. Presidents get paid well, but the job is demanding; they are on call 24/7/365. Depending on the size of your college or university, you may not meet the busy president until you shake hands at graduation. Later, though, I'll tell you how you can get to know him or her if you want to.

Reporting to the president will be some VPs. A typical set of VPs is presented in the organizational chart on the previous pages along with an example of the offices that may report to the various VPs. Also, there may be other VPs depending on the size, mission, and history of the college (e.g., one for medical and health affairs if your university has a medical school, or a VP for research if research a part of the core mission of your school). Your campus organization may differ some from this example; you likely can find a list or a chart showing it on your campus website.

Again, you may never have occasion to meet the VPs, but they too are always on call and are important to the smooth functioning of your university. The people you actually deal with will report to one of them, either directly or indirectly. For example, the dean of students probably reports to the VP for student affairs; and the department chair reports to the college dean who, in turn, reports to the VP for academic affairs. In most universities the library is also a part of the academic affairs office.

The VPs' decisions definitely affect you and your education. Twenty or 30 years ago they were all students like you; most of them cherish the idea that what they do is helpful to students. Of course, on occasion the students will disagree—for example, when the finance VP recommends that tuition needs to be raised to pay the college expenses. Such differences of opinion are part of normal university life.

The University Staff: More Problem Solvers

While we're up here, let's scan again some of the other staff members who affect students. I've mentioned those who work in academic departments. The ones I'm now talking about typically work within a different part of the university's organization. For example, the people in the parking office probably work, directly or indirectly, for the VP for finance. The same is true for those who keep the buildings in good repair. On the other hand, those who work in the residence halls, including the resident assistants, normally will be part of the student affairs component of the university and therefore will report to someone who works for the VP for student affairs. Others who likely report to that office include those who work in the health center, the career center, and the counseling center (where you can and should go for help if your feelings are getting in the way of your work). Some of these offices are shown on the organizational table.

It's possible that you might have difficulty with a university staff member even though you were totally polite and acted with the best of intentions. These things happen occasionally. In that case, spare yourself some hassle and don't over react. Simply tell the person that you don't think the two of you have been communicating effectively and politely ask to speak to his or her supervisor. Given what you now know about the overall organization of the university, you can probably figure out where in the system the person works. Even if you are in the right, though, please don't use the "I pay your salary, so you must do what I say" routine or one of its variants. That rarely works in any setting.

Success: The View From Above

When first discussing Mental Maps to Success in Chapter 2, I mentioned that I was going to introduce some big PICTure maps of the university. We talked then about physical and time "maps." Now we've added maps of some institutional and cultural aspects of the university—though we'll fill in more details when we return to Earth. But while we're up where we can take the long view, let's take a moment to consider what we mean by *success*. As usual, we need a reasonably clear idea of our goals if we want to know whether we've reached them.

There is both a narrow definition of college success and a wider one. From the narrow perspective, you are successful if you make good grades, satisfy the university requirements, choose a rewarding major, and graduate in good time. By calling this a *narrow* perspective, I certainly do not mean that it's easy or unimportant; far from it. Indeed, most of this book is about hitting those narrow targets. But, although crucial, that is not what your college education is really about. The "future you" will be able to accomplish things and to optimistically tackle challenges more effectively than the "current you." If we can list what those things are, we'll have a wider perspective on what will count as success.

The following is my list of characteristics of a "widely successful" person; they are highly ambitious ones, and there are quite a few of them—remember we're listing long-range goals, so why not have bold ones?

You will be a widely successful college graduate if you are

1. Ready to perform at the expected level of professionalism in your first job.
2. Able to communicate clearly, concisely, and quickly in both written and oral formats.
3. Able to set and meet deadlines in both your professional and personal life.
4. Competitive for admission should you choose to apply to a graduate or professional school.
5. Ready to navigate successfully in complex social organizations.
6. Prepared to take up leadership roles appropriate to your experience level.
7. Able to work with a diverse group of people; where diversity includes differences in gender, ethnicity, age, religious preference, political beliefs, and even taste in music or being a fan of the hated teams from Rival U.
8. Able to put current events into a broader social, political, and economic framework. In other words you can see behind the headlines and not just be swept up by them.
9. Committed to lifelong learning to improve your skills and to keep up to date in your career and profession.
10. Ready to make a contribution to your community by being engaged in activities that go beyond your own door.
11. Ready to have mature relationships. You will know how to make and keep friends and know what really counts in making a good marriage or other long-term relationship.
12. Able to enjoy life with a greater depth of understanding. Even being a sports fan is enriched by understanding the history of the game and the role that the sport might have in the current world. That's true for movie buffs, too.
13. Prepared to constructively adapt in a changing world.

This last characteristic, *constructive adaptability,* is one of the most important. An educated person tries to solve the problem of change by finding, or creating, ways to continue to be productive in both career and personal life. This individual can also figure out the boundary between needed recreation and fun, on the one hand, and avoiding one's responsibilities on the other. There are a lot of "walking wounded" out there—people who drink too much, or abuse drugs, or find some other way to avoid the tasks of daily living. They have not found a healthy way to adapt to the normal pressures that arise in a changing world or from the inevitable changes that come as one gets older. You know people like that; they are not fun to be around.

I encourage you to add to or subtract items from my list to make it yours. No matter the details, a college education does not, alas, guarantee that you will constructively adapt and be a success in the wide sense. But as you learn how to "do college," you will gain a set of tools—ways to take action—that will increase those chances. Not all of these tools will be picked up in the classrooms and laboratories. Some are developed by participating in extracurricular activities—that's how leadership skills get honed, for example. Others arise out of interactions with study groups, club and volunteer activities, and late-night talks with new friends.

It's time to land the blimp and return to the practical matters of acing your courses while having time for work, friends, and fun. We'll next examine how to thrive in some challenging classes. That will help build success by any definition.

Summary

All major institutions are composed of smaller units, and these parts are made up of even smaller ones. To make your way effectively inside your university, you will find that it helps to understand its parts and how they are related to one another. A university is a major institution somewhat analogous to a small city. If we focus on the academic part of the university—setting aside for the moment the support components like the health center or career center—a good place to start is the academic department (e.g., the English Department, the Chemistry Department). Faculty members "belong" to departments. Among other things, they determine the courses needed for that major. Faculty members usually start as assistant professors (or instructors) and progress over time to become associate professors and then professors. Other teachers in a department may be graduate students or adjunct faculty. All the teaching faculty—and you—are helped by staff members who work in departments and who help advise students and carry out many other tasks needed to keep things running. Knowing who's who among faculty and staff can help you find answers to your questions and solutions to your problems.

Each department has a faculty member who serves as its *chair* or *head.* A set of related departments make up a *college,* which is headed by an academic dean. The department chairs report to the relevant dean, who in turn reports to the VP for academic affairs. The other vice presidents are in charge of other aspects of the university; for example, there may be a VP for student affairs who is in charge of nonacademic aspects of student life. The dean of students may be part of this office. He or she helps plan positive campus events and, as well, is typically the person in charge of handling nonacademic offenses such as sexual harassment. Both types of deans (academic dean and dean of students) are excellent resources when you have an issue you must deal with. This chapter has provided thumbnail sketches of the university's organization and who is responsible for what. By using the particular table of organization for your college or university, you can track down the office that can best help you with your issue in a timely way.

TAKE ACTION— NAVIGATE YOUR STANDARDS FOR SUCCESS

Spend a few minutes constructing your own list for what constitutes wide success. College is a good time for reviewing and reflecting on what success means to you. Then, next to each item on your list, add an action step that you think will help increase the chances for you to meet that goal. The action may be as simple as investigating what courses will assist you, or committing to a particular off-campus activity. Once you've done that, then block out some time for next semester to carry out those actions.

EXPLORE YOUR CAMPUS

Find the organizational chart for your campus. Tie some of the key offices to the physical office location so that you'll know where to go if you want to get help from that office. For example, find the location of your academic dean's office, the student health center, and the financial aid office.

Try to determine the academic rank of each of your instructors. Are any of them full professors? Adjunct professors?

SELF-TEST ITEMS

1. What responsibilities do faculty members have for determining the required courses for your major?
2. If you must drop a course for a compelling nonacademic reason (e.g., a serious illness), and if the deadline for dropping courses has passed, how would you go about it on your campus?
3. What is an adjunct professor?

CONQUERING CHALLENGING COURSES | V

Solving the Mathematics Course

11

My only class that I wonder about is calculus. I thought that since I took it last year that it would be easy, but that doesn't seem to be the case right now . . . I'm hoping that I can just use what I learned last year to get by.

I found out that my math class was so hard for me to handle that the first thing I thought of is to call my parents. Ask them what I should do. I told them that I feel so bad because I did not know anything on the notes from my math class and almost started to cry.

—Students' reflections on starting college

Where Are We Going?

Mathematical "talent" has virtually nothing to do with success in college algebra and calculus courses. In contrast, the role of proper study skills and problem-solving techniques is huge. Plus you do have to have a grip on some basic math facts. Thus, to become a successful math student you need to redouble your commitment to use effective study methods. In these courses it is important to be extraordinarily diligent in assessing your current knowledge and skill level and to seek appropriate help as soon as you need it. By the end of the chapter, you will be able to describe the confidence-building steps that will improve your math performance. You will also be

http://dx.doi.org/10.1037/14181-011
Your Complete Guide to College Success: How to Study Smart, Achieve Your Goals, and Enjoy Campus Life, by Donald J. Foss

able to describe an effective overall approach to solving math problems that will allow you to have something concrete to try when you get stuck. In addition, you'll be able to explain how anxiety has its effects on math performance.

T rue story: "Ron, I'm done for," I said over the phone late one evening to a good friend who was in my math class. "I'm completely stuck and cannot begin to do the homework problems. Do you have a minute?"

Not being able to do the work, even when I'd set aside the time to do it, was a chilling experience because I thought for a short while that I might be a math major (among other majors!). But there is nothing like a skin-of-the-teeth, barely passing grade to convince one that maybe this topic is not the golden key to the future. My late-night call to Ron was a sign that I was lost. Not the call itself, so much, as the fact that I had waited to make it until I was in mathematical quicksand up to my brain's frontal lobes. And in those days I simply didn't know how to deal with something like that. I thought that if I could just carry on, could move to the next topic, I would somehow catch on and catch up.

My problem wasn't that I was afraid of math—until then, I wasn't; it was that I didn't know how to get myself out of trouble once I was in it. Fundamentally, I didn't know how to be a true problem solver. Struggle, struggle, toil and—yes, trouble was the result. Ron tried to help, and for way more than a minute, but he didn't have the time to tutor me, nor did he know how to diagnose my problem. I wouldn't have blamed him if he had simply told me that I'd come up against my level of intelligence. I imagined him saying, "Don, from now on only people who are smarter than you are can do this." And though I went once or twice to the instructor's office, I was too foolish to get the real help I needed when I needed it. Like the student quoted previously, I hoped that I could "just use what I learned last year to get by." At the college level, that's a fool's wish.

Much later I figured out what my problems were. First, I had failed to understand and master a couple of really basic mathematical points—ideas and techniques that much of the rest of the material was based on. Second, I did not regularly and rigorously test myself—or take seriously enough the results of the class quizzes—to fully appreciate the holes in my knowledge. I was avoiding honest self-assessment, so I did not repair those holes nor even understand what needed repair.

As you know, a lot of math is cumulative. You must understand W to understand X, you must understand X to be able to understand Y, etc. Therefore:

If your knowledge doesn't cumulate, your troubles will.

And then you begin making sad little late-night calls to your friends. Calling for help is okay—more than okay—you should do it; I should have done it. But as I now understand and certainly want you to know, you should make such calls early and often, and to the right people.

Perhaps math is not a problem for you, nor will it be; perhaps you have no more anxiety about math than about other college courses. About half of the students entering college feel that they are ready for math and confident about it. If that's you, that's great; some of what I say in the next few paragraphs may not apply to you. But other tips on how to think about problem solving will be useful in other environments, including work settings, and for problems other than strictly mathematical ones.

Recognizing and Acting on a Problem—In Math and Elsewhere

Like many college students, you may be reluctant to admit that you need help at the moment when it will do you the most good—when you've first wandered off the path of comprehension. It's understandable why. You may still be establishing your independence, a very important step in your personal development, and you are likely engaged in the process of self-discovery. Therefore, you may wonder, "How can it be 'self discovery' if I have to ask someone for help in figuring out what to do next?" Or you may ask yourself, "How can I be independent if I have to look for help at the first sign of trouble?" Or you may simply be reluctant to admit you have a problem for fear of appearing dumb; or because you're afraid that you're wasting the professor's or teaching assistant's time.

Instead of asking yourself those questions, you should instead tell yourself the following, which happens to be true: The most effective people are not those who always go it alone, but those who know when to confer with others and how to build a team. Those people end up being successful and being leaders. Because that is one of your goals, this is a good time, and a relatively safe place, to practice the art of consulting. As you go along, you'll need to find the right balance between head-down, individual, concentrated work, on the one hand, and seeking assistance and building a support team on the other. My advice is straightforward: It's better at first to err on the side of seeking too much assistance rather than too little. Think of it as setting up a private, personal "consulting firm" where you are seeking the consultation rather than providing it. Given the common reluctance to ask for help, you may even have to give yourself a little pep talk to take the first steps. Still, you should:

> **Seek out help—from your instructor or teaching assistant, or from your study group, friends, etc.—if you cannot understand the material after working a couple of extra hours on it.**

Of course, the first step in dealing with a problem is acknowledging that you have one. To recognize that you have a problem, you need to be frequently tested, or to test yourself, to ensure that you really have learned what you need to know. We discussed this a lot in Chapter 3, but I want to underscore it here: Avoiding honest self-assessment is deeply unwise; such self-deception stunts your intellectual development and can destroy your ability to function in areas that are important to you. That is particularly true in cumulative courses like math.

MORE ON STUDY GROUPS

We also discussed in Chapter 3 some advantages of forming or joining a study group, and I provided tips on how an effective group works. I believe that study groups can be particularly useful in courses that require "correct answers," such as mathematics, aspects of science, engineering, accounting, etc. For example, I had virtually no training in music when I signed up for a basic course in music appreciation. Among other things, the exams presented brief musical samples and we were asked to name the time period when each was written. Partway through the course I joined a study group whose members tested each other on course topics, including the ability to identify the time period of a musical selection. Those assessments gave me a wake-up call. I thought I had kept up but found out I was way behind the others in developing a "trained ear." Alas, the exam confirmed this, though I surely did better on it because of the help I got from the group.

A major advantage of study groups is that they can provide feedback about your state of knowledge and where you stand relative to others. The group can also help keep you on task and increase the likelihood of your spending the right amount of time on the subject. Too, members of the group can help one another as soon as someone begins to falter, carrying out the role of a good tutor by diagnosing what's not understood and providing the missing information (see Chapter 9 for how tutoring best works). With respect to mathematics and similar courses, members of a study group also can help you learn *how* to solve the problem at hand, which of course is better than just providing the solution.

Finally, joining or forming a study group is a good way to expand your set of friends on campus. All in all, getting involved with fellow students around a course is usually a very positive experience. Two warning flags, though: First, group work does little good unless the members have the appropriate agenda—one that focuses on testing and giving honest feedback to each other and helping each other actually learn the key concepts and techniques needed to succeed in the course. Meetings do little good if they amount to critiquing the instructor or simply restating what was covered in the book or in class. Second, remember that on exams you have to be able to do the problems alone. Don't assume that you can solve a problem just because your group can.

HELP CENTERS

> Physics and Precalc remain difficult because it has been very hard to find help in both subjects. Giving up isn't the answer to it, but I feel as though I have nothing else to do . . . I have heard of tutoring somewhere on campus and I think it's time to check that out. Why are these subjects so hard since I have taken them in previous years?
>
> *—A student's reflection after starting college*

Math departments generally are very good at providing extra help for their students. A scan of Internet sites suggests that it is the norm for community colleges and universities to have a free math help/tutoring center. Indeed, it's hard to find a school that doesn't. With high probability your college will have one. Do not hesitate to visit it at the first sign of struggle that you cannot resolve after a couple of extra hours studying your notes and text and doing the homework problems.

Math support centers vary in the degree to which the helpers are able to be genuine tutors in the sense we discussed in Chapter 9. Many math centers have only enough available staff to answer direct questions, correct obvious mistakes, and provide general guidance on problem solving. That's a lot, though, and in many cases it can be enough to get you over a rough spot or confirm that you are on the right track. Frequenting such a center is therefore a very good idea. Happily, some centers may have enough resources to provide one-on-one assistance to the point where the helper gets to know what you know and what you don't. In that case, he or she can act as a real tutor. That's a tremendous benefit, and you should definitely make use of it.

Mathematics: Hard or Easy?

Mathematics is both hard and easy. It's hard for certain people because, well, some of it *is* hard—though so is playing the piano; writing an engaging term paper; or, for that matter, learning to drive a car with a stick shift. In other words, it's hard in just the normal way that lots of things are. But an important reason why it's hard for some students is that they *believe* it's unusually hard. That belief creates enough anxiety to fill a supertanker.

The anxiety may arise for some students because they did not have expert math teachers in high school or earlier. Or they might have had good teachers but nevertheless failed to master some basic high school math concepts, even though they managed to pass the course with a decent grade. Whatever the cause, that now makes things difficult because of the cumulative nature of math. Also, the sense of difficulty associated with math often arises from the simple fact that you do have to put in significant, mindful time to grasp the material. You can't fake it. That requirement—the need to be a diligent student—is then interpreted as making the math itself difficult. This amounts to confusing the difficulty associated with any challenging task, on the one hand, with the topic or content of that task (in this case, mathematics), on the other. But whatever the source of the fear, if you believe now, or at the time of the upcoming exam, that math is super hard and even scary, we need very quickly to get you past that self-defeating attitude.

Mathematics is easy. Or perhaps better: Most of it can be easy enough if you are willing to work at it—and you already know how to do that. To learn basic college math, and therefore to do well in those courses, you simply use the study techniques we've already discussed, with a few modifications. Before we get to them, though, let's first dispose of the Number One Math Myth. I've asked numerous college math instructors what leads to success in college algebra or calculus courses. Not one of them ever said a word about mathematical "talent." Even if there is such a thing:

Mathematical talent is not what it takes to do well at this level.

This is an extremely important observation. Many, many students, starting in high school or even before that, will say that they just don't have a head for math, that they don't have the talent for math, or some similar statement. You should never say such a thing to yourself. Here is a truth:

Many students much less prepared than you are have mastered college algebra and calculus.

Here is another truth:

Many students much more anxious about math than you are have mastered college algebra and calculus.

If you say to yourself that you can't master math because you don't have the talent for it, then you give yourself an excuse for not doing what has to be done to actually learn it. You can easily turn your self-defeating attitude into a real-life defeat. What good is that? It's no good, of course, because you then close the door on a large number of options for what you can accomplish later in your college years. More important, you restrict your options for what you can do after college. This is big.

You can do math.

HOW TO BUILD CONFIDENCE
(AND HOW TO TEAR IT DOWN)

The number one key to learning college mathematics is to carry out the study program I've already described, but with extra diligence and with a few additions. Here I'm going to be just as direct as possible (take this medicine!):

1. You must go to class every day.
2. You must do the homework every day. Put time on your master calendar for daily math homework to help guarantee yourself that you'll get it done.
3. Do the homework in a mindful, reflective fashion, paying attention both to what you are doing and to how you are doing it as you work toward the math goals described in the syllabus or the textbook.
4. Be very concrete about your subgoals—about what you should be able to do at the end of each section of the book.
5. Take all the quizzes and exams on time.
6. Take seriously the feedback you get from the homework, the quizzes, the pop quizzes, and the exams. Use that feedback to ensure that you really can do the work and that you understand the basic concepts. Or to put it in a now familiar way: Be totally honest in your self-assessments.
7. And as we've already discussed, ask for help at the first sign of confusion that doesn't clear up after a couple of extra of hours of work. Also, ask for help whenever your confidence wavers.

This is a long list, and I know I'm nagging a bit. But I'm being extraordinarily direct because if you do these things, you can do well in your math courses. It doesn't matter what you think about your level of math "talent," you can learn mathematics. I know about a college math program that tracks students very thoroughly—how often they attend class, whether they turn in the (very frequent) homework every time on time, whether they take the (frequent) pop quizzes, how often they visit the help center, and other measures as well. The director of this program told me that students who are diligent in doing all these things have a very, very high chance of doing well in the course. If you had any doubts to start with, your confidence will build if you carry out this approach to the subject. You will find out: You can do math. Not only that, you will enjoy the feeling of accomplishment that comes from mastering it.

In contrast, here is a way guaranteed not to build confidence: A friend of the family knew that I had once studied college math and asked me to help her daughter, Miranda, a high school student who was in danger of flunking a course. When we met, Miranda told me that she was really worried about the class and very serious about learning the subject matter—and that she had one week to do so! She had managed to put off 90% of the course until there was less than 20% of the grading period left. Miranda was, at last, dedicated, and we worked on math every evening; but it isn't possible to cram successfully to that extent. There was too much material to cover in too short a time, and by then she was so anxious that I had to spend time each day just calming her down.

Miranda squeaked by (that is, she didn't flunk the course), but that's more a comment on her teacher's grading standards than it is on what she learned. Also, whatever she tried to pour into her head when we were working together then drained out like a flash flood—this was massed practice with a vengeance—so virtually nothing was done to help her long-term knowledge of math or her confidence that she could do it. She was probably more anxious next time she "had" to take math, not less. The obvious moral of this story is:

It's much better to keep up than to catch up.

HOW MATH ANXIETY AFFECTS MATH PERFORMANCE

One of your self-management goals is to keep from having high levels of anxiety about math (and other topics, of course) if you are subject to such feelings. We talked in Chapter 7 about anxiety and attitudes, and how to get control over them. It's appropriate to bring that topic up again here, though, because we now know some important things about how anxiety has its negative effect on mathematics. In particular, when you're doing math, you make use of something that psychologists call your "working memory." It's a bit like a mental scratch pad. Suppose I ask you to multiply 27×18 in your head. Go ahead, try it.

However you go about such mental multiplication, you have to keep track of some intermediate numbers, and there is a limit to how many of them you can hold onto at any given moment. That's your *working memory capacity*. People differ, but working memory is quite limited for nearly everyone. You might be okay with doing 27×18 in your head, but few of us can manage mentally multiplying 694×847; in that case, working memory gets swamped, we lose our place, and we get an incorrect answer.

Psychologist Mark Ashcraft and others (e.g., Ashcraft & Krause, 2007) have shown that the very act of coping with anxiety requires working memory. In other words, high anxiety leads to more strain on working memory. As a result, there is less space available on the mental scratchpad to carry out mathematical operations. In simple summary:

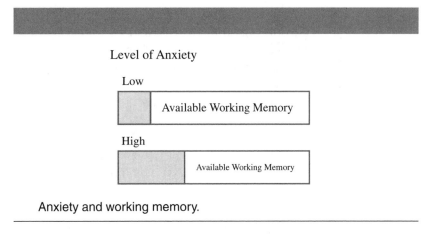

Anxiety and working memory.

High anxiety leads to a reduction in available working memory, which leads to poorer performance in math. This finding gives us another reason to avoid anxiety—not that we needed one. And it's no surprise now to hear that one of the best ways to avoid anxiety about math is (drum roll!) to be on top of the material by using the most effective learning techniques.

Having said that, it is true that some students do have excessive anxiety about math tests even when they've used the proper study/ self-assessment methods and done their best to master the material. Recall that we discussed test anxiety near the end of Chapter 6; please review the advice given there if a math course is stimulating such anxious feelings.

THEOREM: MATHEMATICIANS LIKE PROOFS

It will help if you know a few additional specifics about doing math. First, mathematicians put a premium on precision and economy in their work and their writing. Many math textbooks follow this tendency, and therefore are very focused on the theorems (a statement, usually in formula form, that something is the case, e.g., a triangle contains 180°), and a proof that the theorem is correct. Each line of such a proof is a "sentence" in the language of mathematics, but the number of standard English sentences in these math textbooks tends to be small. In consequence, the printed work is very dense. As you already know from high school, you cannot read a math book the way you do other texts, even science books. It usually doesn't make a lot of sense to highlight or underline in a math book. The book is already tightly packed with information, and the most important points are highlighted in some way right in the text. Even though it is getting more common for math texts to be available in online versions (in some universities that's the only way they're available), the author's dense style probably will be similar to that of a printed version.

Some math textbooks do have a more informal style. That is, they contain more English sentences and thus are somewhat more readable. These texts provide more instructions about the steps involved in getting from one line to the next in a proof and contain hints about how to solve the example problems. In other words, they try to show more about the process of doing the math. If your course uses a traditional, formal book (a terse text), you'll have to acquire and use it, of course; and it may be perfect for you. However, you might also want to take a look at a book or website that covers the material using a style that pays additional attention to the problem-solving steps—that is, a book that is more process oriented.

You can find such books by going to the library stacks and looking in the section that holds books cataloged as QA—in particular, look near QA 150 and QA 300 for algebra and calculus, respectively. (Incidentally, college libraries use the Library of Congress system for cataloging books; your high school and public library probably use the Dewey Decimal system.) If you spot a process-oriented book that looks like it might help, check it out or consider going to an Internet book site and purchasing a used copy as a supplement to your text. For this purpose you don't need the most recent edition (algebra and calculus really haven't changed much in the past few years!). I found just such a book in good condition for $1.00, plus shipping.

Even a process-oriented "informal" math book is far from chatty, though, and it can be a problem to separate the really fundamental, forest-sized points from the details. When I went back years later to review some math, I found very helpful the attitude and approach of an award-winning math professor, Michael Starbird. He pointed out on a DVD/Internet course he offers (Starbird, 2007) that "calculus is the exploration of just two ideas—the derivative and the integral—both of which arise from a commonsense analysis of motion. He also said that "all a 1,300-page calculus textbook holds are those two basic ideas and 1,298 pages of examples, variations, and applications." It's obviously important to be sure you understand those two fundamental ideas, which he and others present with great clarity.

Mathematicians believe in truth—in getting things right and in proving that they've gotten them right. In many math courses you will be asked to follow those proofs and to reproduce or to verify them. It is important to get clear about how much of the proof process your instructor expects you to know—do you have to verify that a proof is correct, or are you expected to reproduce it? The answer will affect how you study.

After your text or your instructor proves a theorem, that result can be used in solving new problems. Problem solving is usually the heart of the course.

How Math Problems Work and How to Work Math Problems

Following proofs is one thing; working problems is another. Like you, perhaps, I was usually able to follow along with the book or the professor when the theorems were being proved (which is certainly not the same as saying I could then prove them on my own!). But I often got stuck doing problems because I didn't know how to approach them effectively. I did not have a set of mental tools that allowed me to tinker constructively with a problem until I worked it out. There is a difference between what is shown in most (especially the terse) mathematics textbooks—the theorems and their proofs, the example problems and their solutions—and the mental processes that you carry out to solve new problems. Most math books do not spend much time discussing what you need to do to actually work the problems. But that is what you have to learn.

In his book, *How to Solve Problems,* psychologist Wayne Wickelgren (1974) wrote:

> In college I was enormously irritated by the hundreds of hours that I wasted staring at problems without any good idea about what approach to try next in attempting to solve them. I thought at the time that there was no value in those "blank" minutes, and I see no value in them today. (p. ix)

It's true; staring blankly is frustrating and not a good problem-solving strategy. We do not have space here to comprehensively cover the effective ways to attack math problems (see, e.g., Dahlke, 2008, for a more extended discussion). We can, though, provide an overall strategy for what you can do.

To be successful in working math problems, you need a mindful plan: a set of instructions that guides you in figuring out what to do. In broad outline, such plans have two major parts:

- First, you must recognize (or figure out) what kind or type of problem is in front of you; and
- second, you must carry out a sequence of mathematical operations to solve that problem.

By *operations* I mean things like "adding a constant to both sides of an equation," or "dividing both sides of an equation by x, where x is not zero." In other words, operations are legal changes or rearrangements you can make to a formula. In theory, then, it's straightforward: First, recognize the type of problem; second, apply the proper operations to get the answer. In practice, of course, it's not so simple.

MATHEMATICAL OPERATIONS WITHOUT PAIN

For the moment, let's talk about the second aspect of the overall plan, the operations component. The chances for successful problem solving will increase as you get comfortable and confident with applying various mathematical operations across a variety of problems. Some solutions (or parts of solutions) require you to recall and use the most basic mathematical operations (e.g., do you remember that multiplication distributes over addition?), whereas others require you to apply new operations that you are just learning. Without doubt, you do have to learn, and learn how to use, a small briefcase full of mathematical operations.

For each problem you have a starting point, the problem's "givens," and a goal, the end point where, for example, you now know what x is or you know how long it took to fill up that odd-shaped container described in the problem. You move from the starting point to the goal by a series of steps, the operations, each of which you can explain or justify.

Frequently you can adopt the technique of working on subgoals, first breaking down the initial problem into a set of smaller or simpler ones and then solving them—once again using the old strategy of divide and conquer. In this case you might say something like this to yourself: "If I can get from the starting point to knowing what y and z are, then I might be able to get from y and z to x. When I do that, I'll have solved the problem. Now, what operations can I apply to get from the starting point to knowing the values of y and z?"

GROUPING OPERATIONS AND "WORKING BACKWARDS"

Reaching a subgoal often involves grouping together a set of operations that move you from the givens to that subgoal—which, recall, you think is a point along the way to the solution. To pick up a familiar analogy, grouping mathematical operations together is like typing the word *the* rather than typing *t* followed by *h* followed by *e*. Of course, *the* requires three keystrokes, but it probably doesn't feel that way; the three keystrokes (operations) are so well learned that they roll speedily off your fingertips as one. When solving a math problem, you pull out and try operations that meaningfully go together—those that have led to past success in reaching a subgoal. You do have to work on lots of problems before you learn which operations you can fruitfully group together in this way, but recall that you didn't learn to type fluently in one evening either.

In some cases, you can adopt the strategy of working backwards from the goal state to the starting point, again by using appropriate operations. In this working-backwards strategy you try to see if you know how to move to the goal from some point that (you think) is in between the starting state (the givens) and the goal. You begin by assuming that the intermediate point is a subgoal. If you can get from it to the goal, that's half the battle. Then you try to see if you can move from the starting point to that subgoal. If that works, eureka! You've solved the problem.

As the course goes along, you will be asked to learn more and fancier operations and to string more operations together to move from the problem to the solution. Once you think you know the problem type, you can begin to apply the appropriate operations to solve it. It takes practice, but after a while you will develop an ability to judge which operations are the best ones to try first, which to try next, etc. Learning the operations and the order in which to try them is very important, but for me, at least, that was the relatively easy part.

WHAT'S YOUR PROBLEM?

The harder task is the prior one: recognizing the type of problem that you have in front of you (e.g., is it a mixture problem?). Recognizing or identifying the problem type requires, first of all, that you realize that that is what you are trying to do (it's the first step of your plan).

It helps if you make a list of the problem types that are covered in each unit or chapter. You can then try them out to see which one of them fits the current puzzle. This list will be of manageable size. When you have such a list of problem types (a very good thing to write in your notes), you can directly attack the task of problem identification by actively going through that list. You also can use a process of elimination, narrowing down the problem type by convincing yourself that because it is not type A, B, or C, then you should try out D and maybe E. You first make an educated guess about the type of problem in front of you and then apply your operators to see if you can solve it. This is a sophisticated trial-and-error technique: You're not trying solutions at random; you try each candidate only after doing some preliminary funneling down. You can be fooled, of course, because the subject matter may be similar to an earlier problem even though they are different types of problems. To take a simple example, not all problems involving liquids are "mixture problems."

It often helps to rewrite what is being asked to help ensure that you understand the problem and therefore what type of problem it is. Also, many students find that drawing a picture—representing the problem's givens in a spatial format—helps them recognize what problem type they are faced with. Mindful practice will help teach you to recognize problem types, though you'll make mistakes. Sometimes you have to try out your bag of operations and find that they don't work before you realize that you've misidentified the type of problem you're facing. That happens to everyone.

Not surprisingly, the problems at the end of a chapter or a section of a textbook tend to be taken from the problem types introduced in that chapter. That narrows it down. Exams will often present problems from more than one section or chapter, though, so you must test yourself to ensure that you can recognize all the problem types that might be on the exam.

If you are having difficulty recognizing the problem—that is, difficulty in determining the type of problem that is in front of you—it is a good idea to visit the professor or the teaching assistant to ask for help. During the visit you want, first, to get a list of the problem types that the course currently is focused on, and second, to ask for help in recognizing the clues that tell you what type of problem is in front of you. Because recognizing problems types gets easier with mindful practice, the experienced teaching assistant (TA) might not even appreciate that spotting the problem type can be a source of struggle for the relative beginner. The TA may not have thought much about how he or she recognizes such "simple" types of problems—simple to him or her, that is. However, if you frame your question along the lines outlined here—you're having a problem with problem identification—that will help the TA or the professor guide you.

Just as a musician comes to recognize musical phrases rather than individual notes, or the way an experienced point guard in basketball comes to recognize at a glance the types of defenses facing him or her, you will get faster and more accurate over time at recognizing problem types. Slowly—but surely—your confidence and even your enjoyment will increase because your knowledge lets you move from just "following the ball" to assessing how well you executed the particular play. You get to the point where you recognize patterns; you "see" what the problem is, and then you get good at carrying out the operations to solve it. But such fluency does not happen immediately in sports, or music, or driving a stick shift—or in math. Success requires you to put in the hours of reflective practice, with feedback.

THE END OF THE BLANK STARE

You are building a mental storehouse containing specific actions you can try when approaching any new problem. If you have such a set of actions, and a plan for which solution technique to try first and which one to try next (because you begin to recognize problem types), then when faced with a problem you will always have something to do. Recall that there is no value whatsoever in those "blank" minutes you spend staring at a problem. You are neither solving it nor learning anything useful. If you find yourself staring, that's a sign that either you don't know enough to recognize the type of problem or you don't have enough mental actions (operators) stored up. You need to acquire some additional recognition and action skills—do that instead of staring. It's a time to get some help.

In summary, there are two major mental phases involved in solving math problems: (a) recognizing the problem type and (b) applying operations to the problem such that you can move from the givens to the solution. Each phase involves acquiring knowledge and learning a set of guidelines for applying that knowledge. In practice, things are not so simple because when you attempt to apply your operations (solution steps) to a problem, you may discover that they don't in fact apply as you expected them to and that the problem is of a different type than you first thought. So the two phases of problem solving do not necessarily follow one after another in all cases. That's okay; you may take a few added steps, but you will get to the solution.

What we've discussed in the above paragraphs may sound abstract at this point; I'd be surprised if it didn't. My suggestion is that you mark this section for rereading during, say, the third or fourth week of your next math class. It will likely connect with what you are doing then.

Homework, Quizzes, and Exams

> Do as many problems as possible. The more you do, the better your chances that a similar problem will appear on the exam.
> —*A student commenting on Calculus I*

If you watch a great tennis player hit a thousand serves, will your serve improve? If you submit your math homework problems to an Internet site that solves them and even shows you the solution steps, will your ability to solve such problems improve? In both cases, the answer is no, not very much, if at all. You have to participate in the process, not just observe it. However, you might improve if you know enough to really understand what you're seeing and, in the case of the math problems, if you carefully follow the steps and then test yourself on whether you can repeat them without looking. And you can improve if you then test yourself on whether you can carry out the steps on a new problem of the same type. In other words, learning will occur if you actively practice, get feedback on how you're doing, and assess yourself to ensure that you're getting closer to the goal of being able to carry out the operations yourself. Yes, it's true; we've heard that before.[1]

Without the feedback on how you are doing in carrying out the steps, and especially without the self-assessment, it's too tempting to just scan the steps—to hum them rather than sing them. So my take on the value of such homework websites is that the good ones can provide feedback, but that you should do the homework first, and if you go to such a site, you should use it as a check on how you are doing. In his extensive book on *How to Succeed in College Mathematics*, an experienced college math professor, Richard Dahlke (2008), agreed with our grand overall theme: "You need to know when you know, and when you don't know." He then went on, "Access to too many answers and solutions hinders this. It stifles development of *internal checks* [italics in original] to see if your thought process for working a problem is correct" (pp. 348–349). He also provided this quote from a Calculus student repeating the course: "The more I used the solutions manual, the less I learned (absorbed, understood, and could relate to)" (p. 360).

Like most math professors, Professor Dahlke asks that you be sure you can justify each step in the solution process, that you check your logic and your computational work, and very important, that you check whether your answer seems reasonable. If you mix two containers of water, a large one having a temperature of 50° and a smaller one at 60°, it doesn't matter how big either container is, you know that the answer has to be somewhere in between those two temperatures. If you get caught up in doing computations involving different amounts of water and come up with a temperature of 63.5°F, you know you've made a mistake. It's surprising how often students fail to make the "reasonableness" check.

Of course, you should follow your instructor's rules when it comes to the resources you're allowed to use when you do the homework.

---

[1] As far back as 1945, a distinguished mathematician, G. Polya, recognized that teachers should help students develop the kinds of problem-solving skills we've been discussing. In his book *How to Solve It*, Polya (1945/1957, p. 2) states that he is presenting the *"mental operations typically useful for the solution of problems"* (italics in original). And his approach is strikingly modern:

> First, we have to *understand* the problem; we have to see clearly what is required. Second, we have to see how the various items are connected, how the unknown is linked to the data, in order to obtain the idea of the solution, to make a *plan*. Third, we *carry out* our plan. Fourth, we *look back* at the completed solution, we review and discuss it. (italics in original; pp. 5–6)

Polya even made an analogy identical to the one we've used. He said, "Solving problems is a practical skill like, let us say, swimming" (p. 4).

Your book may have its own resource site on the web, for example, and the instructor may set out some guidelines for using it. I doubt that you'll find a site that your instructor doesn't know about, so don't be too clever when it comes to turning in material that isn't really your work.[2]

Finally, remember that everyone makes mistakes when doing homework and quiz problems. An award-winning math instructor at the University of Houston, Leigh Hollyear, alerts her students to a distinction between what she calls "normal" errors and "heart-stopping" ones. To quote her:

> I point out errors that I think are normal for a student to make—errors that can easily be avoided with practice. I often reassure a student by pointing out "How normal you are! This is a normal mistake." And I go on to tell them about the "heart-stoppers" . . . the mistakes that reveal so fundamental a misunderstanding that massive amounts of help and tutoring might not be enough . . . they get really happy to be normal after that discussion.

If you mindfully practice and do tons of honest assessment, you can help ensure that your mistakes will be normal and, happily, that your professor's heart keeps beating.

Summary

Learning mathematics is an instance of learning. You can learn; therefore, you can learn college mathematics. Put another way, the core techniques needed to do well in math courses are the same ones that work in other subjects. In that sense, math is not special. Nevertheless, many students hit rough weather in college algebra and calculus courses. It's a happy fact, though, that almost every college has resources to help calm those waters. In particular, math help centers and tutoring opportunities are commonly available. You should make use of these college resources (including a study group you've joined) as soon as you determine that you are not making progress toward the course goals or when you find that you don't have a good toolkit of problem-solving techniques for the homework or end-of-chapter quiz items. Frequent and accurate assessment is common in math classes but will help only if you take the results to heart. Students who acquire effective techniques for solving problems have less anxiety, which in itself helps them to do even better.

---

[2]One website that deservedly gets a lot of traffic and that can be helpful when working on many topics (including, but not limited to, mathematics) is WolframAlpha (http://www. wolframalpha.com/examples/). As with any such site, use it wisely as an aid, not a crutch.

Problem solving has two major components: recognizing the type of problem and carrying out steps to take you from the "givens" to the solution. Both of these major components require substantial and mindful practice to get comfortable and quick when you implement them. Homework will help to the extent that you use it to develop knowledge and skill around these two core components.

TAKE ACTION

1. If you haven't already done so, set up a study group of two to four students from your math class. Test one another on recognizing types of problems, and give each other feedback. Discuss what you each look for as a clue to the type of problem in front of you. Also, have a focused discussion on the list of steps or operations you try out when (you think you are) faced with a problem of each type.

2. Visit with the TA or the course instructor if you are uncertain about recognizing problem types and the initial operations you should try with each type.

3. Check your master calendar to ensure that you have booked enough time to do your math homework each day or every other day. Your goal is to keep up in the course.

4. Find out (by asking the instructor or by looking at previous exams or quizzes) how much of the exam will require you to prove theorems or reproduce those proofs. Modify your study time accordingly.

EXPLORE YOUR CAMPUS

Find out where you can get help with mathematics if you feel that you're hitting a snag. Drop by that help center early in the term so that you will be comfortable going there.

SELF-TEST ITEMS

State in your own words:

1. What is (are) the most important study technique(s) that allow you to master mathematics?

2. What are the two major components of problem solving in mathematics? How do you get better at applying them?

3. Explain how anxiety has its negative effect when trying to solve math problems.

4. Evaluate the claim: Doing well in college mathematics courses requires a talent for the subject.

Comprehending the Writing Assignment | 12

Writing is easy. All you do is stare at a blank sheet of paper until drops of blood form on your forehead.
—*Gene Fowler (as cited in R. T. Kellogg, 1994, p. 47)*

Why can't I do that? Why can all these other people do that? They just pick out their little topic sentence and then they write their paper.
—*Student writer "thinking out loud" while working on a paper*

I like the school, except I don't like the fact that you can't just wing papers and get *As* and *Bs*. It'll take some getting used to.
—*A student's reflection on starting college*

Where Are We Going?

Successful writers pay attention to the writing process as well as to the writing product. By so doing, they—and you—can write clearly and creatively, and can meet deadlines. In this chapter, you will learn how better to think about writing assignments and how professional writers get the job done. We adopt a modified problem-solving approach to dealing with a

http://dx.doi.org/10.1037/14181-012
Your Complete Guide to College Success: How to Study Smart, Achieve Your Goals, and Enjoy Campus Life, by Donald J. Foss

writing assignment. By the end of the chapter, you will be able to take positive, concrete steps to "solve the writing problem," including generating ideas, constructing the written paper, and making it easy for the reader to understand your written work. Along the way, you will learn how to avoid the "blank stare" phenomenon, also known as "writer's block." You will also be able to determine whether you've "solved" the assignment.

Writing assignments, like math problems, can cause the blank stare phenomenon: You gaze at a sheet of paper or the computer screen and nothing happens. Time spent spinning your mental wheels while staring at a blank page is time wasted. In this chapter, I'll describe techniques that will make your writing time productive.

Your high school teachers instructed you on how to organize writing assignments, taught correct grammatical structure, probably tried to get you to use information sources in addition to Wikipedia, and gave you feedback on your writing. Those lessons may have given you confidence that you can write a thoughtful and coherent paper. Your mental wheels can bite into writing assignments and move you along—no spinning for you. If so, terrific! Many students feel that way—until they get back their first college writing assignment. "There must be some mistake," a student may think, "I've never gotten back a paper this marked up or a grade this low." Eventually they may discover that writing a paper does not work quite the way they thought it did, and that the familiar writing guidelines are often unhelpful and even misleading. To understand the useful ones, let's put writing in its proper context.

Both speaking and understanding spoken language are easy for us; they are natural acts. All humans—except those with serious neural disabilities—learn to speak and to comprehend spoken language. In contrast, writing is not a natural act. Many people do not learn to write well. Indeed, it is a recent historical phenomenon that great numbers of people learn to read and write at all. Unlike learning to speak, writing is an acquired skill that requires diligence and effort. Once again, then, it is appropriate to draw an analogy between learning to write, on the one hand, and learning a musical instrument or mastering a sport, on the other. Therefore, like all skills, mastering the art of writing requires . . . what? By now you know the rough outline of the answer—mastering a skill requires mindful practice, dividing the task into parts or subgoals, conquering them, and learning from honest assessment and feedback. In short, it requires a version of Goal-Oriented Active Learning.

Writing Skill and the Writing Process

Writing is a high-level skill. Much of what you do when you write cannot be learned to the point of being automatic and easily carried out. In contrast, some aspects of relatively lower level skills such as fingering on the piano, or shifting from second to third gear in a stick-shift car, or shooting a free throw can become automatic with practice. Similarly, signing your name or typing common words like *the* can become automatic in the sense that you don't have to think about them as you do them; they are low-level writing skills. But planning a 2,500-word paper on an assigned topic never becomes automatic. Creating that paper—especially creatively creating it—poses a problem for you. Therefore, it helps to think about writing as a goal-directed activity that amounts to problem solving. That problem requires your attention as well as your time. Even if you can accomplish a writing assignment without excessive emotional churning, the problem-solving perspective can help you improve.

Most of what you've been taught about expository writing has focused on the product—the final paper. What your teachers told you about how that paper should look is generally accurate. The paper should have a focus, usually stated up front in a topic sentence. It should have clear organization. Its sentences should flow from one to the next without jarring discontinuities. Often, it should have a summary. Each sentence should be grammatical and its words should be spelled correctly. It should contain exactly 2,500 words. Oh, wait, maybe I got carried away on that last one.

Mentioning the exact word count, though, points out that most of us have developed (because we've been taught to have) an intense concern, I'll even call it a fixation, with the product. Writing tutors report that students who come in for help may initially insist that the first paragraph should contain a topic sentence and three supporting sentences. Even if this is good advice (sometimes it's not), thinking about it as you begin to write may give you more trouble than help. The chances are good that you will cause yourself brain freeze, or end up staring blankly at the screen, if you concentrate on the paper's final form to guide your initial writing attempt. You may spend a lot of time thinking about the topic sentence when, in fact, you don't yet know what you actually think about the topic!

It's fine, of course, for you to have some idea about the form of the final product—and if you've thought in advance about the paper's subject and have a good topic or thesis sentence and an outline in mind, that's great. Go for it! But that's an unusual event, not the typical one. So rather than start with the end product clearly in mind, you will find it more useful to have valid tips about producing that product.

A key to successful writing is to focus on the process and not just on the product.

Psychologists and others have studied the writing process, and we should take advantage of what they've discovered. Some studies have tracked both what students do and what they are thinking about as they attempt to write. The investigator gets at the conscious thinking process by asking the writer to "think out loud"—to describe in words what's going on as he or she tries to write. With a little practice, people can do that. Let's listen to an actual student talk out loud; she is describing what she's thinking about while working on a paper. We tune in as she finds herself stuck and frustrated:

> Why can't I do that? Why can all these other people do that? They just pick out their little topic sentence and then they write their paper. If I just stuck to the topic sentence, maybe, and I just let the topic sentence govern all my thoughts and let that dictate what I was gonna talk about. (Flower & Hayes, 1981b, p. 48)

The first thing we discover is that this student thinks that others follow a relatively simple rule for writing and that when they follow that rule, the organized words just flow out. Here's their rule as she imagines it: First, they think; second, they get a topic sentence (and usually an outline); and third, they write. If they are really sophisticated, they will wait a day and, fourth, polish the work or even rewrite parts of it. She also thinks that the process she should be following directly mirrors the product she is trying to produce. Quite a few writing guides are based on this rule.

HOW THE PROS CREATE PROSE

The best writers in the world do not follow that rule for writing. If they don't, how can you be expected to? You can see this for yourself by watching an excellent creative writer at work. Robert Olen Butler (2001), who won the Pulitzer Prize for fiction, carried out a remarkable exercise by writing a short story live on the web over 17 days, 2 hours per day. The project is archived at http://www.fsu.edu/~butler; you can look at it anytime. Professor Butler talks about what he is thinking before and sometimes while he writes, and you can listen in on those thoughts. You also can watch his computer screen and see the words as they come out of him. The story as it existed at the end of each writing session is also shown—all 17 versions of it. By looking at them you can see how the author modified the story as he developed it across the 17 days.

During the first day's webcast, Butler says explicitly that he is not sure what emotional effect he is looking for and, amazingly, that he is not even sure what ideas or themes will guide him! He doesn't have them as he starts; he works them out over the next few days.

Many other experienced writers have confessed that they, too, do not usually have their theme and ideas completely worked out as they begin writing. A dramatic example comes from author and Pulitzer-Prize winning historian Daniel J. Boorstin, who said, "I write to discover what I think" (quoted in Trimble, 2000, p. 166). Relative to the commonly stated writing "rules," that certainly seems backwards—even though it's not. Similarly, the late TV commentator and author Andy Rooney said in one of his books, "The best ideas are the result of the same slow, selective, cognitive process that produces the sum of a column of figures. Anyone who waits to be struck with a good idea has a long wait coming" (Quoted in Trimble, 2000, pp. 182–183).

Professional writers do not wait for inspiration. Like you, they have deadlines. If they don't have an externally imposed one, they impose one on themselves. This is true for creative writers as well as for writers of expository prose, including journalists. A deadline forces them (and you) to have a plan to solve the writing problem. Andy Rooney added this to the passage previously quoted: "If I have a deadline . . . I sit down . . . and damn well decide to have an idea." These writers solve the writing problems as they go along. How do they do it? And what processes will work for you? In other words, what plan will actually work? Let's create a map for writing that you actually can follow.

SOLVING THE WRITING PROBLEM

I've already said that writing is a goal-directed activity that amounts to problem solving. You start at what I'll call your *current state*—with instructions for the assignment at hand and a blank screen in front of you—and you need to get to the *goal state,* where you submit your fine paper by the due date. This goal, though, is different from the goal you have when solving a math problem. Math problems are well-defined. You want to get an answer that is correct—and it's clear what correct means. In contrast, a written paper does not have such a definitive answer. It is neither correct nor incorrect in an exact sense. When the end product is not clear-cut, the goal is said to be ill-defined. The goal of writing an *A+* paper is vague, though it does reflect an optimistic and ambitious attitude. Your instructor will provide guidelines that will constrain the paper—for example, it needs to be on a Civil War topic, it needs to be at least 2,500 words long, and it needs to cite at least five original sources not including Wikipedia. That helps because it adds some well-defined criteria for success. You'll have to add more of them as you go along—but you can't write them all down right away.

We now know that it's unrealistic for you first to write the focus or major point of the paper. The plan to start with a focus is not an operational plan; it doesn't properly tell you what to do. Your goal includes finding your focus and your thesis. You typically will work them out as you proceed. On many occasions the focus and thesis may change during the problem-solving process. It is liberating to have that perspective. Hooray!—it's okay not to know right away what you're going to say. Therefore, it's not so scary to begin working. It's also comforting to know that professional writers work that way.

The Paper Versus the Reader

Thinking about concrete ways to generate ideas and turn them into a paper naturally leads us to concentrate on the paper itself. But consider another perspective, that of your reader (I'll call this person "My Reader"). Ask yourself: Who is My Reader, and what does he or she know about the topic? What are My Reader's attitudes and beliefs about my topic? Will My Reader agree with what I have to say or object to it? If you imagine that he or she disagrees, or doesn't have an opinion, ask yourself, "How can I convince My Reader that my viewpoint is the correct one?" Also, you want to engage your reader—above all, to communicate with this person—so that he or she will actually want to continue reading your work, not read it just because of an obligation to do so.

Instructors who read many student papers are familiar with something I'll call the "'Now it's your problem' problem." A student writes a paper that meets the superficial requirements of the assignment: It has the needed 2,500 words, it cites five sources, and it has a thesis sentence and a strong concluding sentence. When the student reaches that point, he or she considers it finished and turns it in. Either consciously or unconsciously the student thinks that it's now up to the reader to figure out what the paper is saying throughout—it's now the reader's problem. However, all too often the work skips around and fails to provide support for the main points. It also lacks continuity and a sense of flow. The reader frequently has to struggle to figure out the connection between the current sentence and prior ones, and believe me, it's an annoying chore to do that. In other words, the paper isn't clear. What is clear is that the author didn't put enough thought into ensuring that the paper is a vehicle for communicating.

The most successful papers take the reader into account. To do that, you have to make some assumptions about what the reader knows. If your reader isn't knowledgeable about your topic, then it's your job to provide enough contextual information so your points will make sense. You can quickly get to your point for a knowledgeable reader, but for a less knowledgeable one you must first fill in the blanks. If you are unsure, it's better to err on the side of providing more information or context than might be needed rather than too little. Think about the teachers you've had. The best ones take into account how much you know about the topic and provide information that is neither too simple nor too complex—they find the "just right" level and bring you along from there. Teachers who assume too much, lose you; teachers who assume too little, bore you. When you write a paper, you are in the teacher's role. You don't want to lose your reader or to bore him. Therefore you must take him into consideration. When you craft your paper, then, you cannot think exclusively about the paper itself; nor can you think just about the reader. Instead:

Successful writers think about both the reader and the paper. They develop plans that deal with both.

A Four-Step Solution to the Writing Problem

There is no single, golden-rule technique guaranteeing that you will write a fine paper. Various writers use various methods. But there are good tips that can keep you going and keep you on track. Following the work of Linda Flower and John R. Hayes (1981a), and others who have studied the writing process extensively, we can divide your writing plans into four parts—which, as I've already hinted, are not totally separate from each other.

GENERATING IDEAS

The first part of the writing plan is *idea generation*. You should get down on paper, in whatever form works for you, your initial thoughts about the paper topic (e.g., single words or phrases, complete sentences, quotes from others that you find while you are reading about it). Note that this is not the same as starting with a focus sentence. You can also jot down your immediate reactions to those ideas. Your first reaction could be as simple as drawing a frowning face or a thought that is more thoroughly worked out. Some people are helped in the idea-generating phase by coming up with key words or features of the topic and then writing bits and fragments as they follow up on the feature and react to it. For example, if the topic is the effect of railroads on the outcome of the Civil War, you might ask yourself how the trains were powered, or

Some Tips for Generating Writing Ideas

1.   Write down initial thoughts and reactions; let them flow.
2.   Pursue an interesting feature or features of the topic.
3.   Engage in thinking by conflict (pro/con, agree/disagree, etc.).
4.   Try to narrow down the topic rather than broadening it.
5.   Use WIRMI, WIRKI, WIRBI: What I Really Mean / Know / Believe Is . . .
6.   Ask: What would My Reader think about this?

what they carried, or how many of them there actually were, or even whether they brought the wounded back from the battleground. That is called *pursuing an interesting feature* of the topic. You may or may not use these initial thoughts, but at least you are working and not staring.

Another way to help generate ideas is to adopt a pro versus con, yes or no, agree or disagree attitude. Jot down your thoughts, first one way and then the other. I've found *thinking by conflict* to be a very helpful technique because it forces me to figure out what I think or believe about a topic. At first that sounds odd, but by using this technique you may find that you have an opinion that you were not even aware you had. That's an interesting discovery, and it may be quite important for the work of the paper.

A common concern of beginning writers is that they do not have enough to say. However, if you spend time freely generating ideas on the topic using the above aids, you will (a) produce a lot of raw material, (b) find that the topic is more complex or interesting than you first thought, and (c) discover that you have many directions you can go with it. Relative to a lack of ideas, having more than enough is definitely a better problem and an indication of progress. I also find that narrowing my topic helps me produce more ideas, not fewer. For example, I find it easier to come up with ideas on the question "Should undocumented immigrants have the right to in-state college tuition?" than on "Should we extend democratic privileges to undocumented immigrants?"

Still, you need to get the topic straight and to figure out what you think about it. Flower and Hayes (1981b) coined the acronym WIRMI, standing for "What I really mean is . . . ", and a close relative, WIRKI, for "What I really know is . . . " They recommended that to boil down a complex issue you start a sentence or short paragraph (in your notes) with these phrases. That will force you to condense and clarify. I'll add that in your notes you can also start a sentence with WIRBI, "What I really believe about that is . . . " to get your own reactions out in the open. If you have a strong feeling, that too may be important for your paper.

When we talked in Chapter 6 about writing effective answers on essay exams, I said:

> Be sure that you understand the question. Are you asked to describe, to compare, to contrast, to explain, or to evaluate or criticize? Are you asked to report what others have said, to give your own opinion, or to speculate about what might have happened next? The grader will notice and mark you down if you don't address the question that was asked.

Similarly, the nature of the writing assignment—that is, what you explicitly are asked to do—constrains what will count as a successful paper. Those constraints help turn the assignment from an ill-defined problem into a more well-defined one. As you are generating ideas, it helps to aim for some that speak to those constraints; they'll likely fit in the paper somewhere.

Also, you can—and should—produce ideas from the perspective of your reader. What should you assume about his or her initial knowledge state? Will the reader share your beliefs about the topic? If not, how are you going to convince him or her? What supporting evidence can you present? If you write down what you discover when you ask these questions, then along with the other idea-generating aids, you will get lots of notes. These notes can guide you to other reading you may have to do (and, anyway, you need to get at least those five references that are part of the assignment). Plus, of course, the ideas you get from that further reading will also add to your notes.

Finally, you should know about a free resource on your campus—one that can help you find references that are more impressive and on point than those you'll likely find when doing a web search yourself. This resource is your campus reference librarian—just ask at the front desk of the library. A reference librarian can be a fantastic help when it comes to locating high-quality, relevant material on almost any topic. He or she can introduce you to information sources (e.g., professional databases) that you may be amazed to learn even exist. Furthermore, the reference librarian can show you how to sort through these databases quickly to get the clinching information that supports your point and gives your paper the punch it needs.

CONSTRUCTING THE PRODUCT

The notes and reference materials you have collected are not yet organized. They resemble a web more than an outline. In addition, you still may not be sure what your paper's focus will be. Such uncertainty, even a little mental chaos, is normal. But soon you'll have to string words together in a particular order—to convert parts of your developing web into a linear stream that flows smoothly. The second major part of your writing plan is the *paper construction* phase. At this point you begin (or continue) to order your ideas—you are ready to make a loose outline (or perhaps you've already started doing that because an original outline helps you produce ideas; that's fine, there is no golden solution to getting to the goal). Also, you may be ready to write your tentative focus or thesis sentence. Try it. Then see if your materials, along with the first pass at the outline and the first attempt to state your focus, can lead you to a more structured outline. It's still too early to worry about sentence structure and ways to connect the sentences so that they flow. Don't get distracted from your job of the moment: getting the paper organized. You want the sections and the paragraphs to connect with one another and to appear in a logical, persuasive order.

Don't forget about your reader. Your developing outline certainly should take the reader into account; for example, how will the second section of your paper move the reader to understand your point of view? Is it presenting evidence or offering another main point? If you can't see how that section is changing the reader's state of mind, that's a sign you should spend time coming up with ideas for how better to communicate with him. If you pay attention to what you want to accomplish and how to do it, and if you work back and forth between your writing product, your concern for the reader, and your stock of ideas, then you will make concrete progress.

LOOPING BACK

I call the third phase of the writing plan the *G ↔ C loop.* The **G** stands for **G**enerating ideas, and the **C** stands for **C**onstructing the paper. As we've known for a long time, **G**enerating ideas helps you with the plan to **C**onstruct the paper. That's the **G → C** part. We now know that the opposite also takes place, the **G ← C** part: As you try to construct the paper, you will often discover that you need to get additional ideas or to look up some facts—the raw materials from which you build the written product. Go ahead. That's what professional writers do. It is not a one-way street from idea, topic sentence, and outline to constructing a finished product. Just as your thinking affects what you write, now your writing will help you think—in other words, your writing helps you discover what you think and even how you feel about your topic. While this is going on, your focus and your overall plan for the paper may even change; that happens quite often and it can be a moment of creative discovery for you. Soon you will settle on a focus, a point of view, and a basic organization. As I've been saying, though, these are the results of the process, not the initial stage of it. The loop analogy is a much more realistic picture of the writing process than the idealized "idea → outline → paper" version found in many guides to writing.

You will notice something remarkable as you work back and forth within the G ↔ C loop. As you tighten up your outline, write some initial paragraphs, put down your initial main idea, generate some more ideas to support it, and think about how you move the reader along, you won't get stuck—at least not for long. You now have a set of things you can do, a set of operations that can move you and your paper from the initial state to the goal state. When you pay attention to the various writing processes we've discussed, you can use them to do something relevant to your task—they keep you on track. If you feel that you're not getting anywhere, you can ask yourself whether you need to use our tips to generate some additional ideas, or whether you can fiddle with the basic organization, or whether your work at this point moves your reader along, etc. Using these techniques means the end of the blank stare.

Many college writing assignments ask you to evaluate a topic under discussion. The techniques we've already discussed will help make your evaluation clear—first of all to yourself, and then to the reader. You want to end up with a clear idea or opinion about your topic. As I've noted, the writing process often sharpens and clarifies your viewpoint. When appropriate, and that depends on the assignment and the goal of the paper, stating an opinion and providing support for it can add a great deal to your finished product. You can show commitment and even passion—assuming you can defend your point of view in the flow of the paper. Doing so almost always adds interest and helps motivate the reader to stick with you. I recommended earlier that you try starting a sentence with, "What I really believe about that is . . . " and see where it takes you. Recall what Daniel J. Boorstin said, "I write to discover what I think." Writing can also sharpen your attitudes and beliefs. Too, your creative side will have extra room to express itself when you're clear about what you mean.[1]

THE FLOW MAKES IT GO

So far I have not said a word about sentence construction, subject–verb agreement, punctuation, or anything else related to the mechanics of good writing. And I'm not going to say much about these topics. There are many fine writing guides that cover them. However, I do want to make three quick points about the mechanics of writing because they fit with what we've been saying about the usefulness of keeping your mind's eye on the writing process.

---

[1]Even lab reports or a paper presenting the results of a scientific study usually have discussion sections in which the results are put in context or compared with what was expected. These sections are, in effect, evaluating the work presented earlier in the report.

First, the mechanics will not be correct in your first draft. That's common and you don't have to be concerned about it. It is much more important that you first solve the organizational and focus problems discussed above. But, of course, at some point you do have to pay attention to the paper's mechanics. Getting things right at this level allows the reader to sail through your paper instead of being forced to "figure it out."

Second, keeping the reader in the forefront of your thoughts will help you with the mechanics of your paper. Imagine your reader (e.g., the instructor, your friend, the stranger out there) making his or her way through the paper—just the way I'm imagining you right now. You want to present your ideas so he or she easily can follow them, so that they flow from one to the next without causing the reader to stop or to have the "Huh?" experience. Your reader should not have to puzzle over what you mean, or to have to figure out how this sentence connects to the previous one.

The desire to keep your reader moving along will help you solve problems with your paper's flow. You will divide it into reader-friendly chunks (e.g., sections, paragraphs), you will punctuate it to signal the reader to pause and take a mental breath at just the right points in each paragraph, and you will use the "connective-tissue" that the language provides (words and phrases like *however, therefore, in addition to, consequently,* etc.) to guide the reader through the logic of your arguments. In other words, if you concentrate on the reader's state of mind as he or she moves through your work, you will more easily make your paragraph and sentence choices, and make them well.

Third, it's not easy to master the mechanics of flow. As noted, virtually no one can get it right the first time. The main reason you rewrite your paper is to get the flow straightened out. Sometimes that means you have to move, maybe even delete, whole sections. (I've concluded that deleting a section requires a certain bravery—those are your lovely words you're pitching away! But the reader didn't need them, so out they go.) Rewriting certainly means reworking the sentences and the connections between them.

After you have a draft of your paper, it helps to get some distance between it and you. Something as simple as printing it out and reading it in a paper version, editing pencil in hand, can help you see it in a fresh light. Even better, reading it aloud and *listening* to how it sounds nearly always reveals places where the paper doesn't flow. Really—go into a room by yourself, with no distractions, and read the paper aloud. Read every word, just as it appears on the page. When you do this, you will hear things—subject–verb mismatches, number mismatches (e.g., "The main purposes is to . . . ")—that we tend to gloss over when we read silently. Simply said: Never turn in a first draft.

Volunteer for the Draft

In his fine book, *Writing With Style*, John Trimble (2000) wrote that clear writers have "accepted the grim reality that nine-tenths of all writing is rewriting . . . " (p. 9). That sounds harsh after you've done all the previous work, but the rewritten paper can tower above the first version in the positive effect it has on the reader. You probably won't write half a dozen drafts of your papers, as some professional writers do, but to repeat, you never want to approach a deadline such that you have to turn in a first or even a second draft. Directors of composition courses and writing centers know that most students typically write papers at the last minute. It shows, too.

Listen to a fine and witty professional writer, Anne Lamott (1995), in her book *Bird by Bird: Some Instructions on Writing and Life*. She is commenting on the first drafts of her own articles:

> The whole thing would be so long and incoherent and hideous that for the rest of the day I'd obsess about getting creamed by a car before I could write a decent second draft. I'd worry that people would read what I'd written and believe that the accident had really been a suicide, that I had panicked because my talent was waning and my mind was shot. (p. 25)

In other words, she would not dream of turning in the first draft, and she writes and teaches writing for a living.

Another great way to improve your paper and its grade is to have a classmate or friend read the draft and give you honest feedback. When you ask for your friend's opinion, stress that you are not looking for compliments but rather for complaints, uncertainties, and concerns. You want to know about the speed bumps that block the paper's flow. One problem with being your own editor is that you know what you meant to say. Therefore, it is easy for you to read into your paper the meaning you intended, even if you didn't clearly write it in there. Joseph Williams (2009) convincingly makes this point in his book *Style: The Basics of Clarity and Grace:*

> The biggest reason we write unclearly is our ignorance of how others read our writing. What we write always seems clearer to us than it does to our readers, because we can read into it what we want readers to get out of it. Instead of revising our writing to meet their needs, we send it off as soon as it meets ours. (p. 8)

When we do that, our reader may get lost or fail to see the meaning that was oh-so-clear-to-us. When that happens, you know you need to clarify by rearranging and adding markers and signposts to show the way. Writers are mapmakers.

Your helpful reader usually has to know about the purpose of the paper. Is it an evaluation of something you've read in a literature course, a paper summarizing what we know about a topic from your economics class, a chemistry lab report, or something else? Whatever the purpose, you need to conform to the style of that course and discipline. In such cases, another student from the course is your best editor. You can trade off reading each other's drafts, each of you providing and getting honest feedback.

The Successful Product

Earlier, I said that writing is a goal-directed activity that amounts to problem solving, and I noted that in contrast to solving a math problem the writing goal is a relatively ill-defined one. A written paper does not have a definitive answer; it is neither correct nor incorrect in an exact sense. However, by the time you turn in your written assignment you should evaluate whether it meets the following criteria:

1. Your paper has a focus or a central point that is easy to recognize.
2. The paper has an organizational framework that anchors the arguments or points you're trying to make. We've seen that expert writers don't necessarily start with an outline, but the finished product should be well organized.
3. Your paper takes into account the level of knowledge and the point of view of the typical reader. In other words, your work respects your audience.
4. Your paper satisfies all the explicit criteria stated in the assignment (yes, it does "compare and contrast"; yes, it does have 2,500 words!). By checking your writing product against these criteria, you can transform an ill-defined goal into a more well-defined one.

In addition, before you turn the paper in, you will have tested it by having someone else read it and give you honest feedback. By doing that, you reduce the chance that your reader will get lost or have the *huh?* experience.

Many colleges have writing centers that can help you determine whether your paper is a success. This support is in addition to the help you can get from your course instructors. The goal of such resource centers is to help you develop and structure your ideas and to organize your thoughts. The staff in such centers provide feedback, guidance, and encouragement. But most do not provide a proofreading or editing service to correct the mechanics of your work. As the website (http://

Typical Stages in Writing a Paper

1. Generate ideas.
2. Develop initial organization.
   a. Pick organizational framework (e.g., historical, problem-oriented, autobiographical).
   b. Consider your reader's point of view.
3. Use the G ↔ C loop.
   a. Revise organization.
   b. Get new ideas.
   c. Construct paragraphs.
4. Check current product against the stated assignment.
5. Check for flow of sentences. Revise as needed.
6. Check for focus, main point. Check for compatibility with the knowledge level of your reader. Check organization again.
7. Get feedback on the draft.
8. REVISE in light of the feedback.

www.uh.edu/writecen/Students/Gen-Con/) of one such center notes, "They will not simply proofread the paper for grammatical errors." Clearly, these are valuable places to know about. But, again, don't wait until the day before the paper is due to drop by the writing center.

There is, however, one writing "resource" you must avoid—namely, using the exact work of other writers, unless you cite the source(s). The Internet has made it spectacularly easy to copy the work of others. That's okay, as long as you explicitly indicate that someone else created the material. From time to time in this book I've copied materials from other sources and used them word-for-word, as in the preceding paragraph. But I'm up front about it, using quotation marks and indicating the sources I copied from. I'm not pretending they are my words. If I do copy—or very closely paraphrase—without indicating that I've done so, I've committed *plagiarism*.

Some now believe that the concept of *authorship* is out of date and that it's all right to copy without citing the source. As far as I know, no professor at any university accepts that view. Taking someone else's writing, or a close paraphrase of it, and pretending that it is your work does not teach you how to think or how to solve the writing problem. Too, it can lead to bad outcomes, all the way from getting a zero on the paper to dismissal from the university. Plagiarism is not honorable.

One last point: Writing is a complex process, and learning to write well is itself a process. I've asked you to become aware of that process in the belief that paying attention to what you do will lead you to write better—a belief that is supported by the professional literature. However, don't scare yourself by thinking that you have to be perfect;

perfectionism as well as procrastination can be the enemy of getting things done. But you do want to get better, and as usual, that takes mindful effort coupled with feedback about how you are progressing toward your goal. There are many books on this topic that can continue to help you. I've mentioned two of my favorites. One is John R. Trimble's (2000) *Writing With Style: Conversations on the Art of Writing.* Reading his little book will repay you many times over. And at a somewhat more technical level, Joseph M. Williams's (2009) book, *Style: The Basics of Clarity and Grace,* is worth buying and keeping at hand. Both of these books talk about process as well as product, and that's a big reason why I recommend them.[2]

Summary

You increase your chances of producing a superior writing product when you adopt superior writing techniques. Such techniques allow you to solve the writing problem, which is an ill-defined one, and they generally make use of the same processes used by professional writers. Most good writers work back and forth between generating the ideas they hope to convey, on the one hand, and constructing the written product, on the other. They normally do not begin by having an outline and a focus sentence; instead, these important milestones are developed as they go along. I call this process the G $\leftrightarrow$ C loop (generating ideas and constructing the paper are intertwined with one another).

To produce a superior writing product, you should take the reader's knowledge and perspective into account, and you have to work on the paper's flow such that the reader does not get stuck or bogged down by the *huh?* experience. Two steps are important to ensure that your paper flows. First, you need to test it, preferably on another reader. Second, you have to be willing to rewrite and revise it. A first draft is never a winning one.

Good writers test their product against a set of criteria that include those specified in the writing assignment, whether the paper has a focus and central point, whether the role of the supporting material is clear, whether the work takes into account the reader's knowledge and point of view, and whether the material flows. However, these same good writers know that those criteria do not determine how they get to the final product. Finally, wise students take advantage of campus resources that will help them become confident and accomplished writers.

---

[2]The book by Butler (2005) provides a stimulating discussion on writing fiction, a different topic than writing expository prose, the one I've been discussing.

TAKE ACTION

1. Make arrangements with a classmate to read one another's papers (assuming that is acceptable to the instructor). Be sure to have a clear understanding about the type of feedback you will provide each other. It is much more useful to provide and to accept honest, polite, critical feedback than it is to get compliments.

2. While working on a writing assignment, take notes about what you are doing as you go along. It may even help to indicate the time spent on the core writing processes. Then take a look at the notes to see that you've spent time on each of these processes.

EXPLORE YOUR CAMPUS

1. Find out whether your campus has a writing center. If so, find out what their rules are and the type of help and feedback they provide. Then make an appointment to discuss one of your first writing assignments.

2. For your next paper assignment, visit with a reference librarian at your campus library. Ask him or her to direct you to online resources relevant to your topic, and for tips on how to search those sources in an effective way. For the vast majority of students, even including tech-savvy students, this resource person will provide excellent recommendations that will help enrich your project and impress your professor.

SELF-TEST ITEMS

State in your own words:

1. What are the core writing techniques?
2. What is meant by the $G \leftrightarrow C$ loop?
3. At what point in the writing process do you expect to have a completed outline of your paper?
4. Evaluate the claim: A professional writer is one who can write a polished and complete first draft.

YOUR CAMPUS/ COMMUTING LIFE VI

Your Campus Life
The Dorm and the Drive

13

Friendliness, youth, freedom, sexiness, sociability, irreverence, fun, humor, intensity, eccentricity, lack of limits, spontaneity. These are the values of undergraduate life.
—*Rebekah Nathan (2005, p. 27)*

I think I have only one friend here and that's my roommate. He drives me crazy sometimes with his music and the way he acts. He's like a child sometimes. It seems he always needs attention. I'd hate to be like that.

I will be working from 8 a.m. to 4 p.m. and then have a long day ahead of me. After work I have to pick up my daughter, go home, take a shower, eat, and then attend two birthday parties I got invited to. By the time I get home I will have to sleep to get rest for work the next day. After work I will have to work on homework and start studying for an upcoming test. I am starting to get nervous about all these tests coming up.

Coming to campus has been an ordeal. I miss my girlfriend, the classes are harder, and I have to do my own laundry.
—*Students' reflections on starting college*

http://dx.doi.org/10.1037/14181-013
Your Complete Guide to College Success: How to Study Smart, Achieve Your Goals, and Enjoy Campus Life, by Donald J. Foss

Where Are We Going?

Your college experience is significantly affected by your overall responsibilities, your living arrangements, and how well you shape them and adjust to them. In this chapter, I'll describe issues you'll face as you move from home to residence hall or apartment, or—if you continue to live at home—what you can do to maximize the chance of positive outcomes for all concerned. I'll extend the problem-solving approach to include dealing with problems you might have with others. Your college experience is also deeply influenced by the social networks and friendships you develop, and I'll describe ways to improve your chances of good outcomes there, too. By the end of the chapter, you will be able to describe ways to reduce the chances of conflict with, for example, your roommates or your family, and you will acquire a four-step process for dealing with conflict when it arises. Commuter students will also learn why they should set up two campus "headquarters."

One day in the middle of the fall semester, Lucy and I fell in step while walking to a class I was teaching. In response to a casual question about how things were going, she said that the university was not what she expected. "Oh, what did you think it was going to be like?" "Well," Lucy said, "I'm not friends with my roommate, and there's too much pressure!" As we walked, I learned that Lucy was the first in her family to go to college, and I suspect she got her initial beliefs from friends and from the movies (and maybe from the university brochures). Popular films have presented views of campus life, especially its social life, that mold expectations and no doubt affect actual behavior.

Some film versions of campus are rather dark, emphasizing hazing or sexual harassment (or even serial killers and vampires!), and other versions seek to reflect the "youth, freedom, sexiness, sociability, irreverence, fun, humor, intensity, eccentricity, lack of limits, [and] spontaneity" that author Rebekah Nathan (2005, p. 27) says are the values of undergraduate life. Is one perspective correct and the others not? Vampires aside, it's appropriate to have a variety of college movie themes—there is great variation among actual groups and subgroups on almost any campus. Too, there is considerable variability in the conflicts that students must cope with. In this chapter, we'll cover some common issues that come up as students, perhaps including you, adapt to college life and make their contributions to it. We'll start with a big change, living on campus—or at least away from home. Commuter students who continue to live at home have a somewhat different, but no less important, set of changes to deal with; we'll also discuss them.

Life in the Residence Halls: *Imaginary or Real?*

I think the worst aspect of college that makes it feel like a cold and intimidating place are the dorms. I still have not gotten used to sharing a room with a stranger. . . . I hate the community baths. I feel like I am in one of those prison films. The best thing so far has been the atmosphere of students around campus.

I love my new friends. I'm in the dorm under 3 weeks and we've connected so well it's strange. I love it here—it doesn't feel like home but it feels better than home."

—*Students' reflections on starting college*

After being accepted to the university, Lucy chose to live in a campus residence hall her first year. If you are like her in choosing on-campus housing, you'll get a great deal of information about the residence halls directly from your university. I won't try to repeat that information here; you will get specific guidance about what (and what not) to bring and when to bring it, among other topics. I'm also skipping here much of the "standard" advice about survival skills. (But here's a shorthand list so I can say I told you so: don't mix colored clothes with whites in the laundry [http://www.wikihow.com/Do-Your-Laundry-in-a-Dorm], eat healthy foods in sensible portions, exercise regularly, and get at least 7 or 8 hours sleep per night. Also, be alert when walking alone after dark, never let someone you don't know into the residence hall, and don't drive after drinking. Actually, I'll return to some of these topics in the next chapter.) Instead, I want to discuss the overall approach to living on campus and to look at some aspects of it that can greatly affect your success there.

The decision to apply to a residence hall determines much about your initial college experience, including your original expectations. By now you may be aware that those expectations can mislead you, just as they did Lucy. First there is what I'll call the "imaginary roommate" problem. I suspect that most students no longer share a room at home, so the whole experience of having a roommate is new to them. But if your residence hall was built before the 1990s, it probably will have shared rooms and even communal bathrooms. If built or remodeled after that time, the residence hall may have a suite arrangement whereby two to four bedrooms are arrayed around a common living area; those bedrooms may each have a bath, or maybe not. With high probability, then, you will have a suitemate or a roommate. What's he or she like?

The imaginary roommate is the ideal best friend forever. You move in and the two of you truly bond: you both love Nails on the Blackboard's music; you both like (or hate) the college sports scene; neither of you care about keeping a room picked up (or are neat freaks); you both like to party and to bring guests over, and instantly agree about how and how often you can signal to have the room to yourself (or this whole concept insults you both); and so on and on and on. Our imaginary roommate and new best buddy is really an excellent person in every way. We'll do anything for each other.

Of course, you know that reality rarely matches imagination, so in fact your roommate will have annoying flaws. Or maybe you both will. Most universities make an effort to match prospective roommates on some key attributes, knowing that similar values and habits tend to result in better relationships. (Of course, with regard to race and ethnicity the matching is done in a color-blind fashion.) Nevertheless, some pairings work better than others. I know people who have been good friends for decades with their college roommates. Making a lifetime friend is a fairly common outcome; let's hope it happens in your case. But some roommates do not mix as well, resulting in feelings that vary from friendly (but not friends), through tolerance, to plain hostility. These feelings usually show up pretty quickly and may lead to real conflict.

DEALING WITH CONFLICT

An early college challenge may involve dealing with such conflict— in other words, you might have a people problem. By analogy to our previous approaches to problem solving, the *current state* involves your negative feelings and behavior, and the negative feelings and behavior of another person; your *goal state* involves having a different, more positive set of feelings and behaviors. How do you move from the current state to the goal state, that is, how do you solve such problems? Adding the other person to the mix complicates matters: Effectively moving from the current state to the goal state typically requires change on both your parts, and facilitating those changes usually works best if you are direct and nonconfrontational.

The request to handle a conflict by dealing directly and in a nonconfrontational way with a person outside your family may be uncomfortable for you; it is too many students. Nevertheless, you need to handle it, even though "handling it" can be as scary to the person who raises the issue as it is to the person hearing it. It is easy to get defensive in such circumstances and for conversations to escalate. Imagine, for example, that you actually hate Nails on the Blackboard's music and that your new roommate loves to play it loudly when you're there, or that she tosses her wet towels on your bed. If you complain, you fear that your roommate's snap reaction will be, "Don't be ridiculous, everyone

loves *Nails*!" or, "I'll toss my towels where I please; it's my room, too."
Where do you imagine this "discussion" will end?

Fortunately, the residence hall staff members have seen such
clashes before and they've taken an important step (a) to help avoid
the problem, and (b) to facilitate solving it if the problem occurs. In
particular, they will ask you to come to an agreement with your new
roommate either before or just after you move in. The agreement will
specify such things as your policy toward guests; whether you will keep
things clean and, if so, who will clean what; and the boundaries around
use of the other person's property (e.g., clothes, food, computer). Such
"roommate contracts" can be renegotiated, but it's very good to start
with one because it sets up reasonably clear expectations about how
you will deal with issues that can lead to annoyance and worse. It's wise
to take time right away to work out your roommate agreement. It will
help you get to know one another, and it can help avoid problems later.
If you don't come to such an agreement, and if issues do arise, dealing
with them will take up much more of your time and emotional energy
than will making an agreement up front.

If your roommate is not living up to the terms of the contract and
it's driving you crazy, you need to communicate with him or her in a
nonconfrontational way. That requires calm talk. One of the simplest
aids to doing that, and one that's frequently ignored, is the realization
that neither of you is a mind reader. If you don't make your concern
known, your roommate can't know that something is frustrating you—
and vice versa, of course. The worst thing either of you can do is to let
such matters go; in that case, one or both of you will walk around tick-
ing like a time bomb.

A FOUR-STEP FORMULA FOR PROBLEM SOLVING
IN RELATIONSHIPS

One helpful skill—good for dealing with your roommate and with others
throughout life—is to learn how to assert yourself in a nonconfrontational way. Lots of people have trouble doing that. As a result, they fume
inside and become unhappy, or they get angry and explode, perhaps ending up name-calling or in a shouting match, or all of the above.

Here is a relatively easy-to-learn alternative. Suppose you have
agreed that your room will be picked up every Saturday, each of you
putting away your "stuff" that makes for visible clutter. And suppose
you've put away your stuff but your roommate has not. And finally,
suppose this is starting to drive you crazy. There is a four-step "formula"
that can be effective:

- First, *describe the situation* objectively and calmly. ("Mike, it's Saturday and your clothes are scattered all over the room.")

- Second, *state how it affects you* and others. ("The clutter is in the way and I'd like to arrange for the guys to play cards in here later.")
- Third, *state how you feel about the behavior.* ("I feel that we should do what we agreed to about picking up the room on Saturday.")
- And fourth, *describe what your roommate should do to fix things.* ("I would like you to put away your stuff.")

Such a direct approach has the advantage of being clear, and it often works. If your roommate says, "Yeah, I know, I'll do it later," that just avoids the issue. You can either let him get away with it (again?), or better, simply *repeat the core of the message:* "I understand, Mike, but we agreed to this and I'd like you to put away your stuff." If you stick to this routine while staying calm, you'll increase the likelihood that the room will get picked up. The resident assistant (RA) can help facilitate such conversations, if needed. He or she isn't solving the problem—you are—but another pair of ears can help keep emotions in check. Rather than avoiding the issue, ask for the RA's help if the first strategy does not lead to a change that fits the agreed-on contract.

Here are the lessons: First, prevention is preferable to problems. Therefore, make the agreements up front. Second, if something doesn't seem right, be honest with yourself about how much you care about it. Third, don't pretend your roommate is a mind reader; communicate. Fourth, if you discover that your feelings are getting frayed, make a plan to deal with the causes of the bad feelings in a nonconfrontational way—the four-step process and repetition can help you do that.

I don't know about Lucy's roommate experience, but if her adjustment to college meant she had to give up the imagined ideal one, that can be difficult. No one expects that interpersonal conflict will be part of his or her first months on campus. If such conflict is not resolved, and if it's paired with any kind of academic struggle, including difficulty in managing time, the resulting mix can be poison to your college commitment.

Your Home Away From Home—Or Is It?

Residence halls are a combination of home and not home. Your expectations about college life can be shaken if you are not aware of that ambiguity. Let's call it the *Is-this-my-home-or-not?* problem. It comes to you courtesy of your RA. The typical RA is a senior or junior who has been trained for the position; your RA will live nearby, help organize activities, and be on call to assist you. The RAs try to help you develop a sense of belonging and community. In most colleges they normally do not take a moral position on what the residents do; instead, they view them (including you) as adults who make decisions and are responsible for them. In short, they try to make it like home for you, where people in that home treat you as an adult.

However, from time to time the RA simply must act as an enforcer of policies. Certain behaviors cannot be tolerated; for example, anything involving intimidation or force is nonnegotiable. You really wouldn't want it any other way. In real life, anarchy is no fun. Also, the RAs on most campuses are required to act if they have knowledge of law-breaking (including underage drinking in the rooms) or major university policy violations. Students who blatantly flaunt such laws or policies are asking to be busted, and the RA has to accommodate their request.

More generally, though, the RAs take a "rights" perspective. That is, they expect and probably enjoy the eccentricity, spontaneity, and irreverence of undergraduates, and they know to tolerate a certain lack of limits. Furthermore, it wasn't long ago when they were in your flip-flops, and they readily recall how easy it is to get confused about aspects of academic and residence hall life. However, their tolerance for spontaneity and eccentricity only goes up to the point where it infringes on the rights of others in the residence hall—the right to a night's sleep, some study time, clean common spaces, etc. The RA should and will intervene when behaviors occur that stomp on the rights of other residents. Once again, that's really what you want. If you are the one asked to change some behavior, the RA may at first seem annoying or worse. But—how shall I say it?—in more sober moments you know that a rights perspective is necessary for the residence hall to work at all. Thus, living on campus can involve some tension between the home and not home perspectives. Once you see the role of the RA from the rights point of view, though, that tension will evaporate.

COED LIVING

Many residence halls now involve coed living coupled with substantial freedom of interaction. Officials in most universities (excepting some religious-sponsored schools) do not tell students how to behave in terms of sexual interactions, though they often sponsor educational programs on aspects of sex and romance; they want students to be safe and to make sound decisions. Some residence halls have same-sex students segregated by floors, others by hallways on the same floor. Some share bathrooms, others don't. In general there is a lot of gender mixing.

In my conversations with RAs I have found variations in the extent to which local cultures discourage or ignore sexual and romantic relationships between students in nearby living quarters. One RA said it was just fine in her building; the students felt it was "handy," and that students in a relationship could keep an eye on one another. At another university an RA said that such relations constituted "dormcest" and were frowned on; students there are expected to confine such relationships to individuals living in a different building.

I don't know of any published research on the topic, but I have an opinion: The dormcest perspective is the healthier one. Powerful emotions can get released in these relationships. When one goes bad you probably won't want to see the other person in close quarters every day, or to take the stairs to avoid riding in the same elevator. Incidentally, this is also the most common view among students who have commented on the topic, as revealed by a web search. I also find it creepy that someone in a sexual/romantic relationship might want to "keep an eye" on the other person—that's not the sign of a healthy relationship.

SPECIALIZED RESIDENCE HALLS

Many campuses have residence halls that have a focus or specialization. Some involve specific interest groups, for example, a hall for prospective music majors or for women interested in engineering or science. Others may be more general, for example, a dorm for students in an honors college or for students who want additional opportunities for faculty interaction.

There is evidence that such learning communities help keep students engaged in college life when they have good programs. Living in such a dorm even lowers the chances for dropping out. However, specialized residence halls, even those with the same supposed focus, differ across schools in the extent to which they arrange for meaningful student involvement. It's hard to tell from brochures which ones will do a lot to engage you and which just do an acceptable job. This is where asking good questions of current students during a campus visit might teach you a lot.

When I was dean of the Arts & Sciences College at Florida State University, the college helped sponsor a "living/learning" community in a newly renovated campus residence hall. The freshmen students who lived there got to sign up for a small class (maximum of 20) that was taught right in the building. In addition, groups met with professors to learn about the projects the professors were working on. There were other programs, too—for example, the university president visited most years to talk with the residents about his job. A study conducted by an associate dean and fellow psychologist, George Weaver, found that students who lived in that setting (it was not an honors dorm) had a 5% to 10% higher chance of persisting in college and of graduating than an equivalent group of students who did not live there. That's a big effect. I recommend taking advantage of such living/learning opportunities if they are offered on your campus.

Although residence hall living is not to everyone's taste, the great majority of students who live on campus recommend it to others, even if it means cramped quarters and the loss of some privacy. The experience normally stimulates personal development, especially if you are attentive to what is going on in your relationships. First-year students can share insecurities and ask the RA how a "street smart" student gets things done. That's a big advantage. Also, living on campus involves you in campus life, which has been shown to increase chances for success.

You may be tempted to live in an apartment or a "private" dorm your first year in college. Unless the private dorm has resources equivalent to those in a university residence hall—for example, RAs and comprehensive programs that introduce you to campus life—it's not a good idea to give in to that temptation. The absence of such support systems deprives you of useful help and thus increases the chances that you will drop out or find yourself on academic probation.

DIVERSITY

As mentioned earlier, colleges make roommate assignments without regard to ethnicity—and also without regard to numerous other characteristics that you may regard as personal. For most students that provides a big opportunity for growth and learning. It would be less than honest, though, if I didn't add that for some students it also yields initial anxiety and discomfort. They're not sure they can live in such close quarters with _____ (fill in the blank).

There is no doubt that your roommate affects the quality of your college experience. If you get paired up with a person who has a negative approach to life (*dysphoric* is the five-dollar term for this characteristic), it might on the one hand cause you to reject the person, or on the other, it might stimulate you to adopt something of a caretaker role. In any case, you won't be able to ignore the dysphoria.

Suppose you are assigned a roommate who appears to be out of your comfort range—say it's someone from a wildly different financial background or someone whose ethnic identity is different from yours. What's most likely to happen, and what should you do? The first thing to know is that these characteristics are much less important to the success of your relationship than, say, whether the person is dysphoric. The properties of the individual are more important than the category label. A second thing to know is that there is a tendency for roommates to become more similar in their views. For example, one study (Boisjoly, Duncan, Kremer, Levy, & Eccles, 2006) showed that students became more skeptical about policies proposing to redistribute wealth when their roommates came from families with a lot more money than their own families have.

The research on roommates has also shown that ethnicity differences do not have big effects on the success of the relationship, and the effects they do have fit with the previously described observation. For example, if an Anglo student and a Black student are assigned as roommates, they both are likely to become more comfortable with such "between-group" interactions. Working together and living together generally has a positive impact. To quote from one of the best studies I could find on this topic:

> Whites assigned minority roommates are also more likely to say that they have more personal contact with and interact more comfortably with members of minority groups. Minority roommates appear just as likely as non-minority roommates to remain close friends of white students beyond their initial year. (Boisjoly et al., 2006, p. 1902; see also Paluck & Green, 2009)

Boisjoly et al. also stated, "Taken together, these results suggest that students become more sympathetic to the social groups to which roommates belong" (p. 1902). All in all, these are positive findings, though the authors moderate them by also saying that its conclusions should be viewed as suggestive rather than definitive.

WHAT HAPPENED TO YOUR FAMILY?

Leaving home usually involves mixed feelings on everyone's part. Your family will tell you they're sorry to see you go, and that they're proud of you—and they are. They'll miss you, mostly, but they'll also think to themselves that they've done what they can to help make you ready to be more or less on your own—at least until Thanksgiving! And you feel what you feel. After you've unpacked, you're free to cry out, "I'm free!" And you are. But what are you free to do, exactly?

Your vision of college may emphasize the supposed "values of undergraduate life" we've previously pointed to: meeting people; being spontaneous, irreverent, and humorous; staying up as late as you like; eating and drinking what you please; etc. Meanwhile, your parents and others who love you are worried about your safety and security, whether your new place is clean enough, whether members of the opposite (or same) sex have visitation rights in your room, whether there is proper supervision of the other students around you, and what will happen if you get sick. It's not clear that these two lists come from people who live on the same planet.

This two-planet problem is particularly acute if you are the first person in your family to go to college. In that case, your family members have no personal reference point for what college is actually like; their perception of it may come from the movies and other popular media, their own imaginations, or what some older student told them, whether it's true for you or not.

To keep your family's anxiety level in check, all you need do is let them know something about what you are up to. If you keep in mind their concerns, you'll realize that just hearing from you proves you are safe, which is important to them. In contrast, a communication blackout invites dark thoughts. In this age of hyper-communication capabilities, it's easy to ping your parents. Most students do keep in touch—there is some evidence that the average student sends home multiple messages per week.

We have not talked about homesickness, but such feelings are experienced by a significant number of students who leave home for college, and can be a real problem for some. Homesickness—"defined as a negative emotional state characterized by recurrent thoughts of home, missing friends, the desire to go back to the familiar environment and often co-occurring physical complaints" (Nijhof & Engels, 2007, p. 710)— passes in a few days or weeks for most but the most severe cases. If you feel homesick, you can speed the process of getting past it by getting involved in campus activities and working diligently to meet and make new friends. There is some evidence that keeping in touch with family members also helps speed the process rather than slowing it down (Tognoli, 2003).

When to Send an SOS

To your surprise, at some point during the first year you may find yourself wishing that a family member was around to help solve a problem. This is a tricky matter. You want to be able to solve problems for yourself, a viewpoint shared by the faculty and leaders of your university. But what if a faculty or staff member is the source of the problem? For example, what if a clerk in the financial aid office isn't helpful to you or is rude to you even though you're certain they've made an error? Or what if a faculty member will not relent on the time for the final exam, even though you've purchased a nonrefundable ticket for a flight that leaves the morning of that exam? You may come from a family with savvy family members who will stick up for you. There's a big temptation to call them for help.

Resist that temptation, at least for a while. If you immediately call in the family guns, you won't develop the personal firepower you'll need later in life. Here's your chance to solve a problem for yourself and to expand your useful skills. Remember that you are dealing with a complex organization operated by people not that different from yourself. Remember, too, that you now understand the basics of this organization—recall the material we presented in Chapter 10. To start, seek advice from the street-smart people you know; that might be your RA, an upper classmen, a teaching assistant for your lab section, a department advisor (assuming he or she is not the source of the trouble), etc. You want to be (very) politely assertive. You know that if you don't get a plausible reason for the decision, you can go up to the next level in the organization.

Here is where making those contacts I've been recommending can really pay off. If you've been to the advisor's office, or to the professor's office hour, you have someone who is getting to know you. In that case, you comfortably can ask him or her for advice and help. Your familiar face will usually stimulate a positive response from that person. A telephone call from the faculty or staff member can go a long way toward removing roadblocks. If you were in my class, and especially if you've made yourself known to me, I'd call the financial aid director in a minute if I heard a story that sounded like a mistake might have been made—and I'd trust that the director would put someone on the case who is competent and fair-minded. You might or might not get what you'd hoped to, but you certainly would get a hearing.

Sometimes, though, it's just not going to work out—what you want is unreasonable in the college culture, and neither you nor your advocate will be able to make it happen. Though disappointing, you can learn something from the experience. For example, if on the first or second day of class your instructor hands out a syllabus that specifies the date of the required final exam, then he or she simply may not be sympathetic later when you say that you've bought a ticket for a flight that leaves the day before. You've just flagrantly ignored the ground rules and created your own difficulty. You should plan on paying the rebooking fee and getting to your destination after the exam. And it probably will not matter if it's you, a family member, or the state governor who is requesting special treatment for you. Nevertheless, the important fact is that you will have dealt with the problem yourself in a sensible way, which is good preparation for the thousands of other occasions in life when you'll have to do so.

Of course, contacting your family is the smart thing to do for some types of problems. If you get ill at anything above the level of a bad cold, or if you need stitches, or break a bone, you should let them know. Similarly, if you become pregnant or get someone pregnant, you likely will find your family more supportive than you fear. Most families want to know, and (perhaps after their initial reactions) they want to worry about you and with you in such cases.

Commuter Life

It's hard coming from my parents' house where I eat like a king all summer to my apartment where there is usually only ketchup and condiments in the fridge. I really need to go get some groceries. It is always such a good feeling to have a stocked up fridge. Why is it so hard to go to the store?

—A student's reflection on living off campus

Millions of students commute to college. Commuters have different challenges than do dorm residents, and their particular challenges may vary depending on whether they live in off-campus apartments or at home. Those in off-campus apartments may have more freedom of a certain sort, but they often face more of the responsibilities of daily living: things like cooking and paying bills, though many students who continue to live at home also have similar responsibilities. It's surprising how much time these take (though you can be relatively quick at them by being organized—there are many books and websites on efficient cleaning and managing clutter, some of which will even teach you how to sew on a button). That's why I said that apartment living comes with freedom of a "certain sort." Living in off-campus housing (and recall that I've recommended against apartment living during the freshman year) means you can come and go without parental scrutiny. At some point that's desirable for those at both ends of that particular telescope. But it also means you have to add time to your schedule (and master calendar!) to carry out the duties of daily living. Residence hall living comes with cooks; apartment living does not.

Commuters who live at home may enjoy a certain amount of security and even psychological support, and perhaps someone who cooks. A lot of bills are paid, too. But if you live at home and commute, how do you ensure that you become a college undergraduate rather than a glorified high school student?

It's a good idea to have a direct, calm talk with your family about mutual expectations as you embark on this new phase in your life. Remember the two-planet problem? It applies here, too. If you understand and explicitly acknowledge your family's fears and concerns up front, you'll be off to a good start. Agreeing to communication guidelines to let them know that you're safe will, I predict, go a long, long way toward devising house rules you can agree to and that are consistent with your being a college student. Remember, even though you think that fears about your safety are blown way out of proportion, that's the planet they live on and you are not going to rocket them to another one. Of course, you have to keep up your end of the communication bargain, even if you've been partying.

It's also a good idea to discuss and work out expectations with respect to your time. Consistent with meeting the obligations you have at home, I'm on your side in this one: You are responsible for your schedule, day and night. Also, let your family members know that you need time to study, more time than you needed in high school, and that some of it will be spent in your quiet spot at home. Especially if you are the first in your family to go to college, you may have to think carefully, and even enlist some help, as you figure out how to talk about the increased time demands college makes on you. Our discussion of "class time" and "course time" (see Chapter 2) may help you frame that conversation. It's clear, though: If you are going to succeed in college, then it has to be a priority in your life. Because the rest of the world does not stop, you and your family need to recognize that some adjustments will have to be made in order to meet your college goals.

This last point is an important one that too easily can be minimized as you think about the place that college plays in your life. Because many things have stayed the same—you are living at home, perhaps working at the same part-time job, maybe even socializing with the same people—you may be tempted to reduce your commitment to college if the going gets rough. College is the "add-on" to a familiar routine. Therefore, dropping out or stopping out ("taking a break") may seem the easy way out. In the long run, though, that decision may lead to regret (see the list in Chapter 2 for a reminder about the main sources of regret in life).

Finally, it is reasonable that you continue to have responsibilities for keeping up your home. You definitely benefit from being able to live there. If you meet those obligations in a timely manner, the hassle factor will be minimized.

YOUR CAMPUS HEADQUARTERS × 2: A STUDY SITE

After that, you need a headquarters on campus. Actually, you need two. By *headquarters* I mean a place where you are comfortable and that you will repeatedly return to—a place to call your own. Your first headquarters is the place you will study before, between, and after classes. The obvious place is the campus library.

The library contains a wealth of resources, not all of which are obvious or even known to many students. One such resource is space that is reasonably quiet. Most campus libraries are larger than they first seem, with room in the back, or around the corner, or up a couple of floors. These out-of-the-way locations are often lovely. I'd look for one with a comfortable chair, decent lighting, and a nearby power outlet. Find a spot that is out of the line of sight where people come in and out—it's too tempting to check out the newcomers and get distracted.

When you are at your campus study headquarters, you are doing just that—studying. Do not use that location as the place to meet friends and chat them up. Don't use it as the place where you browse the Internet—except when you're doing it for a project or when taking a quick break from studying. Don't use it as the place to catch a quick snooze. If you need to put your head down, move your stuff and find a different spot, one with a comfortable lounge chair. Why? It's been shown that we learn to respond to certain aspects of the environment in more or less consistent ways. These aspects of the environment are called *cues*. When you are in a social group, your friends and the setting provide cues for you to engage in certain kinds of behaviors such as joking around. You want all the cues at your study headquarters—that desk, that chair, that view—to be associated with and to point you toward a different kind of behavior: mindfully working on your courses.

As noted, the library is an obvious choice for your study headquarters, and it's where you should originally set one up. But there are other possibilities that may be even more attractive and convenient, and you can move headquarters if you find one you like. A campus art gallery may have its own library; similarly, some academic departments may have libraries or commons areas. Many of these are quiet and handsome locations that provide you the proper inspiration to study. My campus office is on a floor that has only two small classrooms on it so there is not much foot traffic. The hallway has a sitting area with a comfortable couch and some tables and chairs. I notice that a couple of undergraduate students are "regulars." They've made this area their study headquarters.

YOUR CAMPUS HEADQUARTERS × 2: A SOCIAL SITE

If you're a commuter, you also need a social headquarters on campus. That's where you can hang out, talk, send messages, wait for someone who is going to ride with you, have coffee, etc. The student union is an obvious spot, though there are other possibilities including religious/cultural centers such as a Hillel House or Newman Center, or an ethnic studies center, or for some, a Greek house.

In addition, commuters—and all students—should take steps to get involved in campus activities. We'll further discuss campus involvement and other topics in the next chapter.

Summary

Changing where you live involves making adjustments to your social life and nearly always involves some stress. That's certainly true for the change you make when you go to college. Moving into a residence hall or an off-campus apartment is an exciting experience, but it can lead to disappointment if, for example, you have an incompatible roommate. You can reduce the chances of that occurring if you agree to terms on a roommate contract right away—and then stick to the terms. The RAs will expect you and your roommate to try to make it work. Sometimes there is a rough patch resulting in conflict that threatens to escalate and make your experience very unhappy. In that case, there is a four-step formula for dealing with the conflict in a mature way. The steps ask you to describe the situation objectively, to describe how it affects you, to state calmly how you feel about it, and to describe what the other person can do to improve the situation.

On-campus living both is and is not like living at home; students in the dorms have substantial freedom, but there are limits. The philosophy that most residence hall assistants bring to their positions amounts to a rights perspective: You are free up to the point at which your behavior negatively impacts your neighbors. Many campuses have "interest" dorms, residence halls for students with common interests. If such dorms exist on your campus, living in one that fits you will expose you to programs that will help get you involved and therefore will help you persist in college. Students who room with someone outside of their normal comfort zone often develop attitudes that move closer to that of their new roommate. In common with most students who offer advice on this topic, I recommend not getting passionately caught up with someone who lives "too close."

Commuters need to work out new arrangements with their families if they continue to live at home. It is important that they create a study headquarters on campus, as well as a social headquarters.

TAKE ACTION

If something is not working well for you in your living arrangements—whether you live on campus or off campus—make a plan to deal with the problem and set up a timetable for putting the plan in action. Your goal, of course, is to reduce the problem while minimizing conflict and maximizing the good relationships with the other persons. Try to set up an agreed on set of goals as a first step in solving the problem.

EXPLORE YOUR CAMPUS

If you haven't already done this, find a good spot to study during those odd hours you are on campus and not in class. Literally exploring the campus can result in finding excellent locations. Recall that some organizations (e.g., Newman Center, Hillel House, African-American Studies Center) may have areas set aside for reading and study. Too, if your campus has many commuting students, there may be special lounges or study rooms set aside for them. And, of course, student unions are likely to have quiet spots as well as areas for socializing.

SELF-TEST ITEMS

1. What are the four steps in the four-step formula for conflict resolution?
2. Describe the two types of "campus headquarters" recommended to commuter students.
3. Describe in your own words the "rights perspective" adopted by most campus living communities.

More Campus Life
Steps to Social, Financial, and Physical Success

14

The one thing that really surprised me was that I didn't do as well as I thought I would. I know I might have partied a little too much, but that couldn't have been it.

I was a "goody-goody" in high school. Because I'm going to the university, people think I'm going to change. Well, it hasn't happened yet. I'm still a virgin and I've never been drunk. I am still a nice person to everyone . . .

I do know I want to do something with medicine, but that is going to be very hard and STRESSFUL with all the payment plans and stuff going on now.
—*Students' reflections on starting college*

Where Are We Going?

Your lifestyle choices affect your prospects for college success. One important predictor of success (and enjoyment) is the extent to which you get involved on your campus. By the end of this chapter, you will be able to describe various types of campus organizations and know why and when it's advantageous to join them. I'll also describe

http://dx.doi.org/10.1037/14181-014
Your Complete Guide to College Success: How to Study Smart, Achieve Your Goals, and Enjoy Campus Life, by Donald J. Foss

the pros and cons of different types of Greek-letter organizations. It's no secret that paying for college, and managing finances generally, provides a challenge to many. In the following pages, you will also learn about *opportunity costs* associated with going to college and why such costs are a huge and largely invisible determiner of the real cost of college. You will also be able to describe what we know about the effects of outside work on college performance and when it makes sense to borrow money. The opportunities for *behavioral misadventures* come in two basic flavors: failing to do things that help keep you strong and smart and solvent, and doing things that make you weak and dumb and poor. The chapter presents information you should have as you make your choices. Some of your current beliefs may not be consistent with what we know about these matters—and inaccurate beliefs can affect your decisions. By the end of the chapter, you will know about the actual frequency of alcohol use on campuses, for example, and more about keeping fit physically and psychologically.

Campus Involvement

Both commuters and dorm dwellers benefit from getting involved in campus activities. Being engaged in campus life is fun: It provides opportunities to meet new people and to get experience working in groups or organizations that appeal to you. Being involved also helps keep you motivated toward your goal of graduating in good time. After examining the factors that predict college success, one group of researchers concluded:

> Other things being equal, the greater the individual student's level of integration into the social and academic systems of the college, the greater his or her subsequent commitment to the college and the goal of college graduation respectively. (Pascarella, Smart, & Ethington, 1986, p. 49)

I mentioned earlier that living in campus housing is a plus because it helps ensure campus involvement. And now we know that campus involvement is related to academic success. Given that result, commuter students might feel at a disadvantage. However, researchers have also found evidence that students who live off campus do as well as those who live on campus when they take advantage of opportunities to get involved (Inman & Pascarella, 1998).

If you look, you'll likely find dozens of interest groups, student clubs, and organizations—including (on many 4-year campuses) sororities and fraternities—that focus on a wide variety of topics. For example, the website of the University of Houston (where I teach) reveals more than 500 campus groups. Some are interested in politics, many in community service activities, some in academically related subjects such as the German club, some in club sports (everything from ice hockey to fencing), and some in film and even in very special topics within film: "We're a small anime community based on the campus of the University of Houston," says one group. "We have showings and meetings to introduce and promote Japanese Animation to the general public." Something on your college's list surely will appeal to you.

I've already noted that interacting with faculty and staff can be beneficial to you. These benefits are greater than you might first think. In a study of commuter students, Judith Johnson (1997) found that one of the most important characteristics distinguishing students who stayed in college from those who dropped out was whether they had interactions with, and developed connections to, faculty and staff members. That's a compelling result. Of course, such connections can't make up for a lack of goal-oriented studying, but her research underscores how desirable it is for you to manage your own motivation by doing something that is fun anyway: getting to know people and getting involved.

Making new friends with fellow students has many benefits. Some of them will last a lifetime and be more valuable to you than treasure. Also, we know that loneliness and trying to go it alone predicts all kinds of negative outcomes. To speed up the friend-making process, you can do two things. First, put yourself where new friends might be. That's why getting involved in campus organizations is a plus. Also, do other things that put you with other people; for example, go to the campus gym to work out rather than jogging solo. Strike up a conversation with someone doing what you like to do. Second, after the "warm up" conversations, share a bit of yourself; for example, mention something you like to do or that you are worried about. Take the risk that others will find you interesting! Don't overdo it, though; as you know, new people will be put off if you show evidence of being terribly needy or a whiner. Often the person will share an appropriate amount back. In such ways friendships develop and deepen.

ADVANCED ACTIVITIES

You may have heard of Phi Beta Kappa (a top honorary society), or Tau Kappa Epsilon, or Alpha Chi Omega (a social fraternity and sorority, respectively), but have you heard of Delta Sigma Pi or Psi Chi? These are groups that support the interests of students once they've advanced a year or two and once they've selected a field of study.

The latter differ in their criteria for membership and in how they are structured.

For example, Delta Sigma Pi (DSP) is a "Professional Fraternity for Men and Women Pursuing Careers in Business." Joining DSP or some other professionally related undergraduate organization in business, engineering, social work, pharmacy, etc., brings additional opportunities for networking, learning more about your field of interest, and a good possibility of taking on a leadership role—something that provides valuable experience (and that looks good on a résumé). Psi Chi is the "National Honor Society in Psychology." Membership requires a certain number of hours completed in psychology along with a GPA requirement (see the Psi Chi website). Students who join have regular meetings that may involve visiting interesting sites, having guest speakers tell them about job prospects, and many other topics. Pizza is common.

Page forward on your calendar to the spring term of your sophomore year and put in a notation to look up the appropriate organization for your major. The departmental advisor can tell you when they meet, but if you keep your eyes open when going to class, you'll probably see announcements from these groups posted in the hallways.

Another fine way to get involved is to become active in student government. On many campuses it is quite possible to rise to a leadership position in such organizations, which again is good experience. Your campus student government association likely has a website that describes its mission and will let you know how to participate (often involving an election) and when meetings occur. Student government leaders may meet regularly with senior administrators of the campus, including the president. That is one way you can meet the president before you shake hands at graduation.

On another front, I believe that exploring alternative cultural opportunities not related to your major or your prospective career will also help connect you to your school, allow you to meet interesting new people, and also may give you a lot of enjoyment. For example, go to a play instead of a movie. Although some students are bit by the theatre bug in high school or even earlier, others don't know what they're missing. Many colleges have theatre groups that mount enjoyable and sometimes mind-stretching plays. Also, poke your head inside the campus art gallery from time to time. I've mentioned that a beginning course in "art appreciation" that I was more or less forced to take has added greatly to my enjoyment of life and travel. Similarly, take someone to a musical event outside your normal comfort range—a jazz concert, say, or a symphony. If these are somewhat new to you, you may get intrigued by what you hear and decide to learn more—again leading to lifetime enjoyment.

GREEK LIFE AND LIVING

Greek letter organizations (the social ones) provide both recreational and residential opportunities on many 4-year campuses. Few groups are as subject to quick, stereotyped judgment as "the Greeks": on the one hand, parties are their reason for existing; they cheat like mad; they—the fraternities, anyway—engage in harsh, even sometimes deadly, hazing; and living in a Greek House is equivalent to moving into a sports bar. But also, they provide lifetime bonds of friendship, brotherhood, or sisterhood; they generously raise money for charities; and they help keep their members engaged in campus events and therefore more likely to stay in school. Which picture is accurate?

Neither. Both. It depends. When dealing with stereotypes, it helps to remember that we are talking about millions of people. There is great variability among members of Greek letter organizations, though not as great as the variability among college students overall. So knowing that someone is a member of fraternity Alpha or sorority Omega doesn't tell you a lot about that person as an individual. But, on the average, it does tell some things.

For example, fraternities and sororities attract students with somewhat more traditional and relatively conservative attitudes and values than students who do not join these groups (Pascarella & Terenzini, 2005). Having said that, it is also known that those who join fraternities have, on average, a history of greater alcohol use (and problems) in high school than those who do not join. Although fraternities may not be the initial source of such problems, they can reinforce them to the extent that they glorify drinking and provide additional social pressure to do it. And living in a fraternity house appears to accelerate these effects; it is "related to more frequent alcohol consumption and greater negative consequences even after accounting for family history, expectancies, and high school drinking rates" (Larimer, Anderson, Baer, & Marlatt, 2000, p. 53). There also are studies showing that self-conscious women who join sororities may drink more—especially if the sorority tends to glorify drinking—perhaps in a desire to fit in. I'll quench your thirst for more information about alcohol in just a moment.

One sometimes hears that sororities attract women with a history of eating disorders and that a sorority reinforces the problem. However, to my eye the evidence for these claims is not convincing. Similarly, I've heard it said that sororities affect women's self-esteem (and I've heard it both ways: Sororities help increase it; sororities help decrease it). Again, though, in my judgment the current evidence for any such effect is not convincing.

Serious hazing continues to be a problem on numerous campuses, even though in many states it's illegal and the history of hazing has led many colleges to dismiss the offending fraternities and sometimes the entire Greek system. Here's the kicker: There isn't any real point to hazing—we know from studies of social psychology that one's dedication to a fraternal group can be just as strong following a commitment of time to safe activities as it will be following time spent on dangerous or illegal activities. And, of course, the consequences of the latter can be severe. I'm sorry to report that I've been on campuses when pledges tragically died. You do not want to feel even remotely responsible if that happens.

GRADES AND GROUPS

> I have also realized that I am not at the university to attend school but to go through pledgeship. Basically what I'm saying is that all I really want is just some time to kick back and relax, and as far as I can tell the only time to do that is during class.
> —A first-year student (who probably won't be a second-year student)

Does membership in a Greek organization affect grades? The evidence suggests that there is a negative effect, though not a huge one (about 10% of GPA on average). This effect shows up both in grades and on standardized tests of critical thinking, especially in the first year in college (and it is more pronounced for men than for women). However, the effect gets smaller and in some cases disappears in later years. Its importance from your point of view is this: If you are a marginal student, the 10% effect might push you too close for comfort to the edge of success. And if you aspire to medical, law, or graduate school, you want to be sure that you take extra steps to avoid the possible nick in freshman GPA that joining a fraternity or sorority can lead to (Pascarella & Terenzini, 2005).

On the plus side, Greek life leads to campus involvement. As I've already noted, such involvement predicts college persistence, and that predicts college success. Too, building relationships with new friends adds a tremendous amount to the college experience. If the particular fraternity or sorority you consider joining promotes respect among its members, and if it values activities that lead to real accomplishments, then it likely will be a force for your positive change and growth, and a source of legitimate friends. If its main claim to fame is the glorification of alcohol and sex, then it won't be.

Having emphasized the importance of being a part of campus life, I want to issue a quick caution: Don't overdo it. I once worked with a student government (SG) president who got so absorbed in that job and in campus politics that he became seriously at risk for flunking his final semester. In effect, he had to stop being the SG president and concentrate mightily on his studies to pull his college career out of the drain. Your master calendar and constant self-assessment should keep you honest with respect to your priorities.

Financial Health:
Money Is Nice

> I now am living independently, thank God, as long as I keep getting money from home.
> —*A student reflecting on his "independence"*

It costs money to go to college. Yes, this is another stunningly obvious *Duh*! comment. There are probably 500 pounds of books on the topic of money and college, from those that focus on financial aid—a complex topic, unfortunately, and therefore one that needs its share of books— to making a budget and tips for living within it. We can't cover all that ground here. I'm just going to make four simple points. My aim is to help you see the topic of money with a fresh eye and to help you keep on track toward your real goals, including your financial ones.

OPPORTUNITY COSTS

Although it costs money to go to college, there is an important source of the cost that students and their families often miss. There are two distinct sources of cost: the obvious one, namely, what it costs out-of-pocket (for tuition, books, room, board, etc.), and the not-so-obvious one, that is, what you don't earn because you are going to college and are not in the full-time work force. What you don't earn is called an *opportunity cost*. By doing one thing (going to college), you lose the opportunity to do another (go to work in a decent-paying, full-time occupation). Eventually, of course, you will start your career and, with high probability, earn more money each year because you've been to college. On the average, college graduates earn much more per year than high-school graduates—though the amount varies greatly across occupations. In the meantime, though, we need to count the money that you don't make as a cost.

People don't like to talk about opportunity costs; it's tough enough just to deal with the out-of-pocket expenses. However, suppose we ask whether college is "worth it" when we include the opportunity costs. I'm now talking about costs and benefits from a strictly dollars-and-cents perspective. College will also provide a multitude of intangible benefits over your lifetime, but I'm leaving them out of the picture for now. This worth-it question has been studied, and the answer is yes. Now suppose, though, that you take 6 years to finish college instead of 4 years. What will it cost you to stretch out your time in college, and is it worth it then? Remember, you have to figure in both the out-of-pocket costs (an additional 2 years of tuition, room and board, etc.), plus the opportunity costs (the lost income). How about if you take 8 years? 10? You can see that at some point whether college is "worth it" gets questionable or even silly—again, from a strictly dollars-and-cents point of view—because the total cost, especially the opportunity cost, gets really high and you might never recover it even though you will eventually have increased annual earnings because of your college education, and even though you will work for decades.

It costs money to go to college. The thing you can do to increase those costs the most is to stretch out the time it takes to finish. Therefore, to keep the cost down you want to finish on time. This is probably the smartest financial advice I know about controlling college costs, but it doesn't get the attention it deserves. The simplest way to finish on time is to take the proper number of credits each year. Some students think that 12 semester credit hours is a full-time load. But if you only take 12 hours each semester and don't go to summer school, it will take 5 years for most degree programs (some take longer).

Each year you delay your graduation adds both direct and opportunity costs—probably in the multiple tens of thousands of dollars. These numbers overwhelm other, belt-tightening steps you can take. Thus, even though most people don't think about it in this way, delaying graduation is a very costly decision. That's the first point:

Make timely progress through college. Delaying graduation is very, very expensive.

EFFECTS OF WORKING FOR PAY ON COLLEGE SUCCESS

The second money point concerns the amount of time you work for pay while you are in school. I was surprised to find only a few high-quality research reports on this important topic, so my conclusions and recommendations have to be somewhat tentative. What is clearly established, though, is that many college students are working a lot. Estimates are that more than 60% of students work for pay and that on the average they work about 25 to 30 hours per week.

How does this affect their college performance? There is evidence (e.g., DiSimone, 2008) that working part time—up to about 10 hours per week—leads to slightly improved grades. There is also evidence that working more than 20 hours per week has a negative effect on grades compared with not working at all (Pascarella, Edison, Nora,

Hagedorn, & Terenzini, 1998). These are not very big effects on the average, though they seem to hold for students of all ethnic groups and economic backgrounds.

There are many possible explanations for these results; here is mine. Working a few hours per week may not cut into "college" time (going to class, to labs, active studying, working on projects). Instead, those work hours may be stolen from recreation time or—and this likely would be a good thing—from such activities as playing video games. So some work can be beneficial. If the average student works more than 20 hours per week, though, it does cut into college time and therefore affects his or her grades in the wrong direction.

Whether that is the correct explanation or not, I recommend against working more than 20 hours per week. I especially recommend against it if it leads you to take less than the course load you need to graduate on time. You have to earn a lot of money in that part-time job to make up for the opportunity cost of stretching out your education. I'd consider making an exception to my recommendation, though, if the job very directly relates to your career goals and provides network-ing possibilities that can help you later. And I also would temper my recommendation some if you can work on campus. There is evidence that an on-campus job may contribute to student success. Nevertheless, here is my second main money point:

> **If you work to help support your education, limit the hours. Also, do not steal the work hours from the college hours.**

BORROWING MONEY: DOES IT MAKE SENSE?

"Forget about getting married and buying a home," blared a news report on college-student loans. The headlines are full of stories about students who graduate with mountains of debt. Unfortunately, some do. Student loan debt can be a major handicap, like strapping a 20-pound weight on each foot as you begin the postcollege race of life. To make my third point about money, let's look at the facts about student loans and see what makes sense.

About one third of the students walking across the graduation stage have no debt. Good for them, and a tip of the hat to their families. The vast majority of the other two thirds have debts that I would call reasonable—by which I mean that they will earn enough by being a college graduate to pay off that debt without major strain. Indeed, for those students who graduate with debt, the average amount owed is about equal to the average additional amount a college graduate will earn in 1 or 2 years compared with what the average high school gradu-ate will earn. Economists who study this topic agree that it *is* sensible to borrow money if you need to in order to get your degree. Some make even stronger statements: Anthony P. Carnevale, director of Georgetown University's Center on Education and the Workforce, said, "From an economist's point of view, debt is the very best way to pay for education because you're shifting the cost forward until you'll be earning more money. You borrow cheap money. It's really a very good bargain" (as cited in R. Wilson, 2009, p. A1). Michael McPherson, another expert on this topic, put it simply: "Most people borrow a reasonable amount of money, they pay it back, and they are better for having gone to college" (as cited in R. Wilson, 2009, p. A1). As is common, the headlines focus on the unusually bad cases—the normal is not the news.

Paying for college is probably the best investment you will ever make in your life. I hope you don't have to borrow money to make those payments—"free" financial aid (e.g., scholarships and fellowships) is obviously the best kind. But if you do have to borrow money, and if you do it in a smart way, it's highly likely that loan will be worth it to you. People take out loans to buy a car, which becomes less valuable every day. The value of a college education does not depreciate.

Even so, you have to pay back the loan. Therefore, you should borrow as little money as you can, consistent with getting through college *on time*. That's the smart way. The headline-grabbing problem cases occur when the student borrows too much money, which happens for one of two reasons. In one case, the student picks a college that is too expensive; typically it is the student's "dream college," usually a private school or an out-of-state public university with high cost. If the dream college does not offer enough free financial aid, then, I'm sorry, but reality requires that cost factors enter into the decision of where to go. Just as you may not be able to afford your dream house or dream car right away, you may not be able to afford your dream college. However, and as you may already have discovered, odds are you will love the alternative, more affordable, school.

In the second case, the student borrows money simply to support a lifestyle. He or she is borrowing money to pay for, among other things, a fancy new portable electronic device or the pleasure of frequent and expensive coffee concoctions. This does not make financial sense. I know that to many I sound completely out of touch, worse than a killjoy. But if you insist on having a high standard of living while in college, and if you borrow money to support it, that decision will negatively affect your standard of living for years after college. Here, then, is another stunningly obvious, but often ignored, conclusion: You won't need to borrow as much while in school if you don't spend so much. To summarize this third point:

Invest in yourself by borrowing money to get through college on time if you need to.

But only borrow for that reason. Do not borrow to support a college lifestyle. Your lifestyle will be much better in the long run.

The U.S. Department of Education has a website (http://www.ed.gov/finaid) that contains much useful information and many useful pointers about paying for college and financial aid, including a calculator that can help determine in advance how much federal financial aid you may qualify for. Also, the website http://www.college.gov provides additional information about student loans and related topics.

SHOULDN'T YOU GIVE YOURSELF CREDIT?

My fourth money point results from holding a magnifying glass up to the topic of borrowing, specifically to the topic of credit cards or credit purchases using portable electronic devices. Students under 21 need a family member to cosign an application for credit. Even so, many students still get in trouble by misusing their ability to borrow money. These "credit enablers" (whether plastic cards or electronic devices) are psychologically interesting objects. Research has shown that people are more willing to spend money when they can put the purchase on plastic than if they have to pay by taking cash out their wallets. The card/device provides some "distance" between the desired item and the fact that you have to pay for it. That sense of distance is misleading, of course; it has contributed to getting millions of people in serious financial trouble.

It's both easy and expensive to forget that every time you buy something on credit you are borrowing money at a very high interest rate. Really, these plastic aids to temptation should be called "loan cards" rather than credit cards; it's a more accurate description. Over time, and unless you pay the balance in full each and every month, you can easily pay more in interest charges for the "double Alaskan-ice latté with cinnamon whipped chocolate on top" than that overpriced confection cost in the first place. You may even be paying twice what you think you are. Same is true for tickets to the Nails on the Blackboard concert.

Here is a simple test: Will you still be paying for the tempting item after it is gone? As a rule of thumb it makes no sense to do that. Thus, borrowing to buy textbooks may be a sensible decision; the books will outlast the loan, and they are needed to reach your main goal. But if the item (e.g., the concert) does not outlast the loan, that's a sign you are borrowing money to support a lifestyle. The credit card (loan) companies are happy for you to do that. Those who care about you are not. Bottom line: Pay cash for "short-term" items or use a debit card rather than a credit card.

To summarize this fourth point: See the summary of the third point.

THE B-WORD

Finally, because you need to get ready for the rest of your financial life, you should start now. Therefore, and as you already know, you do need to have a budget. How much income do you have? What are your expenses? One piece of paper with two columns is all you need to figure it out. Or maybe two pieces: one for a monthly budget and one for a yearly one. The two columns must balance. (Typing "making a budget" into a web browser will lead you to numerous helpful sites that give more details and useful tips.) This is pocket science, not rocket science. The income column includes what you take from savings, what you get from your family, how much you take home from employment, and any free financial aid you get. For budget purposes, the expense side involves just the out-of-pocket costs, not the opportunity costs. But you must be honest with yourself about what you include on the expense side (e.g., did you remember car insurance?). It is a good idea to keep detailed records for, say, a month. By which I mean that you write down every nickel you spend and what, exactly, you spent it for. That can lead to surprising revelations about yourself (possibly including the revelation that you really don't want to know how you spend your money). If expenses exceed income, you need to get them in balance.

There are two basic things you can do: get more income or have fewer expenses. One last time: *Duh!* It makes sense to start on the expense side. Here's my sob story: I had to sell my car after my freshman year, something almost unheard of even then. If I hadn't, though, I would have had to work more, or go to school less, or study less, or all of the above. I wasn't as smart about these topics as you are, but somehow I did realize that stretching out my time in school, or threatening my then not-spectacular GPA, were not good ideas. So I waved goodbye to my beloved jalopy—and survived it. I got in a car pool and even occasionally took public transportation. (Though thanks to my family I had fairly regular access to wheels in the evenings and weekends, so this was not a vow of total poverty.) Cutting down on expenses can be done if you list what you spend money on and then ruthlessly and honestly decide what you can postpone.

On the income side, you can decide to work more—but then you must watch out for (and include) the opportunity cost if working slows down your progress toward your degree. And last, you can borrow to invest in yourself. Of course, you will do so judiciously after you've reduced the expense side of the budget ledger. Your budget will help you discover what your real priorities are, and it will remind you that money is the means to (some of) the things you value, not an end in itself. That realization is part of the college experience, too.

This is the start of the rest of your life: Make a budget.

Physical Health: Feeling Good and Doing Well

> I am going to take a nap now because I am extremely tired.
> Sleep is not a common word used here, unless it is preceded by
> "I don't."
>
> —*A freshman student*

Believe it or not, someday you will be older than you are now. But the rate at which you get old is not fixed. Your behavior can influence how quickly you age—not chronologically, of course, but in terms of your physical and psychological selves. The choices you make now can dramatically affect both your college performance and how you feel as you age.

One choice involves how much you allow yourself to sleep. As the student quoted previously indicates, and as you know, sleep deprivation is a common college experience. What you may not know is that partial sleep deprivation (the typical college variety) can have a bigger negative effect on cognitive functioning than either long-term or short-term sleep deprivation (Pilcher & Huffcutt, 1996). Also, one of the side effects of sleep deprivation is that we underestimate its negative effects on us (it's like alcohol in that respect). To quote the investigators, "Findings indicate that college students are not aware of the extent to which sleep deprivation negatively affects their ability to complete cognitive tasks" (Pilcher & Walters, 1997, p. 121). Again we come to a simple conclusion:

College success can be affected by the amount you sleep.

Your success will also be affected by what you do in your waking hours to stay healthy. It is well known and well documented that you get back with interest the time you spend exercising; you gain energy and a higher degree of mental alertness. Plus, exercising is fun and provides an opportunity to interact with others. Getting and staying fit takes only a few minutes a day, on average—if you do it in a smart way.

I recommend that you pick your exercise with the long term in mind. Look around; no one plays football after age 30 unless they are paid enormous sums of money to do so—and then they can't walk a few years later. Energetic "old" people engage in activities that maintain and tone their bodies rather than tearing them down, and thereby slow the pace at which they get older. Thus, consider using your university recreation center to learn or improve a lifetime sport—tennis, handball, squash, hiking or jogging, mountain biking, etc. Lessons are usually free or very inexpensive.

You should also consider pairing exercise with eating well. The famous "freshman 15" extra pounds are not inevitable. College eateries often have the typical fast food choices, but also healthy ones (see http://www.choosemyplate.gov/ for the latest on what that means). But you know all that. The one thing I want to flag is the prevalence of eating disorders among college students, especially females (according to statistics from the National Institutes of Health website, nearly 4% of female adolescents have a "severe disorder"). Here, again, complete honesty with yourself is your best friend. An eating disorder does not fit with your life goals. If you have, or have a tendency toward, an eating disorder, seek help at the campus health center right away. If you have a friend with such a problem, help her or him get help.

Some Common Roadblocks to Success

Most students deal just fine with the freedom and responsibility associated with college. But some take serious risks that can increase the likelihood that their college career will veer off the road. Rather than an adventure, they have *behavioral misadventures.*

ALCOHOL IS NOT ANONYMOUS: WHAT STUDENTS ACTUALLY DO

The stereotype of the college student is not entirely wrong; everyone likes to party—and many drink. Drinking is in our culture, and it's not for me to preach about it. We should, though, look at a few things we've learned from the research on this topic. But before going on, please take a moment to write down the percentage of freshmen who drink during a typical week (say we're talking about freshmen at a big football school with a reputation for the party life): _____%. Now write down the percentage at that same school who drink until "drunk" during a typical week in the freshman year: _____%.

Here are some things we've learned from research on this topic: First, we know that many students are not accurate in their assessment of how much other students drink; it's common to overestimate it. That's important because your drinking habits can be influenced by what you *think* others do (Borsari & Carey, 2001). If you're wrong, then you may be drinking to catch up with an imaginary classmate rather than a real one. Loads of students like to put on a front by saying that they drink a lot and never study. It makes for a good story (or, if true, a way out the door).

Let's look at what other students actually do. In one project, a researcher at the University of Texas–Austin (UT-Austin) asked an entire freshman class to participate in a study of drinking and other behaviors. A large percentage of them agreed, and the project continued throughout their college years. The investigators found that about 40% of freshman students basically did not drink at all (the percentage of nondrinkers did drop to about 35% by the sophomore year). Further, the study found that more than half of the students had not been drunk during the fall or spring semesters, nor had they engaged at all in "binge" drinking—defined as five drinks at a sitting for men and four for women (Fromme, Corbin, & Kruse, 2008).

Was your estimate correct? Nationwide, according to the National Institutes of Health (the U.S. government's main health organization), about 60% of students between 18 and 20 years old drink. That makes the UT-Austin freshman close to the national average.

It's easy to lie with numbers, so it's good to keep in mind that averages don't represent each student. There is large variation among individuals—as noted, 40% of freshmen do not drink at all. Others drink moderately. But some are guzzling at an alarming rate. By the sophomore year about half are binge drinking sometime during a semester. It's no surprise that most students who drink in college were already drinking in high school. For some of them, college seems to release the restraints of home, and they experiment with drinking more. The great majority of them will "get over it" by the end of college or shortly thereafter. Unfortunately, though, about 10% of the binge drinkers are developing patterns of behavior that will haunt them and their families well into their adult lives after college (Schulenberg & Maggs, 2002). In effect, they are drowning their career chances before they start. You can decide if you want to take that chance.

Second, we know that drinking occurs at special times. It's also no surprise to you that it goes up on the weekends and on average goes up even more at spring break, on Halloween, and on New Year's Eve. But one of the riskiest days in a college student's life can be his or her 21st birthday (Neighbors, Spieker, Oster-Aaland, Lewis, & Bergstrom, 2005; Rutledge, Park, & Sher, 2008). Here college traditions of "celebrating" the day you become legal to drink can, and all too often do, lead to disaster. A small minority of students report that they (try to) drink perilous amounts of alcohol (for example, 21 drinks to celebrate being 21), which if done in a single evening is literally enough to kill them unless they throw it up in time.

This is way too dangerous. If you are a real friend to someone whose 21st birthday is coming up, plan to keep him or her within a reasonable limit. It's really not compulsory to have a drink in every bar around the campus when doing so runs the risk of alcohol poisoning, even if that's supposedly the college "tradition." Real friends help friends survive past 21.

Third, it follows that you should make real friends. If you are going to look out for them, and I know you will, then choose people who will return the favor, not people who will laughingly shout you on to the next shot after you've had enough. You are subject to social pressures—everyone is—and there is a huge keg of evidence that if you hang out with people who drink to the point where they put their education (or themselves) at risk, you're more likely to do it, too. That is not consistent with your life goals; the cost can be enormously high. Step back just for a moment and ask yourself whether your new acquaintances share your core values and those of your family; will they help protect you? If so, that's great. If not, maybe they don't deserve to be your friends.

Fourth, please don't get killed, or maimed, or do something that can ruin or even reduce your chances for success later. Nearly five college students die every day—*every day*—in alcohol-related events. That's about a 33-student classroom dying every week of the year. Most of them are killed in car crashes, which also injure huge numbers of students (more than half a million each year) and thereby cause enormous amounts of pain and loss; but some deaths are from alcohol poisoning and even from students drowning in their own vomit. Nice image, I know. This is so tragic I can hardly stand to write about it: campus life leading to campus death. Nearly 20% of the UT-Austin freshmen admitted to driving after drinking, as did slightly more than 25% of the sophomores. To me, that's more than scary. If you follow the advice presented in this book, you certainly want to live to enjoy the benefits. See the list on the next page for some common strategies designed to reduce the likelihood of excessive drinking and its heartbreaking consequences. These strategies have been shown to reduce the harmful consequences related to drinking (Haines et al., 2006), and the more of them that are used, the lower the chances of harm. Of course, they are not guaranteed to keep you safe; you always want to err on the side of caution.

ALCOHOL AND JUDGMENT

Alcohol affects judgment. Somewhat amazingly, it is possible to study people who drink alcohol to the point of legal drunkenness and to compare them with people who genuinely *believe* that they've been drinking alcohol but, in fact, have been drinking a nonalcoholic beverage that smells and tastes like the real thing. In one such study, young adults (averaging 23 years old) rated the likelihood of various consequences that would result from risky sexual practices such as having sex without a condom (Fromme, D'Amico, & Katz, 1999). The intoxicated participants had lower perceptions of risk than those who only

Some Common Strategies Designed to Reduce the Probability of Unwanted Consequences

- Alternate non-alcoholic with alcoholic beverages
- Set a limit in advance that you will not exceed
- Put extra ice in your drink
- Use or be a designated driver
- Eat before and/or during drinking
- Tell a friend to let you know when you've had enough
- Keep track of how many drinks you are having
- Pace your drinks to no more than one per hour
- Avoid drinking games
- Drink an alcohol look-alike (non-alcoholic beer, punch, etc.)
- Choose not to drink alcohol

thought that they'd been drinking. This is probably no surprise; if you drink, it rings true. The problem is that a lowered expectation for risk can be quite devastating when it leads to actual risky behavior—and it does.

Although I'm not making moral judgments here, our story does have a moral: You should not trust yourself or others to make a decision about driving after you've started drinking. By then you have poor judgment about how risky it is. And that's risking a ticket to jail or, horrifically, a trip to the morgue. Someone needs to be designated as driver *before the evening begins,* and he or she needs to abstain from drinking that night.

OTHER CAMPUS DRUGS

The UT-Austin study found that marijuana was second to alcohol among risky drugs used by freshmen (slightly more than 15% said they had used it during the semester). It's commonly said by marijuana users that it is a less dangerous drug than alcohol. That's not necessarily saying much. Still, a drug that can lead to difficulty in learning, memory, thinking, and problem solving really can't be recommended as an effective aid to college success. All of the above problems have been documented by research. Also, according to the National Institute on Drug Abuse (NIDA, 2010), "research has shown that marijuana's adverse impact on learning and memory can last for days or weeks after the acute effects of the drug wear off." Increasing the likelihood of memory impairment for weeks should give pause to anyone trying to stay in school and finish on time.

The only other drug I'll mention is related to one that was around when I was a student. In those days some students acquired Dexedrine (dextroamphetamine sulfate), though nowadays a similar drug, Adderall, appears to be more "popular." Adderall has a legitimate use; it is prescribed for some children diagnosed with attention-deficit/hyperactivity disorder (ADHD). Those children show symptoms that may include lack of sustained attention, being easily distracted, forgetfulness, having poor organization, making careless mistakes, and related behaviors. When prescribed, it is often part of part of a total treatment program for ADHD that may also include psychological, educational, and social measures (http://dailymed.nlm.nih.gov/dailymed/drugInfo.cfm?id=1362). Thus, Adderall is used along with other treatments to help these children concentrate.

Some college students believe that Adderall can help keep them alert and to have productive all-nighters. They also think it does so more or less free of cost, except for the extra sleep needed to catch up. It turns out, though, that the "free of cost" part is wrong. An NIH website (NIDA, 2009; http://www.drugabuse.gov/publications/drugfacts/stimulant-adhd-medications-methylphenidate-amphetamines) reports:

> Stimulants [e.g., Adderall] can increase blood pressure, heart rate, body temperature, and decrease sleep and appetite, which can lead to malnutrition and its consequences. Repeated use of stimulants can lead to feelings of hostility and paranoia. At high doses, they can lead to serious cardiovascular complications, including stroke.

Here is a quote from an article in *ColoradoDaily.com*, the student newspaper at the University of Colorado, written by the director of that university's health center:

> Every year at Wardenburg Health Center, I have cases of students who have used Adderall to supposedly enhance their academic performance in the short-term, but who instead induce long-term mental illnesses . . . they must deal with for the rest of their lives.
>
> Some of these unfortunate students respond to treatment, but others do not, as their nervous system has become permanently damaged by the stimulant.
>
> Without consulting a physician about your medical history and genetic preexisting conditions, taking Adderall is literally like playing "Russian roulette" with your brain—the very organ you are working to develop and will be dependent upon for functioning in your life and career . . .
>
> Taking a stimulant does not instill in any student the skill set needed to be successful or to graduate from college. It no more magically creates the skills needed to write a paper or pass a test than would a chef's taking Adderall magically produce the skills to cook a complicated meal.

> Using Adderall to burn the candle at both ends doesn't
> create a sharper mind, it simply creates a very dangerous,
> all-consuming fire. (Methner, 2009)

You can be confident that the author of that piece, Dr. Steven L. Methner, is on the side of student success. Of course, the decision about playing "Russian roulette" is yours—as is your brain.

Mental Health

Finally, we know that college students, like everyone, are subject to mental health and behavioral problems. I am very happy to note that the stigma associated with such problems is much reduced now compared with when I was in college, but it is not entirely absent. If people were aware of how common these disorders are, I think the stigma would be even further reduced. Therefore, you should know that according to the National Institute of Mental Health, the lifetime prevalence of a major depressive disorder is about 17%, whereas the lifetime prevalence of anxiety disorders is over 30% and that of impulse-control disorders is about 25% (some individuals have more than one, so we can't simply add the numbers to get a total).

A particularly acute and scary problem might occur if you or a friend feels suicidal. Suicide is a highly serious problem: It is the seventh most frequent cause of death among males and 15th leading cause among females. In fact, suicide is more frequent than homicide, though the latter gets on the news most nights. Here is the advice posted on the National Institute of Mental Health website (http://www.nimh.nih.gov/health/publications/suicide-in-the-us-statistics-and-prevention/index.shtml):

> If you think someone is suicidal, do not leave him or her alone.
> Try to get the person to seek immediate help from his or her
> doctor or the nearest hospital emergency room, or call 911.
> Eliminate access to firearms or other potential tools for suicide,
> including unsupervised access to medications.

They also note that you can

> call this toll-free number, available 24 hours a day, every day:
> 1-800-273-TALK (8255). You will reach the National Suicide
> Prevention Lifeline, a service available to anyone. You may call for
> yourself or for someone you care about. All calls are confidential.

Mental health and behavioral problems make up a huge fraction of all health issues in the United States, and treating them requires substantial resources. The good news is that there have been very significant advances in the effectiveness of behavioral treatments. It is likely that your college offers access to professionals who can help and who do so at low or no additional cost; the cost is often covered in student fees. If you or a friend needs such help, please take advantage of the college resources, which are likely available at a counseling center or the health center.

To conclude this chapter on a positive note, my recommendations can be summarized simply, if metaphorically: To maximize your social, financial, physical, psychological, and academic success, stretch your body, mind, and heart. They can all take it.

Summary

Everyone benefits by getting involved in campus activities. Getting connected has been shown to increase the chance of persisting to your degree. As your college career progresses, there are additional organizations that open up to you—for example, groups composed of students with the same or similar majors. They can help you both socially and professionally. I described the benefits and the risks of a particular type of organization, Greek letter societies, and provided tips on selecting one that fits with your actual values.

You will have to make decisions about money during your college years. This chapter discussed four financial issues, including the opportunity costs of attending college (a much greater factor than is usually recognized); the effects of working on academic progress and success (it can be a plus but only up to a point, after which it turns negative for most students); the impact of borrowing money (it can be a good thing if it helps you get through college on time); and the impact and proper use of credit (don't use it for items that won't outlast the payment plan).

The chapter briefly reviewed the choices you make with respect to your physical and psychological well-being as a student. It described and presented the facts about some potential roadblocks to your success, including alcohol and drugs.

TAKE ACTION

1. If you have not already done so, search your college website or other sources to find groups whose activities and goals interest you. Arrange to get further information on them—for example, by attending a meeting.
2. Make a budget. Keep records for a month to see how well you live within it.

EXPLORE YOUR CAMPUS

1. Attend a cultural event (e.g., campus play, musical performance) that is different from your usual choice. Do an Internet search before you go in order to get some idea of what to expect and what to look for. Take someone with you so you have a partner to discuss the evening with.
2. Find out whether there is a club or fraternal organization (e.g., Delta Sigma Pi for business students) associated with your major or majors you are considering. Determine the criteria (if any) for joining the group. Go to one of their meetings and strike up a conversation with someone else who is attending.

SELF-TEST ITEMS

State in your own words:

1. What is an opportunity cost?
2. With respect to financial matters, what does the chapter say is the biggest determiner of opportunity costs for a college student?
3. What do we know about the relationship between campus involvement and academic success?
4. Evaluate the claim: Borrowing money to go to college is almost always a bad idea.
5. What do we know about the effect of working off campus on one's GPA?
6. What percentage of students in the typical American university drink alcohol?
7. Evaluate the following claim: The primary risk of stimulating drugs such as Adderall is associated with the lack of appropriate amount of sleep.

COMMENCEMENT VII

Commencement

Now that it is my fourth year I realize that while my freshman year was tumultuous, it was wonderful. I am a completely different person now than I was four years ago. I am more sure of myself and interested in myself and not afraid to do the things I want to do. I love my life . . . it looks to be a great one—thank you to [My College].

—An about-to-be grad

Y ou're walking across your familiar campus, perhaps heading for your graduation ceremony; you took your last final a few days ago. It's glorious outside and, yes, you look the part of a confident new graduate. You're happy to be there, and you should be. But, inside, is that all you feel? Are you sure about your future and where it will take you? Well, of course, not entirely. A mature person can never be certain about these things, and you are vastly more mature than you were the day you first walked across campus. However, I suspect you are convinced about this: Your work and development here, both academic and personal, have equipped you to continue your journey with as much confidence as a reasonable person can have. You know that what you did in college will help enormously as you move further into the world of careers and commitments. You are ready for the test of life.

http://dx.doi.org/10.1037/14181-015
Your Complete Guide to College Success: How to Study Smart, Achieve Your Goals, and Enjoy Campus Life, by Donald J. Foss

The campus somehow allowed you to navigate the seeming conflict between irreverence, lack of limits, spontaneity, and those other supposed freshman values on the one hand, and on the other, the need to understand, work within, and help shape the demands of the university and other components of the adult world. College helped you work out this transition to maturity. You've become a more competent and authentic person, a mission you accomplished in your own individual way. You've mastered the art of mindfulness, of paying attention to process, of self-management, and of being goal directed. Your increased understanding of the physical, social, and humane aspects of life—and of yourself—will, I'm confident, allow you to continue building a fulfilling life in a future that none of us can clearly see.

I wish I could be standing next to the president, so I could shake your hand. Congratulations!

References

ACT Educational Services. (n.d.). *National collegiate retention and persistence to degree rates.* Retrieved from https://www.noellevitz.com/documents/shared/Papers_and_Research/2012/2012-ACT-Retention-Data.pdf

Armbruster, B. B. (2009). Notetaking from lectures. In R. F. Flippo & D. C. Caverly (Eds.), *Handbook of college reading and study strategy research* (2nd ed., pp. 220–248). New York, NY: Routledge.

Ashcraft, M. H., & Krause, J. A. (2007). Working memory, math performance, and math anxiety. *Psychonomic Bulletin & Review, 14,* 243–248. doi:10.3758/BF03194059

Bjork, R. A. (1994). Memory and metamemory considerations in the training of human beings. In J. Metcalfe & A. Shimamura (Eds.), *Metacognition: Knowing about knowing* (pp. 185–205). Cambridge, MA: MIT Press.

Bjork, R. A. (1999). Assessing our own competence: Heuristics and illusions. In D. Gopher & A. Koriat (Eds.), *Attention and performance XVII. Cognitive regulation of performance: Interaction of theory and application* (pp. 435–459). Cambridge, MA: MIT Press.

Bjork, R. A., & Linn, M. C. (2006, March). The science of learning and the learning of science: Introducing desirable difficulties. *American Psychological Society Observer, 19*(3), 29–39.

Boisjoly, J., Duncan, G. J., Kremer, M., Levy, D. M., & Eccles, J. (2006). Empathy or antipathy? The impact of diversity. *The American Economic Review, 96,* 1890–1905. doi:10.1257/aer.96.5.1890

Borsari, B., & Carey, K. B. (2001). Peer influences on college drinking: A review of the research. *Journal of Substance Abuse, 13,* 391–424. doi:10.1016/S0899-3289(01)00098-0

Brown, J. S., & Burton, R. R. (1978). Diagnostic models for procedural bugs in basic mathematical skills. *Cognitive Science, 2,* 155–192. doi:10.1207/s15516709cog0202_4

Butler, R. O. (2001). *Inside creative writing.* Retrieved from www.fsu.edu/~butler

Butler, R. O. (2005). *From where you dream: The process of writing fiction* (J. Burroway, Ed.). New York, NY: Grove Press.

Callender, A. A., & McDaniel, M. A. (2009). The limited benefits of rereading educational texts. *Contemporary Educational Psychology, 34,* 30–41. doi:10.1016/j.cedpsych.2008.07.001

Carver, C. S. (2004). Self-regulation of action and affect. In R. F. Baumeister & K. D. Vohs (Eds.), *Handbook of self-regulation* (pp. 13–39). New York, NY: Guilford Press.

Credé, M., Roch, S. G., & Kieszczynka, U. M. (2010). Class attendance in college: A meta-analytic review of the relationship of class attendance with grades and student characteristics. *Review of Educational Research, 80,* 272–295. doi:10.3102/0034654310362998

Cuseo, J. (n.d.). *The liberal arts, your college major, and your future career(s): Myths & realities.* Retrieved from http://www.uwc.edu/administration/academic-affairs/esfy/cuseo/

Dahlke, R. M. (2008). *How to succeed in college mathematics: A guide for the college mathematics student.* Plymouth, MI: BergWay.

DiSimone, J. S. (2008). *The impact of employment during school on college student academic performance* (NBER Working Paper 14006). Cambridge, MA: National Bureau of Economic Research.

Fisher, J. L., & Harris, M. B. (1973). Effect of note taking and review on recall. *Journal of Educational Psychology, 65,* 321–325. doi:10.1037/h0035640

Flippo, R. F., Becker, M. J., & Wark, D. M. (2009). Test taking. In R. F. Flippo & D. C. Caverly (Eds.), *Handbook of college reading and study strategy research* (pp. 249–286). New York, NY: Routledge.

Flower, L., & Hayes, J. R. (1981a). A cognitive process theory of writing. *College Composition and Communication, 32,* 365–387. doi:10.2307/356600

Flower, L., & Hayes, J. R. (1981b). Plans that guide the composing process. In C. H. Frederiksen & J. F. Dominic (Eds.), *Writing: The nature, development, and teaching of written communication: Vol. 2. Writing: Process, development and communication* (pp. 39–58). Hillsdale, NJ: Erlbaum.

Friedman, T.L. (2011, July 13). The start-up of you. *The New York Times,* p. A27. Retrieved from http://www.nytimes.com/2011/07/13/opinion/13friedman.html?partner=rssnyt&emc=rss

Fromme, K., Corbin, W.R., & Kruse, M.I. (2008). Behavioral risk during the transition from high school to college. *Developmental Psychology, 44,* 1497–1504. doi:10.1037/a0012614

Fromme, K., D'Amico, E.J., & Katz, E.C. (1999). Intoxicated sexual risk taking: An expectancy or cognitive impairment explanation? *Journal of Studies on Alcohol, 60,* 54–63.

Haines, M.P., Barker, G., & Rice, R.M. (2006). The personal protective behaviors of college student drinkers: Evidence of indigenous protective norms. *Journal of American College Health,* 55, 69–75. doi:10.3200/JACH.55.2.69-76

Hartung, P.J., & Niles, S.G. (2000). Established career theories. In D.A. Luzzo (Ed.), *Career counseling of college students: An empirical guide to strategies that work* (pp. 3–21). Washington, DC: American Psychological Association. doi:10.1037/10362-000

Hartwig, M.K., & Dunlosky, J. (2012). Study strategies of college students: Are self-testing and scheduling related to achievement? *Psychonomic Bulletin & Review, 19,* 126–134. doi:10.3758/s13423-011-0181-y

Holland, J. (1985). *Making vocational choices: A theory of vocational personalities and work* (2nd ed.). Englewood Cliffs, NJ: Prentice-Hall.

Huey, E.B. (1968). *The psychology and pedagogy of reading.* New York, NY: Macmillan. (Original work published 1908)

Inman, P., & Pascarella, E. (1998). The impact of college residence on the development of critical thinking skills in college freshmen. *Journal of College Student Development, 39,* 557–568.

Johnson, J.L. (1997). Commuter college students: What factors determine who will persist and who will drop out? *College Student Journal, 31,* 323–332.

Karabenick, S.A., & Sharma, R. (1994). Seeking academic assistance as a strategic learning resource. In P.R. Pintrich, D.R. Brown, & C.E. Weinstein (Eds.), *Student motivation, cognition, and learning: Essays in honor of Wilbert J. McKeachie* (pp. 189–211). Hillsdale, NJ: Lawrence Erlbaum Associates.

Karpicke, J.D., Butler, A.C., & Roediger, H.L. (2009). Metacognitive strategies in student learning: Do students practice retrieval when they study on their own? *Memory, 17,* 471–479. doi:10.1080/09658210802647009

Karpicke, J.D., & Grimaldi, P.J. (2012, November). *Guided retrieval of educational materials with automated scoring.* Paper presented at the 53rd annual meeting of the Psychonomic Society, Minneapolis, MN.

Kellogg, R.T. (1994). *The psychology of writing.* New York, NY: Oxford University Press.

Keynes, J.M. (1964). *The general theory of employment, interest and money.* New York, NY: Harcourt Brace and World. (Original work published in 1936)

Kiewra, K. A. (1983). The relationship between notetaking over an extended period and actual course-related achievement. *College Student Journal, 17,* 381–385.

Kiewra, K. A., & Benton, S. L. (1988). The relationship between information-processing ability and notetaking. *Contemporary Educational Psychology, 13,* 33–44. doi:10.1016/0361-476X(88)90004-5

Kiewra, K. A., Benton, S. L., & Lewis, L. B. (1987). Qualitative aspects of notetaking and their relationship with information-processing ability and academic achievement. *Journal of Instructional Psychology, 14,* 110–117.

Kniering, J. (2010). Colleges: Freshmen looking for career advice now. *Boston.com.* Retrieved from http://www.boston.com/news/education/higher/articles/2010/09/12/colleges_freshmen_looking_for_career_advice_now/

Lamott, A. (1995). *Bird by bird: Some instructions on writing and life.* New York, NY: Anchor Books.

Landrum, R. E. (2009). *Finding jobs with a psychology bachelor's degree: Expert advice for launching your career.* Washington, DC: American Psychological Association.

Laney, C., & Loftus, E. F. (2009) Eyewitness memory. In R. N. Kocsis (Ed.), *Applied criminal psychology: A guide to forensic behavioral sciences* (pp. 121–145). Springfield, IL: Charles C. Thomas.

Larimer, M. E., Anderson, B. K., Baer, J. S., & Marlatt, G. A. (2000). An individual in context: Predictors of alcohol use and drinking problems among Greek and residence hall students. *Journal of Substance Abuse, 11,* 53–68. doi:10.1016/S0899-3289(99)00020-6

Larsen, R. J., & Prizmic, Z. (2004). Affect regulation. In R. F. Baumeister & K. D. Vohs (Eds.), *Handbook of self-regulation* (pp. 40–61). New York, NY: Guilford Press.

Leonard, M. J. (2010). *Major decisions: For students who are exploring majors.* Retrieved from http://dus.psu.edu/md/mdintro.htm

Lepper, M. R., & Woolverton, M. (2002). The wisdom of practice: Lessons learned from the study of highly effective tutors. In J. Aronson (Ed.), *Improving academic achievement: Impact of psychological factors on education* (pp. 135–158). New York, NY: Elsevier Science. doi:10.1016/B978-012064455-1/50010-5

Lifetime "Career" Changes. (2006). *Occupational Outlook Quarterly Online, 50*(2). Retrieved from http://www.bls.gov/opub/ooq/2006/summer/grabbag.htm#C

Light, R. J. (2004). *Making the most of college: Students speak their minds.* Cambridge, MA: Harvard University Press.

Loftus, E. F. (1979). *Eyewitness testimony.* Cambridge, MA: Harvard University Press.

McDaniel, M. A., Howard, D. C., & Einstein, G. O. (2009). The read-recite-review strategy: Effective and portable. *Psychological Science, 20,* 516–522. doi:10.1111/j.1467-9280.2009.02325.x

Methner, S. (2009, May 5). Adderall at CU: Getting high or getting higher grades? Stimulant abuse a prescription for danger. *Colorado Daily.* Retrieved from http://www.coloradodaily.com/ci_12961059 #axzz29cG3r1Y3

Mulcahy-Ernt, P. I., & Caverly, D. C. (2009). Strategic study-reading. In R. F. Flippo & D. C. Caverly (Eds.), *Handbook of college reading and study strategy research* (pp. 177–198). New York, NY: Routledge.

Nathan, R. (2005). *My freshman year: What a professor learned by becoming a student.* Ithaca, NY: Cornell University Press.

National Institute on Drug Abuse. (2009). *DrugFacts: Stimulant ADHD medications—Methylphenidate and amphetamines.* Retrieved from http://www.drugabuse.gov/publications/drugfacts/stimulant-adhd-medications-methylphenidate-amphetamines

National Institute on Drug Abuse. (2010). *DrugFacts: Marijuana.* Retrieved from http://www.drugabuse.gov/publications/drugfacts/marijuana

Neighbors, C., Spieker, C. J., Oster-Aaland, L., Lewis, M. A., & Bergstrom, R. L. (2005). Celebration intoxication: An evaluation of 21st birthday alcohol consumption. *Journal of American College Health, 54,* 76–80. doi:10.3200/JACH.54.2.76-80

Nijhof, K. S., & Engels, R. (2007). Parenting styles, coping strategies, and the expression of homesickness. *Journal of Adolescence, 30,* 709–720. doi:10.1016/j.adolescence.2006.11.009

Paluck, E. L., & Green, D. P. (2009). Prejudice reduction: What works? A review and assessment of research and practice. *Annual Review of Psychology, 60,* 339–367. doi:10.1146/annurev.psych.60.110707.163607

Parsons, F. (1909). *Choosing a vocation.* Boston, MA: Houghton Mifflin.

Pascarella, E. T., Edison, M. I., Nora, A., Hagedorn, L. S., & Terenzini, P. T. (1998). Does work inhibit cognitive development during college? *Educational Evaluation and Policy Analysis, 20,* 75–93. doi:10.2307/1164375

Pascarella, E. T., Smart, J., & Ethington, C. (1986). Long-term persistence of two-year college students. *Research in Higher Education, 24,* 47–71.

Pascarella, E. T., & Terenzini, P. T. (2005). *How college affects students: A third decade of research.* San Francisco, CA: Jossey-Bass.

Pashler, H., McDaniel, M., Rohrer, D., & Bjork, R. (2008). Learning styles: Concepts and evidence. *Psychological Science in the Public Interest, 9,* 105–119.

Pauk, W., & Owens, R. J. Q. (2005). *How to study in college* (8th ed.). Boston, MA: Houghton Mifflin.

Pennebaker, J. W., & Chung, C. K. (2007). Expressive writing, emotional upheavals, and health. In H. Friedman & R. Silver (Eds.), *Handbook of health psychology* (pp. 263–284). New York, NY: Oxford University Press.

Pennebaker, J. W., Colder, M., & Sharp, L. K. (1990). Accelerating the coping process. *Journal of Personality and Social Psychology, 58,* 528–537. doi:10.1037/0022-3514.58.3.528

Pennebaker, J. W., Mehl, M. R., & Niederhoffer, K. G. (2003). Psychological aspects of natural language use: Our words, our selves. *Annual Review of Psychology, 54,* 547–577. doi:10.1146/annurev.psych.54.101601.145041

Pilcher, J. J., & Huffcutt, A. J. (1996). Effects of sleep deprivation on performance: A meta-analysis. *Sleep, 19,* 318–326.

Pilcher, J. J., & Walters, A. S. (1997). How sleep deprivation affects psychological variables related to college students' cognitive performance. *Journal of American College Health, 46,* 121–126. doi:10.1080/07448489709595597

Polya, G. (1957). *How to solve it: A new aspect of mathematical method.* Garden City, NY: Doubleday. (Original work published 1945)

Reardon, R. C., & PAR Staff. (2001). *SDS Sample Report.* Retrieved from http://www.self-directed-search.com/sdspreport.html

Richland, L. E., Linn, M. C., & Bjork, R. A. (2007). Cognition and instruction: Bridging laboratory and classroom settings. In F. Durso, R. Nickerson, S. Dumais, S. Lewandowsky, & T. Perfect (Eds.), *Handbook of applied cognition* (2nd ed., pp. 555–583). West Sussex, England: Wiley.

Robinson, F. P. (1970). *Effective study* (4th ed.). New York, NY: Harper & Row. (Original work published 1946)

Roediger, H. L., & Karpicke, J. D. (2006). Test-enhanced learning: Taking memory tests improves long-term retention. *Psychological Science, 17,* 249–255. doi:10.1111/j.1467-9280.2006.01693.x

Roese, N. J., & Summerville, A. (2005). What we regret most . . . and why. *Personality and Social Psychology Bulletin, 31,* 1273–1285. doi:10.1177/0146167205274693

Rohrer, D., & Taylor, K. (2006). The effects of overlearning and distributed practice on the retention of mathematics knowledge. *Applied Cognitive Psychology, 20,* 1209–1224. doi:10.1002/acp.1266

Rose, M. (1989). *Lives on the boundary: The struggles and achievements of America's underprepared.* New York, NY: Free Press.

Rutledge, P. C., Park, A., & Sher, K. J. (2008). 21st birthday drinking: Extremely extreme. *Journal of Consulting and Clinical Psychology, 76,* 511–516. doi:10.1037/0022-006X.76.3.511

Schulenberg, J. E., & Maggs, J. L. (2002, March). A developmental perspective on alcohol use and heavy drinking during adolescence and the transition to young adulthood. *Journal of Studies on Alcohol,* Suppl. 14, 54–70.

Starbird, M. (2007). *Change and motion: Calculus made clear* (2nd ed.) [Streaming video]. Chantilly, VA: The Teaching Company. Retrieved from http://www.thegreatcourses.com/tgc/courses/Course_Detail.aspx?cid=177&pc=Search

Tangney, J. P., Baumeister, R. F., & Boone, A. L. (2004). High self-control predicts good adjustment, less pathology, better grades, and inter-

personal success. *Journal of Personality, 72,* 271–324. doi:10.1111/
j.0022-3506.2004.00263.x

Tice, D. M., & Baumeister, R. F. (1997). The costs and benefits of daw-
dling. *Psychological Science, 8,* 454–458. doi:10.1111/j.1467-9280.1997.
tb00460.x

Tognoli, J. (2003). Leaving home: Homesickness, place attachment, and
transition among residential college students. *Journal of College Student
Psychotherapy, 18,* 35–48. doi:10.1300/J035v18n01_04

Trimble, J. (2000). *Writing with style: Conversations on the art of writing*
(2nd ed.). Boston, MA: Allyn & Bacon.

University of Minnesota–Duluth. (2011). *Test-taking strategies.* Retrieved
from http://www.d.umn.edu/kmc/student/loon/acad/strat/test_take.
html

Weinstein, Y., McDermott, K. B., & Roediger, H. L. (2010). A comparison of study strategies for passages: Rereading, answering questions,
and generating questions. *Journal of Experimental Psychology: Applied,
16,* 308–316. doi:10.1037/a0020992

Wickelgren, W. A. (1974). *How to solve problems: Elements of a theory of
problems and problem solving.* San Francisco, CA: Freeman.

Williams, J. M. (2009). *Style: The basics of clarity and grace* (3rd ed.). New
York, NY: Pearson/Longman.

Wilson, R. (2009, May 22). A lifetime of student debt? Not likely. *Chron-
icle of Higher Education, 55*(37), A1. Retrieved from http://chronicle.
com/weekly/v55/i37/37a00101.htm

Wilson, T. D. (2002). *Strangers to ourselves: Discovering the adaptive uncon-
scious.* Cambridge, MA: Belknap Press of Harvard University Press.

Wilson, T. D. (2009). Know thyself. *Perspectives on Psychological Science, 4,*
384–389. doi:10.1111/j.1745-6924.2009.01143.x

Wilson, T. D., & Dunn, E. W. (2004). Self-knowledge: Its limits, value,
and potential for improvement. *Annual Review of Psychology, 55,* 493–
518. doi:10.1146/annurev.psych.55.090902.141954

Zaromb, F. M., & Roediger, H. L., III. (2010). The testing effect in free
recall is associated with enhanced organizational processes. *Memory
& Cognition, 38,* 995–1008. doi:10.3758/MC 38.8.995

Index

About the Author

Donald J. Foss, PhD, was the first in his family to go to college. He attended Hamline University and then transferred to the University of Minnesota, where he received both a bachelor's degree and a doctorate. After a postdoctoral fellowship at Harvard, he joined The University of Texas at Austin, rising to be a professor of psychology and the chair of the psychology department. Dr. Foss has also been on the psychology faculty at Florida State University, where he was dean of its College of Arts and Sciences. Presently, he is a professor of psychology at the University of Houston, where he also has served as senior vice president for academic affairs and provost.

Dr. Foss enjoys teaching and interacting with students. He received an All-University Outstanding Teaching Award from The University of Texas at Austin and an Outstanding Achievement Award from the University of Minnesota. His research interests are in cognitive psychology, specializing in how people comprehend both spoken and written language. He has published numerous professional articles and book chapters and has cowritten or coedited seven books. More recently, he turned his attention to the factors that determine success in college. The evidence-based book in front of you is one result of that interest. It provides college students with the best current information and insights on how to succeed in college (and after).